Present Day English
for Foreign Students

BOOK THREE

Please ask publishers for details of
PRESENT DAY ENGLISH:

Students' Books
Teacher's Books
Keys to the Exercises
Work Books
Graded Readers
Language Laboratory Exercises
Recordings of Conversation and Reading Passages
Picture Books

Present Day English for Foreign Students

E. Frank Candlin, B.A. (Hons.)

*Principal of the Oxford College of Further Education.
Formerly Head of the Department of
English, College of Advanced
Technology, Cardiff*

BOOK 3

UNIVERSITY OF LONDON PRESS LTD

SBN 340 09017 0

First published 1963

Third edition copyright © 1966 E. Frank Candlin
Second impression 1970
Illustrations copyright © 1963 University of London Press Ltd

University of London Press Ltd
St Paul's House, Warwick Lane, London EC4

Illustrations by Bill Burnard
Printed and bound in Great Britain by
Hazell Watson and Viney Ltd, Aylesbury, Bucks

CONTENTS

CONTENTS

PREFACE

THIS book completes the *Present Day English* Course, a series designed for teachers who are looking for class-books that will ease their task of lesson-planning and enable their students to make rapid progress in understanding, speaking, reading and writing everyday English.

Book Three continues the general plan developed in Books One and Two. Each Lesson begins with a reading passage dealing with the daily lives of the Brown family and their friends. A piece of conversation follows, so that similar material is treated colloquially and more formally in the same lesson, and there are comprehension questions covering both passages. Next come sentence-pattern drills illustrating points of grammar and usage, introduced by rather fuller explanatory notes than those in the earlier books, together with a list of new words and idioms and a plentiful collection of exercises based on the material of that and earlier Lessons. The composition exercises at the end of each Lesson are introduced by notes on the different kinds of written composition which the student needs to master either for his own use or in order to pass examinations.

The vocabulary includes (with a very few exceptions) the remaining 800 words of the 2,000 *General Service List of English Words* not already covered in Books One and Two, together with an additional 150 words required by the subject-matter of the reading passages. Phonetic transcripts are given for all new words and idioms after each Lesson, and again in the general vocabulary at the end. There is a list of the structures and teaching items exemplified in the sentence patterns. A reference index to the exercises will be found in Teacher's Book Three. Once again, the illustrations not only enliven the text but also provide further material for classroom exercises.

Students who have worked steadily through the three books of *Present Day English* should have mastered the main difficulties which beset the learner of English as a foreign language, and be ready to meet native speakers and writers on their own ground. Much widening of vocabulary will still remain to be done and many of the 'short cuts' in contemporary spoken English may still remain puzzling, but a sound foundation will have been laid on which the student can build by further reading and practice.

E. F. C.

LESSON 1

The Bishopton Flower Show

THE Flower Show is one of the important events of the year
in Bishopton. For weeks before the show all the keen gardeners are getting ready for the great day. Each one likes to
think himself (or herself) an expert in growing some particular vegetable, flower or fruit. And indeed, it is surprising
how often the same people win the prizes for the same things
every year.

Mr and Mrs Brown take a great interest in the show, for
they are both keen gardeners. They are always pleased to
offer advice to new gardeners, and they like to give plants and

cuttings to their gardening friends. For the past five years Mr Brown has won the first prize for the best collection of mixed vegetables; Mrs Brown goes in for flower arrangement, and she, too, has won first prize for three years running. This year she is afraid she will not win because there has been so much rain and wind during the summer that her flowers have not done so well as usual. But, as she says, it has been the same for everyone. Mr Brown hopes to win again this year, because vegetables do better than flowers in a wet summer.

On the evening before the show, or early the following morning, the competitors are busy arranging their fruit and vegetables and flowers on the tables in the big tent in which the show is held. They try to have everything ready for the show to open by eleven o'clock. Then the judges begin to walk slowly round looking at everything very carefully, and making notes in their programmes. Coloured cards are placed beside the winning collections of fruit, flowers or vegetables to show who has won first, second or third prize.

After the judging is over, Mrs Brown likes to go round to see how other people have done. The masses of flowers, roses, carnations and brightly coloured sweet-peas look very beautiful. The vegetables and fruit are interesting, too, and Mrs Brown gets her husband to explain why one has gained a prize and another, which seems to be as good, has not. They like to meet their friends, too, and talk about their gardens, and to invite each other to come and see how this or that is doing this year.

There are competitions for the making of jam and marmalade. Mrs Brown does not usually enter for these, but this year they had such a fine crop of fruit in their garden that she decided to try. She made some very good jam but she did not do well enough to win a prize. But as she managed to win first prize for her flower arrangement and second prize for her roses she didn't mind. Mr Brown was a little disappointed as he only won second prize for his vegetables. He was beaten by a man who had retired from work and was able to spend all day in his garden.

Although the Flower Show is so gay and friendly and full of colour, it is a little sad, too, for it comes at the end of the summer. All the vegetables and fruit have been gathered and stored away. Soon the rough winds of autumn and the cold of winter will kill the last roses. The gardening tools—the forks, the spades, the rake and the trowel—will be put away, and apart from scraping the snow away from the winter cabbages and covering the more tender plants with straw, the keen gardeners will have to put up with sitting by the fire, looking through the seed-lists and making their plans for next year. That is the great joy of gardening—there is always next year!

CONVERSATION
(At the Flower Show)

MRS BROWN: Well, John, your vegetables look very nice! Do you expect to win first prize?

MR BROWN: I shouldn't like to say; but I'm afraid not. The competition this year is pretty stiff. I want you to look at Dick Marshall's collection. None of mine are good enough to beat those.

MRS BROWN: I don't pretend to know much about prize vegetables but they certainly seem a fine lot. Do you expect him to win? Will they give the prize to a man who is almost a stranger? Surely we mustn't allow a new-comer to walk off with the most important prize in the show.

MR BROWN: The judges would prefer their friends to win,

but I'm afraid they won't allow that to make any difference to their decision. And I shouldn't wish them to do
so. Let's go and look at your flowers.

. . . . .

MR BROWN: Your flower arrangement looks very nice. I
think you ought to win.

MRS BROWN: I'm afraid to think about it. Just look at those
beautiful roses with the long stems, over there. I must
remember to get some of that colour next year. They're
almost without thorns, too.

MR BROWN: Your own look very well.

MRS BROWN: They are rather nice, aren't they? I'd love to
win a prize with them, especially as it's the first time I've
shown roses. You'll be able to have your revenge on
Dick Marshall next year, won't you?

MR BROWN: I don't think I shall be showing next year.

MRS BROWN: Oh, John! Surely you don't intend to give up
gardening.

MR BROWN: No, but the Committee want me to be one of the
judges. They invited me to join this year but the rules
won't allow anyone to be a competitor and judge at the
same time, so I had to refuse their request.

MRS BROWN: I think I should prefer you to go on showing.
Can't they get someone else to do the judging? What
would happen if they asked you to judge something I
was entering for and you gave the prize to me?

MR BROWN: They won't ask me to judge the flowers; I shall
do the vegetables. They only give the judging to someone who is supposed to be an expert. But I needn't do it
for more than one year.

MRS BROWN: All right, then. You should make a good judge—
you certainly know all the tricks of the trade. But promise not to give up gardening. I should be afraid you'd
get old and fat. Now help me to get a jug of fresh water for

these flowers—and be careful not to upset it, and spill the water on the tablecloth.

Mr Brown: Hurry up. The judges have started to walk round. We'll go and have some coffee, and exercise the virtue of patience. They don't like people to watch them while they are judging. That's why they have the show tent cleared of people before they start.

. . . . .

Mr Brown: Hello, Dick. Well done! That's a fine collection of vegetables you have there. I told my wife you'd win first prize with them. Where did you learn to grow vegetables like that? Those cauliflowers and cabbages are very fine indeed. I'm afraid I haven't anything as good as those.

Mr Marshall: Thanks very much—but I don't think I could teach you how to grow vegetables, John. I'm pleased, of course, but it wasn't easy for the judges. You've got a very good show, too. I hear you mean to give up showing next year.

Mr Brown (*with a laugh*): Yes, they've persuaded me to join the judges. I'll try to be fair to you, even though you have beaten me this year.

Mr Marshall: I don't think I need be afraid of your being jealous! Your wife did very well with her roses. I must ask her to give me some tips on how she does it.

Mr Brown: How are your fruit trees doing?

Mr Marshall: I shan't get much from them for a year or two, I'm afraid. The apple trees and pear trees are coming on well, but I've had trouble with the plum trees. I hope to do better with them next year. I think I shall have them looked at by an expert—or perhaps you'd come in and show me how to prune them properly.

Mr Brown: We had a wonderful crop of fruit this year. My

wife made a lot of jam. I persuaded her to put some of it
in the show, but she didn't get a prize.

Mr Marshall: I daresay you'll enjoy the jam, all the same.
My wife's waving to me, so I'm afraid I must go. We
hope to see you for a game of cards one evening before
long. We're very busy at the moment having our house
painted.

Mr Brown: Thanks. We shall enjoy a game.

COMPREHENSION QUESTIONS

1. What is 'a keen gardener'?
2. Why does Mrs Brown think she may not win a first prize this
   year?
3. Why is the Flower Show a sad as well as a happy event?
4. What do the keen gardeners do during the winter?
5. What does Mrs Brown mean by calling Mr Marshall 'a
   newcomer'?
6. Why won't Mr Brown try for a prize at the show next year?
7. Why doesn't Mrs Brown want her husband to give up gardening?
8. What other shows have you heard of besides flower shows?
9. Why do you think flower shows are popular in England?
10. What is the meaning of each of the following words as used
    in this passage?

    expert; competitor; crop; judge; prune.

SENTENCE PATTERNS

1.   The Infinitive

(a) A *to*-infinitive is used after certain verbs instead of a separate
    clause, where the subject of both is the same.

    Pattern: subject + verb + *to*-infinitive (+ object)

I didn't want to spend so much money on my holiday.
He decided to visit the Flower Show.
They all started to speak at once.
He hopes to get home before dark.
You ought to know better than that.

Other verbs followed directly by a *to*-infinitive are:

agree, arrange, begin, care, dare, determine, expect, fear, forget, intend, learn, like, manage, mean, need, offer, prefer, pretend, promise, refuse, remember, try, wish.

(b) An object and a *to*-infinitive are used after certain verbs.

Pattern: verb + object + *to*-infinitive

He taught the boys to speak English.
He invited his friends to call on him when they were in London.
I should like you to finish this work before you go.
We want you to enjoy yourselves.
Mr Robinson told Susan to be early every morning.
He asked us to tell him the time.

Other verbs followed by a noun or pronoun as object and a *to*-infinitive are:

advise, allow, choose, expect, get, hate, help, intend, love, mean, order, persuade, prefer, remind, warn.

(c) Some verbs are followed by a noun or pronoun as object and an infinitive without *to*.

Pattern: verb + object + infinitive

Let them come if they are ready.
Make him do his homework more carefully.
We watched him enter the empty house.
I saw him get off the bus.

Other verbs followed by an object and an infinitive without *to* are:

hear, notice.

(d) The expression *how to* followed by an infinitive is used after certain verbs.

Pattern: verb (+ object) + *how to* + infinitive

He did not know how to plant roses.
He showed the child how to ride a bicycle.
I will now explain how to play cricket.
He told us how to get free tickets for the theatre.

Other verbs:

advise, ask, decide, discover, find out, forget, hear, learn, remember, see, show, teach, think, understand.

2.
Indirect Object
(See Book Two, Sentence Pattern 13)

In sentences where the indirect object is short or unstressed, it is placed immediately after the verb and without a preposition.

Pattern: subject + indirect object + direct object

He taught them English.
The judge gave him the first prize.
The teacher asked John a question.

But when the indirect object is long, or is stressed because of its importance, it is placed after the direct object with *to* or *for* before it.

Pattern: subject + verb + direct object + *to* or *for* + indirect object.

To

The judges gave the prize to the best gardener at the show.
The dog brought the ball to his master.
He handed a book to every student in the class.
He promised a prize to anyone who could answer the question.
Susan wrote a letter to her friends in Switzerland.

Other verbs:

lend, offer, owe, pass, pay, read, refuse, sell, show, teach, tell.
For

He brought flowers for all the ladies at the wedding.
Tom is choosing a present for the girl he is going to marry.
You must save some sweets for the other children.
Mrs Brown is making a dress for her niece.
The artist was painting a picture for a rich American.

Other verbs:

buy, choose, cook, do, fetch, get, leave, order, write.

3.   Causative use of *Have*

The following uses of *have* were noted in Book Two (Sentence Pattern 6).

Have (Possessive)
    I haven't a pen.
Have (Customary)
    I have an egg for my breakfast every morning.
Have (Obligatory)
    He has to go to London on Monday.
Have (as Past Tense of *Must*)
    I had to go home early.
Have is also used to express the idea of *causing something to be done*, usually in response to some need.

I shall have my shoes mended next week.
He has his suit cleaned once a month.
She is having her hair done at the hairdresser's.
We must have this grass cut before it grows too long.
They have their house painted every year.

In casual conversation this causative use of *have* is often replaced by *get*:

We must get this tap mended.
For goodness sake get your hair cut, it's nearly down to your shoulders.

We must get these windows cleaned; I can hardly see
through them.

He has got himself elected to Parliament.

Notice that *get* is also used with, but not instead of, *have* in its Possessive and Obligatory uses.

I see Tom has got a new car.

I've got to go now, but I shan't be away for long.

4. *One, Ones*

Notice these uses of *one*:

(*a*) As a Number Adjective.

He took one book and left the other on the table.

I have only one brother.

There is only one biscuit left.

(*b*) As a Pronoun.

All these dogs are clever, but this is the cleverest (one).

We have looked at a lot of houses, but this is the nicest (one)
we've seen.

If you haven't an umbrella, we'll lend you one.

Will you have the black one or the blue one?

If you miss this train you'll have to catch the next (one).

We're still using the old chairs as the new ones haven't
arrived yet.

Keep the good ones and throw the bad ones away.

(*c*) Occasionally *one* is used as a pronoun in a numerical sense.

He sold all his houses except one.

You don't need all those pens; one is enough.

He had a bag of sweets and he gave the children one each.

(*d*) *One* as an indefinite pronoun.

One should be careful when crossing the road.

One often hears a foreigner make this mistake in English.

One cannot always believe what one reads in a newspaper.

Accidents happen when one least expects them.

5.
Afraid

Afraid has two meanings:

(*a*) To have fear.   (*b*) To have regret, to be sorry about something.

It is used in four constructions:

(*a*) followed by *of.*

> Is she afraid of the dark?
> You needn't be afraid of the dog.
> Are you afraid of being hurt?
> You need not be afraid of telling the truth.

(*b*) followed by an infinitive.

> She heard the noise, but she was afraid to go downstairs.
> The clerk was afraid to ask for more money.
> He was afraid to look over the edge of the cliff.
> He was afraid to jump into the rough sea.

(*c*) followed by a clause beginning with *that* (the *that* is generally left out in conversation).

> He was afraid (that) he would be late.
> I'm afraid (that) your English isn't very good.
> I'm afraid (that) he smokes too many cigarettes.
> I'm afraid (that) there's no tea left in the pot.

(*d*) with *so* and *not* to form short answers. (See Book One, Sentence Pattern 69.)

> Has it started raining? Yes, I'm afraid so.
> Has he lost all his money? Yes, I'm afraid so.
> I'm told you have failed your examination. I'm afraid so.
> Shall we be able to stay here another week? I'm afraid not.
> Is she getting any better? I'm afraid not.
> Can you lend me some money? No, I'm afraid not.

In these last two uses, *afraid* has the meaning of *to regret* or *to be sorry.*

NEW WORDS

advice (əd'vais)
carnation (kaː'neiʃn)
cauliflower ('koliflauə)
competition ('kompə'tiʃn)
competitor (kəm'petitə)
crop (krop)
cutting ('kʌtiŋ)
decision (di'siʒn)
expert ('ekspəɪt)
jam (dʒam)
judge (dʒʌdʒ)
list (list)
mass (mas)
newcomer ('njuːkʌmə)
patience ('peiʃəns)
plant (plaɪnt)
plum (plʌm)
rake (reik)
revenge (ri'vendʒ)
rose (rouz)
seed (siːd)
show (ʃou)
sort (soɪt)
stem (stem)
straw (stroɪ)
thorn (θoɪn)
tip (tip)
trick (trik)
trowel (traul)
virtue ('vəɪtjuɪ)
beat, beat, beaten (biɪt, biɪt, biɪtn)

collect (kə'lekt)
compete (kəm'piɪt)
disappoint (disə'point)
enter ('entə)
expect (iks'pekt)
gain (gein)
intend (in'tend)
judge (dʒʌdʒ)
mix (miks)
note (noun and verb) (nout)
persuade (pə'sweid)
pretend (pri'tend)
prune (pruɪn)
request (ri'kwest)
retire (ri'taiə)
scrape (skreip)
spill, spilled (spilt) (spil, spild, spilt)
upset, upset, upset (ʌp'set, ʌp'set, ʌp'set)
jealous ('dʒeləs)
keen (kiːn)
particular (pə'tikjulə)
proper ('propə)
rough (rʌf)
stiff (stif)
tender ('tendə)
properly ('propəli)
surely ('ʃoɪli, 'ʃuəli)
none (nʌn)

Idioms

to get ready for (tə 'get 'redi fə)

he likes to think himself an expert (hi 'laiks tə 'θiŋk himself ən 'ekspəːt)

to take an interest in (tə 'teik ən 'intrəst in)

to go in for (tə 'gou in fə)

for three years running (fə 'θriː 'jiəz 'rʌniŋ)

they haven't done so well (ðei 'havnt 'dʌn sou 'wel)

to put up with (tə put 'ʌp wið)

I shouldn't like to say (ai 'ʃudnt 'laik tə 'sei)

to have one's revenge (tə 'hav wʌnz ri'vendʒ)

the tricks of the trade (ðə 'triks əv ðə 'treid)

Well done! ('wel 'dʌn)

to come on well (tə 'kʌm on 'wel)

EXERCISES

A. *Complete these sentences by adding a phrase beginning with a to-infinitive:*

   1. They wanted . . .
   2. She tried . . .
   3. He promised . . .
   4. I refused . . .
   5. Did you remember . . . ?
   6. Has she offered . . . ?
   7. We didn't like . . .
   8. I don't intend . . .
   9. They haven't begun . . .
   10. Has he dared . . . ?

B. *Complete these sentences by adding a noun (or pronoun) and a to-infinitive:*

   1. Did you remind . . . early?
   2. I can't allow . . . without an umbrella.

3. Did he intend . . . the night at his house?
4. I told . . . very careful.
5. Nothing will persuade . . . to this suggestion.
6. Mr Brown taught . . . a car.
7. His teacher expected . . . his examination.
8. We asked . . . the carriage door.
9. I don't want . . . the train.
10. He invited . . . with him to London.

C. *Complete these sentences by adding a noun (or pronoun) and an infinitive without* to:

1. Did you hear . . . the door?
2. Let . . . the book if he wants it.
3. I watched . . . the money from the drawer.
4. Help . . . her luggage into the car.
5. I didn't notice . . . into the room.
6. She made . . . all the jugs with water.
7. The policeman saw . . . the house at nine o'clock.

D. *Complete these sentences with a phrase containing* how to *and an infinitive:*

1. We asked . . .
2. They discovered . . .
3. He could not find out . . .
4. Have you decided . . . ?
5. I always forget . . .
6. You must learn . . .
7. Can you remember . . . ?
8. Let me show . . .
9. The master taught . . .
10. It is difficult to understand . . .

E. *Use these verbs in sentences in which the indirect object follows the direct object (see Sentence Pattern 2):*

buy; choose; cook; do; fetch; lend; offer; owe; pass; pay.

F. *Rewrite these sentences, replacing the main verb by the verb* have:

    1. There is a cigarette lighter in my pocket.
    2. I drink a glass of beer with my lunch every day.
    3. She must stay at home this evening.
    4. She was told to be home before midnight.
    5. I shall send this suit to be cleaned next week.
    6. It is necessary to know a great deal about flowers if you are to be a judge at a flower show.
    7. He is wearing a carnation in his button-hole.
    8. I shall see that you are punished if you do that again.
    9. They made me show my passport before I went on board the steamer.
    10. We spend a holiday in the south of France nearly every year.

G. *Complete these sentences by adding* one, ones, some, any *as required:*

    1. I don't like these pink roses. Please give me . . . yellow . . .
    2. I have . . . cigarettes here. Will you have . . . ?
    3. Mrs Brown won . . . first prize and . . . second prize, but Mr Brown didn't win . . . prizes at all.
    4. . . . of those shoes has a hole in it. You need . . . new . . .
    5. . . . always feels uncomfortable if . . . hasn't . . . money.
    6. Can you lend me . . . matches, please? I had two boxes, but I gave . . . to John and left the other . . . at home.
    7. " . . . boys are clever, . . . are stupid," said the teacher, "and I usually get the stupid . . . !"
    8. There are . . . sweets in that box. You may have . . . each, but leave . . . for Joan and Mary.
    9. Are there . . . easy exercises in this lesson? I can only do the easy . . .
    10. Have you . . . apples? I want . . . nice, sweet . . .

H. *Write three sentences for each of the following patterns with* afraid *(Nine sentences in all):*

    (a) *afraid of*   (b) *afraid to*   (c) *afraid that*

I. *Put the given* -self *pronoun into the correct place in these sentences, and say whether each is reflexive, intensive or an indirect object:*

1. David enjoyed at the cinema yesterday. (himself)
2. I gave the parcel to the lady and not to her servant. (herself)
3. "I have bought a new coat," said Susan. (myself)
4. We will let David decide what he will do, as it is his birthday. (himself)
5. Look after in this crowd or you'll get hurt. (yourself)
6. The children dressed quickly and came down to breakfast. (themselves)
7. We did the work so we know it was well done. (ourselves)
8. I asked what I should do with the money if my horse won the race. (myself)
9. Find a seat and sit down. (yourself)
10. He killed when he found he had lost all his money. (himself)

J. *Put the word* since *or* for *into these sentences, and put the verb into the right tense:*

1. I (live) in this country . . . four years.
2. How much longer (you stay) here? . . . another three months.
3. I (not see) him . . . last December.
4. How many times (you visit) London . . . you (come) to England?
5. It is a long time . . . we last (see) him.
6. I (wait) for you . . . two hours.
7. I (am) here . . . last Tuesday.
8. They (go) to France . . . a fortnight's holiday.
9. How long that telephone (ring)? . . . five minutes?
10. You (met) Mr Brown lately? Not . . . last Monday.

K. *Put these sentences into the reported form:*

1. "I called on my friend when I was in London," she said.
2. "We wrote to him while he was on holiday," she said.
3. "I have finished my work," the boy told the master.
4. "Where have you been?" she asked the boy.
5. "It is the best book I have ever read," David told his father.
6. "How long have you been in England?" Susan asked the Greek boy.
7. "I have been here since October," the boy answered.
8. "The Browns have bought a new house in Bishopton," Mrs Morton told her friends.
9. "Have you bought a new car?" Susan asked Tom.
10. "We haven't played cards for a fortnight," Susan said to the rest of the family.

COMPOSITION
Writing a Letter to a Friend

In the notes on composition which follow most of the Lessons in this book we shall consider the different kinds of written composition which students will need to master either for their own use or in order to pass examinations. We begin with the personal letter.

The ability to write a clear and correct letter, either to a friend or on a matter of business, is something which everyone should acquire. Think of the number of occasions in life when we are judged by the letters that we have written: in applying for employment, in enquiring about rooms for a holiday, in writing to relatives living at a distance, in keeping up friendships with people who have moved to another town or whom we have met on holiday, and so on.

Study the following letter carefully:

15, Penzance Road,
Torquay,
Devon

16th August, 19—

Dear Joan,

What a wonderful time we are having down here! The weather has been kind to us and I don't think there has been a single day when the sun has not shone. We are all as brown as berries.

I had no idea Devonshire was so beautiful. The green grass, the red cliffs and sand and the blue sea shining in the sun, make a picture it will be difficult to forget. You would love the bathing and the scrambling among the rocks 'exploring'.

On Friday we went into Exeter, and at the end of this week we are going to pay a visit to Plymouth. We went to Exeter by train, and in places the line passes very close to the sea; it reminded me of the time we all went to Edinburgh by the east coast route. Do you remember?

Harry has been doing a lot of boating since we arrived— in fact it is hard to drag him away. He potters about all day in a dirty old jersey with some local boating enthusiasts he has picked up, and we see very little of him. He says he will write to you, but you must expect his letter when you get it!

Now Sonia wants me to come and play tennis, so I will say good-bye to you for the present. We shall be glad to hear from you if you have time.

Yours very sincerely,
Elizabeth

Notice these points:

1. The address, but *not* the name, of the sender, appears at the top of the paper on the right. This address should be properly punctuated.

2. A space is left between the address and the date, and between the date and the 'Dear Joan'. The date should be written in full, in the order: day, month, year. Note the comma before the year.

3. The 'Dear Joan' begins at the left-hand margin and is followed by a comma.

4. The first and all the following paragraphs begin a little to the right of the margin. Each paragraph begins a fresh line of thought.

5. The closing phrase begins about half-way across the page. 'Yours' has a capital letter (but no apostrophe) while the following word ('sincerely', 'faithfully', 'truly', etc.) does not take a capital. Note the comma.

6. There is no reason why a letter should be dull or formal because it is correctly written. An easy, conversational style should be used, and your reader should be made to feel that he or she is in your mind as you write. Remember, it is the little personal details which make what you are describing come to life.

In addressing a letter, you should be careful to space the name and address correctly on the envelope. No writing should appear above an imaginary line crossing the middle of the envelope. The space separating the beginning of the address from the left-hand side should be about equal to the space separating the end of the address from the right-hand side. Here are some examples. Be particularly careful with the punctuation, and notice that *Mr* and *Esq.* are never used together in the same address.

John Northcote, Esq.,
  15, Bristol Road,
    Castlebridge,
      Devon

Brian Jones, Esq., M.A.,
  'The Cedars,'
    Connaught Avenue,
      Stoneleigh,
        Essex

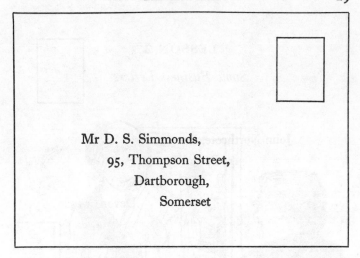

Mr D. S. Simmonds,
95, Thompson Street,
Dartborough,
Somerset

EXERCISES

1. Write a letter from Mary Brown to her friend Joan Morton in which Mrs Brown tells her friend about the Bishopton Flower Show.
2. Write a letter from the Secretary of the Flower Show Committee to Mr Brown, inviting him to act as judge at the next year's show.
3. Write a description of a garden you know well, in such a way that your reader will want to visit it.

LESSON 2

Some Business Letters

ALTHOUGH Susan is only twenty she is very good at her job and Mr Robinson, the Manager, has made her his personal secretary. He knows that he can trust her; if he tells her that he wants something done, he knows that she will do it well. He is hard to please, but he says she is the best secretary he has ever had because she is intelligent and quick to understand what is wanted—and she can spell!

Each morning, Susan goes through the letters that have

come in and separates the important ones from those that are easy to answer. The unimportant ones she pins together and puts in a drawer in her desk to deal with later, the others she takes in to Mr Robinson and he dictates the answers. He does not always tell her exactly what she must write but leaves it to her. Mr Robinson believes that people work best when they are given responsibility. Sometimes on Monday morning Susan finds that Mr Robinson has been into the office during the weekend and has dictated some letters on to a recording machine called a dictaphone. She then plays back the record and types the letters.

Susan is a very careful typist. She agrees with Mr Robinson that letters should be correctly arranged, neatly typed, and pleasant to read. There are other typists and clerks in the office, but the Manager has given orders that no one but Susan may do his letters. There is an accounts clerk who looks after all the money and accounts, a filing clerk who sees that all the letters and other papers are put away tidily so that they can be found easily. And there is a telephonist who works the switchboard. She takes all incoming telephone calls and puts them through to the different departments; she also deals with all outgoing calls.

Susan's firm does quite a lot of business with customers abroad. The Manager is always pleased when he gets an order from abroad because international trade is good for the country as well as for the firm. Britain is a small island with over fifty million people living in it, and unless the country can export manufactured goods to pay for cotton, wool, rubber, wood and—most important—the food it needs to import, her people would not be able to live.

Here are some examples of the sort of business letters with which Susan has to deal. Like her brother David, she is good at languages, and she often translates foreign letters before passing them on to Mr Robinson.

J. FERNANDEZ Y CÍA
General Import Merchants
BUENOS AIRES

6th April, 19—

Messrs James Robinson & Co. Ltd.,
London Road,
BISHOPTON, Surrey,
England

Dear Sirs,

We have frequent enquiries from firms in this country for men's lightweight suits, and your Company has been recommended to us as one from which we could obtain supplies at reasonable prices.

We should be pleased if you would quote for 400 suits in the usual sizes, stating probable delivery date from receipt of order.

An early reply would be appreciated.

Yours faithfully,

JAMES ROBINSON & CO. LTD.

BISHOPTON, Surrey

10th April, 19—

J. Fernandez y Cía,
General Import Merchants,
BUENOS AIRES, Argentine

Dear Sirs,

Thank you for your letter of 6th April in which you enquire about the supply of men's lightweight suits. I have much pleasure in enclosing our current price list, together with details of our terms of sale. Patterns of suitings which we think will meet your needs have been sent to you under separate cover today.

We have a long experience in working for overseas markets and can assure you that any orders you place with us will receive our most careful attention. We can promise shipment within three weeks of the receipt of your order and for the quantity you mention we could allow a discount of 5% on settlement within thirty days of receipt of invoice. Payment may be made in pounds sterling or dollars.

Yours faithfully,
James Robinson,
Managing Director

J. FERNANDEZ Y CÍA
General Import Merchants
BUENOS AIRES

20th April, 19—

Messrs James Robinson & Co. Ltd.,
London Road,
BISHOPTON, Surrey,
England

Dear Sirs,

Thank you for your letter of 10th April enclosing your current price lists and for the samples of men's suitings.

We wish to place an order for 400 men's suits in the sizes given in the enclosed list, and note your terms of 5% discount for settlement within thirty days of receipt of invoice.

Yours faithfully,

J. FERNANDEZ Y CÍA
General Import Merchants
BUENOS AIRES

2nd June, 19—

Messrs James Robinson & Co. Ltd.,
London Road,
BISHOPTON, Surrey,
England

Dear Sirs,

We thank you for the prompt delivery of our order No. 5126, and have pleasure in expressing our complete satisfaction with the quality of these suits.

We should, however, like to draw your attention to a mistake in your invoice, which has also now reached us. The terms of sale quoted in your letter of 10th April offered a discount of 5% for settlement within thirty days while your invoice shows a discount of only $2\frac{1}{2}$%. If you will be good enough to let us have a corrected invoice, we will pass the account for immediate payment.

Yours faithfully,

JAMES ROBINSON & CO. LTD.
BISHOPTON, Surrey

6th June, 19—

J. Fernandez y Cía,
General Import Merchants,
BUENOS AIRES, Argentine

Dear Sirs,

Thank you for your letter of 2nd June.

We are glad that you found the consignment of men's

suits to your satisfaction, and hope that we may have the pleasure of quoting for similar or other lines in the future.

A corrected invoice is enclosed, showing the agreed discount of 5%. Please accept our apologies for this mistake.

Yours faithfully,
James Robinson,
Managing Director

Writing business letters is not easy. The letter must say exactly what we mean: all facts and figures must be correct. The letter must be clearly expressed so that the reader can understand its meaning at a first reading. The letter must be polite, for the reader will judge a firm by the kind of letters it sends out. Last of all, a business letter should be short; it is a mistake to waste the time of a customer, for 'time is money'. These are four things to remember: a business letter should be correct, clear, polite and short.

Years ago, clerks used to use many formal phrases in business letters, so that their language became something quite different from ordinary English. You will find some old-fashioned people still writing like that even now. But today most business firms think it is better to write in the ordinary language that one man would use to another. This does not mean that business letters should be like conversation; they should be more formal than that, but they should be human.

CONVERSATION

(It is ten o'clock on Monday morning. Susan has brought the morning post into Mr Robinson's office)

SUSAN: Good morning, Mr Robinson.

MR ROBINSON: Hello, Susan. Well, what have you got for me this morning? Nothing too terrible, I hope.

SUSAN: It's rather a heavy post today, I'm afraid. There are several circulars and letters asking for price lists, but these I can deal with myself. The bills for payment and the cheques settling accounts I have passed to Mr Hardy. Here are the letters I think you ought to see.

MR ROBINSON: Good. I'm glad you're careful not to waste my time on things that other people can do. Let's go through the important ones, shall we?

SUSAN: This first one is from a firm of import merchants of Buenos Aires, enquiring about men's lightweight suits. It looks like a good opportunity for a new market there.

MR ROBINSON (*reading the letter*): M'm yes, it does, doesn't it? Send them our price list No. 3 and a set of patterns. I think we can promise them shipment within three weeks of receipt of order. Can I leave that one to you?

SUSAN: Yes, Mr Robinson. Now this one is a bit more difficult . . .

(*They discuss the other letters Susan has brought in*)

MR ROBINSON: Right—that's that. Anything more?

SUSAN: No, I don't think so.

MR ROBINSON: What's in the diary for today?

SUSAN: It's a busy day, I'm afraid. You have a Mr Warner coming to see you at eleven. He represents Deacon and Yardley of Bradford who want us to place a larger order with them for woollen cloth. Then you're lunching with the Mayor at the Town Hall to meet the President of the Board of Trade, who's opening the new motor-cycle factory. At three o'clock there's a meeting of the Works Council here and at four you've promised to go with Mr Hardy to look at some new office furniture they have at the Bishopton Furniture Stores. This evening there's the Staff Dance here. Will you and Mrs Robinson be coming?

MR ROBINSON: Well, I'm going to be pretty busy if I get through all that, aren't I? Yes, we shall be looking in at the dance, as usual. I suppose you will be coming with that young man of yours. By the way, someone was talking to me about him at dinner the other night.

SUSAN: Who was that, Mr Robinson?

MR ROBINSON: His Manager, Henry Carter. He said young Tom would do very well indeed—so long as he didn't allow running about with girls to get in the way of his work.

SUSAN: With *girls*, Mr Robinson?

MR ROBINSON: Running about with *a* girl, then. Now, what about some coffee?

SUSAN: It should be ready now. And next time I go out with Tom, Mr Robinson, I'll be careful to *walk*.

COMPREHENSION QUESTIONS

1. What are the qualities that make a good secretary?
2. What does Mr Robinson mean when he says:

   "People work best when they are given some responsibility"?

3. What is a dictaphone?
4. Why is the export trade so important to Great Britain?
5. Explain these phrases, used in Letter 1:

   the usual sizes;
   probable delivery date from receipt of order.

6. Explain these phrases, used in Letter 2:

   sent under separate cover;
   shipment within three weeks of the receipt of your order.

7. Explain this phrase used in Letters 2 and 3:

   5% discount for settlement within thirty days of receipt of invoice.

8. What are the qualities which make a good business letter?
9. What is the Board of Trade?
10. What is a Works Council?

SENTENCE PATTERNS

6.   Gerund in-*ing*—*Swimming*

The gerund is a verbal noun (part verb, part noun). It can be used as the subject or object to a verb or following a preposition.

(*a*) Gerund as Subject

Swimming is good exercise.
Making friends is not easy for some people.
Finding is keeping.
Living in London is expensive.
Spending money is easier than earning it.

(*b*) Gerund as Object

Mrs Brown enjoys cooking.
Mr Brown likes working in the garden.
Do you find living in London expensive?
He has started playing cricket.
Do you prefer swimming to playing tennis?

Among the verbs followed by a gerund in this way are:

begin, cannot help, dislike, enjoy, excuse, find, finish, forgive, go on, hate, intend, keep, like, love, mind, permit, prefer, regret, remember, risk, start, stop, try, watch.

(*c*) Gerund after a Preposition

Susan is tired of typing letters.
He makes a living by writing books.
He is good at driving a car.
She got fat by eating too many cakes.
They went straight home after leaving the theatre.
He washed his hands before having lunch.

(*d*) Gerund with Possessive Adjective

Because the gerund is a noun it can follow a possessive adjective.

> I dislike his answering so rudely.
> We will forgive your coming in late.
> I remember his asking about this.

But in conversation the object form of the pronoun is often used instead of the possessive adjective.

> I don't like him answering so rudely.
> We'll forgive you coming in so late—but don't do it again.
> I remember him asking me about this.

The object pronoun forms are always used after *see, hear, watch, notice.*

> Did you see him doing his homework?
> I watched them swimming.

7.   *That*-clauses

Notice that the *that* is sometimes left out.

(*a*) Verb + *that*-clause.

Here the *that*-clause acts as object to the verb.

> He agreed (that) we should share the cost.
> Mr Robinson believes (that) our foreign trade is important.
> We expected (that) he would be there.
> I hear (that) she is going to live abroad.
> Mind (that) you don't fall out of the window.

(*b*) Verb + Noun (or Pronoun) + *that*-clause

Here the *that*-clause is the direct object and the noun or pronoun is the indirect object to the verb.

> She promised her mother (that) she would be home early.
> I shall remind him (that) I lent him some money.
> We must teach him (that) success comes only from hard work.
> He told me (that) he was going to London for a week.

(c) *That*-clauses forming part of answers to questions are sometimes replaced by *so* or *not*.

> Will it rain tomorrow? I think so.
> > I hope not.
>
> Will this train be late? I expect so.
> > I hope not.
>
> Is he going to Oxford in October? I've heard so.
> > We believe so.
> > He says so.
> > I suppose so.

Sometimes the *so* is put at the beginning of the sentence.

> Tom has bought a new car. So I see (notice, believe, hear, suppose).

8.   Adjective and a *to*-infinitive

(a) The verbs *be, seem* and *appear* are often followed by an adjective and a *to*-infinitive in the pattern: subject + verb + adjective + *to*-infinitive.

> He was surprised to see us.
> I am sorry to hear you have been ill.
> We are glad to know he is doing well.
> He is sure to be home before five o'clock.
> I'm sorry to say we have no cigarettes.
> He was pleased to meet his old friend again.

Among the adjectives that are followed by a *to*-infinitive in this way are:

> *able, afraid, anxious, brave, careful, careless, certain, clever, cruel, delighted, disappointed, excited, glad, good, happy, kind, likely, lucky, nice, pleased, quick, ready, right, rude, sad, silly, sorry, stupid, sure, surprised, unable, wicked, willing, wise, wrong.*

(b) A *to*-infinitive also follows adjectives used with *too* and *enough*.

The patterns are:

subject + verb + *too* + adjective + *to*-infinitive;
subject + verb + adjective + *enough* + *to*-infinitive.

She is too young to go to school.
It is too early to go to bed yet.
We have been too busy to answer your letters.
It is too cold to swim in the sea.
It is easy enough to do this if you try hard.
Is it warm enough to go out without a coat?
Jack is old enough to go to school.
He is not tall enough to reach that high shelf.

9. ## Phrasal Verbs—*Put*

In Book Two we noticed the idiomatic use of some common verbs combined with adverbials to form Phrasal Verbs. Some further idiomatic expressions of this kind are given in this and the following Lessons. Care should be taken to distinguish between phrasal verbs that are used in informal speech only, and those that can also be used in more formal speech and in writing.

Put by

You should always put by for a rainy day.
She has a good deal of money put by.

Put down

Put these notes down in your book.

Put down to

I put his rudeness down to his youth, but I don't like it.

Put forward

The famous player put forward a suggestion for improving the rules of the game.

Put through

"I'll put you through in a moment," said the telephone operator.

Put together

He was clever at taking watches to pieces and putting them together again.

10. *What about ... ?*

A question beginning *What about ... ?* is asked when we wish to obtain someone's response to or comment on a proposal or suggestion. The proposal or suggestion may be added or left implied.

What about a drink? (Do you think we should have a drink now?)

What about Susan? (Shall we take her with us?)

What about the dog? (Do we wish, or shall we be allowed to take the dog with us?)

What about France? (What will the French government do about this matter?)

What about the children? (Will they be all right if we leave them alone in the house?)

What about wine? (Have we got enough?)

NEW WORDS

account (ə'kaunt)
apology (ə'polədʒi)
attention (ə'tenʃn)
cheque (tʃek)
circular(s) ('səːkjulə(z)
cloth (kloθ)
consignment (kən'sainmənt)
dealer ('diːlə)
delivery (di'livəri)
detail ('diːteil)
diary ('daiəri)
dictaphone ('diktəfoun)
discount ('diskaunt)
discussion (dis'kʌʃn)
dollar ('dolə)
drawer (droː)
enquiry (in'kwaiəri)

example (igz'aːmpl)
export ('ekspoːt)
figure ('figə)
import ('impoːt)
invoice ('invois)
mayor ('meə)
merchant ('məːtʃənt)
million ('miljən)
opportunity ('opə'tjuːniti)
pattern ('patən)
payment ('peimənt)
per cent (pə'sent)
person ('pəːsn)
pin (pin)
president ('prezidənt)
quantity ('kwontiti)
reason ('riːzn)

receipt (ri`si:t)
reply (ri`plai)
representative (repri`zentətiv)
sample (`sa:mpl)
satisfaction (satis`fakʃn)
settlement (`setlmənt)
shipment (`ʃipmənt)
staff (sta:f)
suiting (`sju:tiŋ)
switchboard (`switʃbo:d)
telephonist (tə`lefənist)
term (tə:m)
typist (`taipist)
week-end (`wi:k`end)
apologise (ə`polədʒaiz)
appreciate (ə`pri:sieit,
   ə`pri:ʃieit)
assure (ə`ʃuə, ə`ʃo:)
bear, bore, borne (beə, bo:,
   bo:n)
complete (kəm`pli:t)
correct (kə`rekt)
deal, dealt, dealt (di:l, delt,
   delt)
deliver di`livə)
dictate (dik`teit)
discuss (dis`kʌs)
enquire (iŋ`kwaiə)
file (noun and verb) (fail)
line (lain)
manufacture (manju`faktʃə)
obtain (əb`tein)
place (pleis)
quote (kwout)
reach (ri:tʃ)
reply, replied (ri`plai, ri`plaid)

represent (repri`zent)
settle (`setl)
spell, spelt (spelled) (spel,
   spelt, speld)
state (steit)
supply, supplied (noun and
   verb) (sə`plai, sə`plaid)
translate (trans`leit)
waste (weist)
complete (kəm`pli:t)
correct (kə`rekt)
current (`kʌrənt)
exact (ig`zakt)
express (iks`pres)
frequent (`fri:kwənt)
human (`hju:mən)
immediate (i`mi:diət)
immense (i`mens)
incoming (`inkʌmiŋ)
intelligent (in`telidʒənt)
international (intə`naʃnl)
lightweight (`laitweit)
neat (ni:t)
ordinary (`o:dinri)
outgoing (`autgouiŋ)
overseas (`ouvə`si:z)
personal (`pə:snl)
probable (`probəbl)
prompt (prompt)
reasonable (`ri:znəbl)
responsible (ris`ponsəbl)
similar (`similə)
exactly (ig`zaktli)
neatly (`ni:tli)
probably (`probəbli)

EXERCISES

A. *Put the verb in brackets in these sentences into the correct form:*

1. (Dig) in the garden can be very hard work.
2. (Live) in the country is healthier than (live) in the town.
3. I can't help (wonder) where he gets all his money.
4. Most people dislike (listen) to long speeches.
5. You need not go on (work) after you are sixty-five.
6. Mrs Brown hates (wait) for buses.
7. She kept (run) to the door to see if the postman had come.
8. Do you mind (open) the window, please?
9. I don't remember (see) him here before.
10. Please stop (interrupt) me; it's very rude.

B. *Put the verbs in brackets into the correct forms:*

1. She went away without (say) goodbye.
2. I am quite used to (live) by myself.
3. The best way to learn a language is by (live) in the country where it is spoken.
4. He is clever at (talk) himself out of difficulties.
5. Bob has no idea what he wants to do after (leave) school.
6. Please wipe your shoes before (come) into the house.
7. I was nearly run over while (cross) the street this morning.

C. *Put the pronouns and verbs in brackets into the correct forms:*

1. I dislike (you) (arrive) late every morning.
2. Excuse (I) (interrupt) but I think you have made a mistake.
3. I saw (he) (cross) the street, but he was too far away to speak to.
4. We could hear (she) (sing) in the next room.
5. If you will forgive (I) (say) so, you're not a very good cook.
6. They watched (we) (swim) but they would not come into the water.
7. I remember (he) (ask) us the way to the station.

8. We noticed (he) (look) pale during the lecture, but we didn't know he was really ill.

D. *Complete these sentences with a* that-*clause as object to the verb:*
   1. They suggested . . .
   2. He expected . . .
   3. I suppose . . .
   4. She hoped . . .
   5. Tom thinks . . .
   6. We warned him . . .
   7. Susan told her mother . . .
   8. Mr Brown promised David . . .
   9. Parents should teach their children . . .
   10. I reminded him . . .

E. *Answer these questions with a* so *or* not *sentence containing the verb in brackets:*
   1. Will you be away from home for long? (expect)
   2. Do you think it will rain all day tomorrow? (hope)
   3. Has Tom bought a new car? (believe)
   4. It is Thursday today? (think)
   5. Tom won't be going to Birmingham tomorrow now his new car has not arrived. (suppose)

F. *Write sentences in which these adjectives are followed by a* to-infinitive:
   Example: Children are often afraid to go upstairs in the dark.

   able; afraid; anxious; brave; careful; careless; clever; cruel; glad; good; happy; lucky; unable.

G. *Rewrite these sentences, using* too *or* enough *followed by an infinitive:*
   1. She is young; she cannot go to school.
   2. You are not very tall; you cannot reach that high shelf.
   3. You are quite good at English; you can do this exercise.

4. It is very warm; I don't want to play cricket today.
5. This woman is so old that she cannot be left to live alone.
6. He is so rich that he could buy the largest house in the town.
7. It is late; we shall not catch that train now.
8. That case is very big; it will not go into the car.
9. It was so wet we couldn't go out.
10. He is very silly; he will believe anything.

H. *Write sentences, other than those given in the Sentence Patterns, containing the following phrasal uses of* put:

put by; put down; put down to; put forward; put in for; put off; put out; put through; put together; put up with.

I. *Write out in full the question or suggestion which might be expressed by the following:*
(*See Sentence Pattern* 10)

1. What about another game?
2. What about your work?
3. What about the Browns?
4. What about South Africa?
5. What about your bad cold?
6. What about the police?
7. What about Aunt Anne?
8. What about a picnic by the river?
9. What about finding a hotel?
10. What about a holiday?

J. *Use these verbs in sentences followed by a* to-*infinitive:*
(*See Sentence Pattern* 1)

agree; arrange; care; determine; fear; learn; manage; mean; need; remember.

K. *Use these verbs in sentences in which the indirect object follows the direct object:*

get; leave; order; read; refuse; show; teach; tell; write.

COMPOSITION
Business Letters

It is not only those who work in an office who should know
how to write a good business letter. Everyone has to write
to individuals or firms from time to time on matters of business, and it is surprising how few people can do this well.
The difficulty becomes much greater when the language in
which the letter is to be written is not one's own.

Special phrases—almost a special language—were used
years ago for business letters in English, but this 'business
English' has now disappeared from the letters of all big
business houses, and its place has been taken by a simple,
direct style which is friendly and natural without becoming
conversational.

A business letter should be:

Clear. The reader must be in no doubt about the writer's
exact meaning.

Brief. Time is money in business. Leave out everything
which does not help the matter in hand. Choose words
carefully, and use no more words than are necessary.

Polite. Write the kind of letter you yourself would like to
receive. Rudeness is often understandable, but it is seldom
good business.

Correct. Details such as facts, figures, dates, sums of money
must be exact and the spelling, punctuation and word usage
must be correct.

The business letter has a pattern which must be followed.
This is shown in the examples given on pp. 32-5. Where a
business letter is being written by a private person from his
home address, the heading and date are the same as in a
personal letter; a business letter sent out by a firm has the
firm's name and address printed at the top. The writer begins

with the date on the right, and this is written in full. The address of the person to whom the letter is to be sent appears next, on the left, and has exactly the same form as the address on the envelope. 'Messrs' is used in addressing a firm whose name contains the name of an individual (e.g. Messrs James Robinson & Co. Ltd.) but not otherwise (e.g. The Imperial Tobacco Co.). 'Dear Sirs' is used when addressing a company; 'Dear Sir' when addressing an individual. 'Yours faithfully' is the usual ending for a business letter.

The first paragraph states what the letter is about, and refers to any previous letter or letters which may have been written on the same subject. The following paragraphs add necessary details. The last paragraph usually states what the writer thinks should be the next step in the matter.

EXERCISES

1. While visiting London from your home in Manchester you bought a table-lamp in a London store. You paid for the lamp and the firm agreed to post it to you. When the lamp arrives you find it is badly damaged. Write a letter of complaint to the store.
2. Write a letter from an import merchant in London to a manufacturer of shoes in Milan, asking them to send their price lists and terms of sale.
3. Write the Italian firm's reply.

LESSON 3

A Motoring Tour of England—1

SUSAN and Tom have decided to spend part of their holiday this summer going for a motor-tour through the South of England. There are many interesting places they have not been to before, so they will not hurry. If the weather is fine, they think they will have a very pleasant holiday.

Tom is looking forward to taking his new car on its first run. It is a fast and comfortable car, and was rather expensive. But Tom did not pay all the cost of the car at once: he put down part of the money and is paying the rest month by month. This is called 'hire purchase'. In the past few weeks Tom has taught Susan to drive, and she is to take her driving test next week. If she passes the test, she will take out a driving licence, and she can then take over some of the driving on their holiday. Tom is a good practical mechanic, so he can do most of his own repairs.

They have enjoyed themselves planning the tour and choosing which places they should visit. There are one or two places they had decided they must include either because they had friends there, or because the places were interesting. They wanted to visit David in Oxford and hoped to see a play at the Royal Shakespeare Theatre in Stratford. Tom wanted to call on a friend who was manager of a factory near Cardiff and Susan had an invitation to spend a day or two with a schoolfriend who was teaching in a school in Cambridge. So they planned their tour to include these places.

At last the day came for the holiday to begin. They had chosen the middle of June because this is when the days are longest and the weather is most likely to keep fine. They set

off from Bishopton after breakfast, the sun shining as brightly as the paint on Tom's new car. Their first stopping-place was to be Windsor. Tom was anxious that they should avoid the heavy traffic in Central London so they circled round through Guildford and arrived at Windsor in time to visit the Castle before lunch.

The Round Tower of the Castle could be seen on its high hill long before they reached the small busy market-town that has grown up around its ancient walls. The Queen does not usually stay at Windsor except at Easter, so the Royal

Standard was not flying from the tower. Susan and Tom walked round the State Rooms with their wonderful collection of pictures; they saw the splendid Waterloo dining-room, its walls lined with pictures of English soldiers of the early nineteenth century. They visited the beautiful fifteenth-century St. George's Chapel, where the kings and queens of England are now buried, and they climbed the Round Tower to see the fine view. Across the River Thames they could see the Chapel of Eton College, the most famous of all English Public Schools.

After lunch at a hotel in Windsor they drove the forty miles to Oxford. Susan's brother David is in his first year at the University in Oxford, and they had arranged to meet him there for tea. Entering Oxford from the east, they passed the large Morris Motors factory, which has now become part of a larger group called B.M.C. (British Motor Corporation). On the other side of the road they saw the equally large factories of the Pressed Steel Company, which among other things makes bodies for a number of car manufacturers.

At last, crossing the beautiful Magdalen Bridge, they entered that older Oxford which has been called 'the city of dreaming spires'. David is at the Queen's College, which faces on to the High Street. Having parked their car in a side street, they went through the little gate of Queen's, into the peaceful green of its garden, where the street noises could be only faintly heard. Susan was surprised that it was so quiet. Passing from the noisy traffic into the silence of the College grounds seemed like moving from one world into another.

David was waiting for them in his rooms and they spent a pleasant hour over tea while he told them about his life at the University. A friend from the same staircase came in and the time passed very pleasantly. They were to stay at the ancient 'Mitre Hotel' nearby and after dinner they had arranged to go with David to see a comedy at the Playhouse Theatre.

The following morning they spent visiting some of the other colleges: splendid Christ Church set in its wide quadrangles; beautiful Magdalen surrounded by its deer-park beside the river; ancient Merton in its narrow stone-paved street unchanged since the Middle Ages; Wadham and Worcester with their lovely gardens; stately Balliol; New College which was new five hundred years ago, and Jesus College which, because it has remained small, has kept that community spirit which some of the larger colleges are in danger of losing.

After lunch, Tom and Susan drove out of Oxford on the road to the West, turning aside for an hour at Woodstock to visit Blenheim Palace, the enormous country house given by the nation to the first Duke of Marlborough as a reward for his victories. They spent the rest of the day among the grey stone villages in the Cotswolds, lunching in the oak-beamed dining-room of an ancient inn in Burford, and having tea in an old-world garden in Broadway, perhaps the loveliest of all the Cotswold villages.

A pleasant drive as the soft evening sunlight began to fade brought them to the City of Bath, that splendid monument to the elegance and good taste of the eighteenth century. The story of Bath goes back to the days when the Romans ruled Britain, for it takes its name from the Roman baths which can still be seen in the heart of the city. There is a fine church which was built by the monks in the Middle Ages, and is still called Bath Abbey, although there have been no monks there since the sixteenth century. But the glory of Bath belongs to the eighteenth century, when all the wealthy and fashionable people in England gathered here to 'take the waters' as a cure for rheumatism and many other illnesses, and to enjoy the brilliant social life of this elegant city.

Today Bath is a quiet town, the warm yellow stone of its squares and terraces sleeping in the sunlight. But once a year in June, during the Bath Festival of Music, Drama and the Arts, the ancient city comes to busy life once more and for a short time it is again one of the social and artistic centres of England.

CONVERSATION
(In David's rooms at Oxford)

SUSAN: Well, David. You seem to have made yourself very comfortable. I like the pictures on the walls.

DAVID: Actually, they're framed posters. I took them over from the man who had these rooms before me. Sit down and have some tea. This is the most comfortable chair, Tom. Susan, you can sit by the table and pour the tea. It's no use having a woman about the place unless she's useful, is it, Tom?

TOM: Charm can play a part too, David; although as a brother you wouldn't see it in that way. How are you enjoying Oxford?

DAVID: Immensely. There's so much happening that it's difficult to fit everything in. I'm afraid I haven't done as much work as I should—but the thought of it doesn't keep me awake at night. There's always the holidays.

SUSAN: David, where do you keep the sugar?

DAVID: Here it is. All the other stuff you want is in that cupboard. And here are some cakes and biscuits. Can you manage?

CHRISTOPHER: Can I come in?

(David's friend, Christopher Dean, comes in)

CHRISTOPHER: I heard the sound of cups and saucers and

"Chris," I said to myself, "tea—without having to make it!" Oh, visitors?

DAVID: Come in, Chris. Susan, this is Christopher Dean—my sister Susan, and her fiancé, Tom Smith. Chris has the rooms above these—and keeps me awake half the night with his record-player. Give him some tea, Susan.

TOM: What part of the country do you come from?

CHRISTOPHER: Nottingham.

SUSAN: That's where they make bicycles, isn't it?

CHRISTOPHER: Bicycles and cigarettes, lace, boots and shoes, silk stockings, and all the things you can buy in the chemist's shop. A fine city, Nottingham.

DAVID: Go on, Chris, tell them it has the finest cricket ground in the country at Trent Bridge.

SUSAN: We shan't be going through Nottingham, shall we, Tom?

DAVID: They're off on a tour of English beauty spots, Chris. Tom's got a new car, and he's quite taken up with it— dividing his attention between it and Susan. I leave you to guess which is winning.

CHRISTOPHER: I expect you've planned to by-pass all the big industrial towns like Nottingham. But you'll be making a mistake. These are the places where you'll find the real England, where life is a serious business in which people have to work hard for a living. And there's fun and enjoyment there, too; but people don't have to go out and buy it, they make it for themselves. Life's too easy in the South of England—it makes people soft.

DAVID: Now he's off! He'll keep on for ever if we let him. Soon he will start to quote from *Room at the Top*, or *Saturday Night and Sunday Morning*.

TOM: Or *A Taste of Honey*, if that's not too sweet for his sour opinion of us Southerners.

SUSAN: Or more likely *Look Back in Anger*. No, we mustn't

tease him. Chris, you're perfectly right. And I promise you that if we are anywhere near Nottingham we'll pay it a visit. More tea, anyone?

DAVID: Susan the sweet-tempered peace-maker! You've kept that side of your character hidden from me, dear sister.

SUSAN: Do be your age, David! Are you going to live in the nursery all your life?

TOM: When I hear you two arguing, I sometimes wonder . . .

DAVID: And well you may! After all, *I* bring out the best in her.

(*At which point Susan throws a cushion at him*)

TOM: We're going to the theatre this evening. Would you like to join us for a drink afterwards, Chris? Shall we say ten o'clock in the 'Mitre'? Now David, I think we must go. We mustn't keep you two from your work any longer. Thanks for the tea.

SUSAN: See you both later. Good-bye for now. And don't be late!

COMPREHENSION QUESTIONS

1. What is 'hire purchase'?
2. What is a 'driving test'?
3. For what reasons did Tom and Susan decide to include the following places in their tour:

    (*a*) Oxford; (*b*) Stratford; (*c*) Cardiff; (*d*) Cambridge?

4. Why did they decide to take their holiday in June?
    (Add one more reason to those given in the passage.)
5. The Queen usually spends Easter at Windsor. She has two other houses which she visits regularly. Where are they and when does she visit them?
6. Name two other famous collections of pictures in England.
7. What is meant by the term 'Public School' in England?

8. What is Oxford famous for, besides its university?
9. What is meant by the term 'community spirit'?
10. Explain the term 'one of the social and cultural centres of England'.

SENTENCE PATTERNS

11.   Uses of the Verb *Be*

(*a*) To express a state:

> Mr Brown is in London today.
> Susan is a pretty girl.
> He was the best footballer in his school.
> I shall be in England for another six months.

(*b*) As an auxiliary, to form:

(i) continuous tenses—with the present participle.

> She is learning English.
> He was waiting for a bus.
> I shall be working all the evening.

(ii) the passive—with the past participle.

> The book was taken from the library.
> This bell is rung every evening.
> This chicken will be cooked for tomorrow's dinner.

(*c*) With *Do* in the imperative to express persuasion or emphasis:

> Do be quiet, please.
> Do be careful.
> Do be quick; we shall miss the train.

(*d*) To denote that an arrangement has been made (present and past tenses only):

> We were to start our journey on July 5th.
> I was to meet her in London.
> He is to arrive on the 5.30 plane from Paris.
> We are to have a picnic this afternoon.

(e) As an imperative, where the person giving the order or prohibition does not expect it to be questioned:

> You are to be home before it gets dark!
> You are to do exactly as I tell you!
> You are to go straight home!
> You are not to talk to strangers!
> She is not to go there again!

12.   Adjectives followed by *that*-clause
          (See Sentence Pattern 7)

The verbs *be, seem, appear* may also be followed by an adjective denoting awareness or feeling, and a *that*-clause.
Pattern: subject + verb + adjective + *that*-clause
The *that* is usually omitted in conversation:

> He was sure (that) they would miss the train.
> I am certain (that) I have seen him before.
> I am glad (that) I met him.
> We are pleased (that) you have won the prize.
> They were surprised (that) their friends had already arrived.
> David was afraid (that) he would be late.

Other adjectives used thus are:

> *anxious, careful, delighted, disappointed, sorry, worried.*

13.   *Keep*

Keep is a word frequently used in colloquial English. Here are some of its meanings:

(a) *To look after*

> Mr Johnson keeps a hotel in Manchester.
> The Smiths have a large garden, and they keep chickens.
> My friend keeps a baker's shop.
> Keep this seat for me; I shall be back in a minute.

(b) To stay, continue

Will it keep on raining all the morning?
She keeps asking me for money.
Keep off the grass.

(c) To have something and not to give it up

May I keep this?
'Finding is keeping.'
(You may) keep the change.

(d) To store

Where do you keep your car?
Do you keep your money in the bank or at home?
We never keep money in the house.

(e) To remember, take notice of

The English keep Christmas and the Scots keep New Year.
You should always keep your promise.

(f) To stop, prevent, hold back

That noise keeps me from sleeping.
She kept me talking for half an hour.
They kept us up till after midnight.
He keeps her out too late at night.

14. Phrasal Verbs—*Take*

Take along

I'll take you along with me if you promise to be quiet.
I shall have to take him along to the doctor if he doesn't get better.

Take down

Take this down in your note-books.
She took down the telephone message in shorthand.

Take for

What do you take me for?
I was taken for a sales assistant when I was in the stores yesterday.

Take over

This shop has been taken over by a big firm.
I'll take over now. You have a rest.
When does the new manager take over?

Take to

He may be a nice person, but I didn't take to him.
Bob has taken to staying out late at night.
Now that he has taken to golf I see very little of him.

Take up with

He's entirely taken up with his work lately.
He is so taken up with fishing he can talk about nothing else,

15. *Here he is*

Here and *there* are used in exclamations. When the subject is a personal pronoun, the subject comes before the verb; when the subject is not a personal pronoun, the subject comes after the verb.

Here we are.	Here comes the bride.
There they go.	There goes the bus.
There it is.	Here's your coat.
Here she comes.	Here are the scissors you're looking for.
	There goes the bell! We must hurry.

NEW WORDS

agent ('eidʒənt)
anger ('aŋgə)
art (aːt)
beam (biːm)
by-pass ('baipaːs)
chapel ('tʃapl)
charm (tʃaːm)
comedy ('komədi)
community (kə'mjuːniti)

corporation (koːpə'reiʃn)
court (koːt)
deer ('diə)
elegance ('eligəns)
fame (feim)
festival ('festivl)
fiancé(e) (fi'aːnsei)
fun (fʌn)
glory ('gloːri)

group (gruːp)
hire purchase ('haiə 'pəːtʃəs)
honey ('hʌni)
illness ('ilnis)
industry ('indəstri)
lace (leis)
licence ('laisəns)
mechanic (mi'kanik)
monk (mʌŋk)
monument ('monjumənt)
nation ('neiʃn)
nursery ('nəːsri)
opinion (ə'pinjən)
poster ('poustə)
rest (rest)
reward (ri'woːd)
rheumatism ('ruːmətizm)
ruler ('ruːlə)
society (sə'saiəti)
spire (spaiə)
spirit ('spirit)
staircase ('steəkeis)
standard ('standəd)
state (steit)
temper ('tempə)
test (test)
tour (tuə)
victory ('viktri)
view (vjuː)
wealth (welθ)
avoid (ə'void)
bury, buried ('beri, 'berid)
cure (noun and verb) (kjuə)

fade (feid)
float (flout)
guess (ges)
hire (haiə)
include (in'kluːd)
mention ('menʃn)
remain (ri'mein)
surround (sə'raund)
tease (tiːz)
test (test)
actual ('aktjul, 'aktjuəl)
ancient ('einʃnt)
artistic (aː'tistik)
brilliant ('briljənt)
elegant ('eligənt)
enormous (i'noːməs)
equal ('iːkwəl)
faint (feint)
industrial (in'dʌstriəl)
likely ('laikli)
modern ('modən)
practical ('praktikl)
public ('pʌblik)
real (riəl)
social ('souʃl)
soft (soft)
sour (sauə)
stately ('steitli)
wealthy ('welθi)
actually ('aktjuli)
around (ə'raund)
aside (ə'said)
equally ('iːkwəli)

Idioms

to look forward to (tə luk ˈfɔːwəd tə)
to put down the money (tə ˈput daun ðə ˈmʌni)
to set off (tə ˈset ˈof)
to park a car (tə ˈpaːk ə ˈkaɪ)
it takes its name from (it ˈteiks its ˈneim frəm)
to take the waters (tə ˈteik ðə ˈwɔːtəz)
to fit everything in (tə ˈfit evriθiŋ ˈin)
he's quite taken up with it (hiːz kwait ˈteikn ˈʌp wið it)
I leave you to guess (ai ˈliːv ju tə ˈges)
to pay it a visit (tə ˈpei it ə ˈvizit)
Do be your age! (ˈduː ˈbiː jər ˈeidʒ)
And well you may! (ənd ˈwel ju ˈmei)
After all (ˈaːftər ˈɔːl)

EXERCISES

A. *How is the verb* to be *used in each of these sentences?* (*Sentence Pattern* 11.)

1. Do be good children.
2. The college is to move into its new building next year.
3. Edinburgh is the capital of Scotland.
4. Susan was listening to the radio and David was reading a book.
5. Brian is to go to bed at nine o'clock.
6. They were to stay with some friends in Paris for a fortnight.
7. You are not to visit those people again.
8. Tom will soon be the manager of a factory.
9. This castle was built in the Middle Ages.
10. I can't come to the theatre; I shall be working all the evening.

B. *Complete these sentences by adding a* that-*clause. Place a bracket round* that, *if you think it could be left out.*

1. I'm sorry . . .
2. They were disappointed . . .
3. I am very worried . . .
4. We are all anxious . . .
5. Susan is delighted . . .
6. Be careful . . .
7. David was surprised . . .
8. Mrs Brown will be pleased . . .
9. Mr Robinson was sure . . .
10. I'm glad . . .

C. *Re-write these sentences, using* keep *instead of the main verb in each:*

1. I do not want you to return that book to me.
2. Mr Jones has a greengrocer's shop in Bishopton.
3. The rain stopped me going out all day yesterday.
4. Will you tell me where the sugar is?
5. English people do not set aside Sunday as a day of rest as they used to do.
6. You must not interrupt the lesson so often.
7. Many country people have pigs in their back gardens, even though they are not farmers.
8. We can't make her stay here any longer if she wants to go.
9. The boy cut the apple in two but took the larger part himself.
10. She asked me over and over again where I lived.

D. *Write sentences, other than those given in the Sentence Patterns, containing the following phrasal uses of* take.

take along; take down; take for; take in; take on; take out; take over; take to; take up; take up with.

E. *Replace the following sentences by exclamations using* Here *or* There (*Sentence Pattern* 15):

1. They have got here at last.
2. The bus is just coming.
3. The whistle has just sounded.
4. I have found the matches.
5. I can see her hiding behind that tree.
6. He has lost his last chance of winning the race.
7. The Queen is now arriving.
8. He is just disappearing from sight.
9. We have now reached our destination.
10. Be careful. The police are coming.

F. *Write sentences in which these adjectives are followed by a to-infinitive:*

kind, nice, pleased, right, rude, silly, sorry, stupid, sure, surprised.

G. *Use these verbs in sentences followed (a) by an indirect object placed before the direct object, and (b) by an indirect object placed after the direct object:*

buy; cook; give; leave; lend; make; pass; promise; save; show.

H. *Put the words in brackets into their correct forms (Sentence Pattern 6):*

1. (Dance) is pleasant, and very good exercise.
2. Mr Brown enjoys (drive) a car.
3. He said good-bye before (leave) the house.
4. I remember (they) (vote) against me in the last election.
5. We watched (she) (cross) the street with a basket in her hand.
6. Where did you go after (call) on Mrs Jones?
7. Do you mind (open) the window, please?
8. (Find) anyone in this crowd is almost impossible.
9. It's no use (ask) me, because I don't know.

10. Please forgive (I) (interrupt) but can you tell me the time please?

I. *Put these sentences into the passive (Book Two, Sentence Patterns 15, 16, 17):*

1. Someone found these gloves in the garden.
2. People often call the County of Kent 'the Garden of England'.
3. They turned down his application for a gun licence.
4. You can buy a television licence at any post office.
5. We finished all the painting and decorating yesterday.
6. No one has ever spoken to me like that before.
7. In some countries women instead of men work in the fields.
8. The Romans built this wall.
9. Has anyone found those children yet?
10. No one has done any repairs to this house since someone built it.

J. *Put the verbs in brackets into the correct tense (Book Two, Sentence Pattern 21):*

1. No one may go home until he (finish) his work.
2. David does not know what he will do for a living when he (leave) university.
3. You can have this book as soon as I (finish) it.
4. We (call) to see you when we come back from Austria.
5. I (not forget) you while you are away.
6. Make hay while the sun (shine).
7. David will say good-bye to his friends before they (go) on holiday.
8. I (not sleep) until I know he is safe.
9. We will go to the dining-car for lunch after the train (leave) Crewe.
10. Mr Brown will buy a cottage in the country as soon as he (retire).

K. *Put the correct preposition into these sentences:*

1. The train reached Paddington . . . exactly five o'clock.
2. The result was very different . . . what he had expected.
3. I have not been to London . . . last November.
4. I have lived in England . . . four years.
5. The aeroplane flew . . . the town.
6. The small boy ran . . . the road to his friend . . . the other side.
7. It is easier going . . . the mountain than coming . . .
8. The car came . . . the corner and pulled . . . . . . the door . . . the hotel.
9. I met him . . . the station and took him . . . some friends who lived . . . a small village not far . . . the lake.
10. He took . . . his watch, looked . . . it, and put it back . . . his pocket.

COMPOSITION
Telling a Story

We all like listening to stories, and the person who is good at telling stories will always be a popular member of any company. The art of good story-telling covers more than just making up exciting adventures: it includes telling about the doings of living people or famous men and women of the past, about your own travels and adventures and experiences, about the books you have read and the films you have seen. Practising the art of story-telling will help you to think clearly, to sort out and arrange your ideas, to express yourself and to use language effectively.

When you are setting out to tell a story you must first think out the events clearly in your own mind and arrange them in the right order. Story-tellers who interrupt the flow of the story to put in points that have been left out earlier soon lose our attention. Do not give long explanations at the beginning, but start the story at once and keep it moving all the time. Any necessary explanations or descriptions can come in by the way.

Try to see in your own mind the people taking part in the story and the places where events happen; you cannot hope that they will come alive for your hearers or readers unless you can see them clearly yourself. Instead of describing people, make these people do or say things which show what they are like. Some conversation will help, for it gives reality to the story and adds interest and variety.

Be careful not to put in too many details. We all know the tiresome person who tells even the simplest story at great length, giving all sorts of facts about the people or places that do not help at all. Tell your reader what he will need to know in order to follow the story, and nothing more.

The choice of words is important in story-telling. The well-chosen word will often do the work of a whole sentence of description. Try to find the exact colour adjective, the verb which tells exactly what happened or was done, and the adverb which shows *how* it was done. Notice how much the words in italics in these sentences add to the meaning:

She stood there *shivering*, *blue* with cold.
Their faces *shone* in the *warm* firelight.
The dancer *floated* across the stage, *as light as a feather*.
The fog came down on the city like a *blanket*.
The *tall* ship *dropped gently* into the *purple* sunset.
The *rushing* wind *tore* the leaves from the trees.

You must take special care with the most exciting or amusing part of the story—the climax, as it is called. All that the reader will need to know must be told well before, so that when you come to the heart of the story you can make this as effective as possible without stopping for explanations. And when you have passed the climax, finish as quickly as you can, or you will spoil the effect.

EXERCISES

1. Tell the story of something interesting or exciting that has happened to you during the past year.
2. "It was the best day I had ever spent." Give an account of what you did on this day.
3. Describe a castle or other place of historic interest that is well known to you.

Still No Peace

Returning home after attending his mother-in-law's funeral, a man was struck on the head by a roof-tile as he was about to re-enter his house.

"Good gracious!" he murmured, glancing Heaven-ward, "she's there already!"

LESSON 4

The Street of Adventure

BEFORE leaving school, David Brown was editor of the school magazine. He found he could write easily and well, and he became very interested in journalism as a possible career. Now that he is at university he has made up his mind to become editor of one of the student newspapers at Oxford. In order to learn a little more about how newspapers are produced he asked his father if he could arrange for him to visit one of the big newspaper offices in London.

Most English national newspapers are produced in Fleet Street or nearby, and most provincial papers have their London offices there. Fleet Street has been called 'The Street of Ink' and 'The Street of Adventure'. It is the ambition of most British journalists to get a job in Fleet Street, but to succeed there you need ability, courage and determination, for the competition is very fierce. So immense are the costs of running a newspaper today that the newspaper industry has become 'big business' and some people fear that too many newspapers are owned by too few people. There need not be too much harm in this so long as editors and their staffs are given independence and are free to print what they please.

When David arrived at the newspaper office he was taken first to meet the Editor, a customer at his father's bank. From there he went to the News Room. Here news is collected from all over the world. It comes into the newspaper office from the Press Agencies, from the paper's own correspondents in Britain and abroad, and from the reporters who are sent out to 'cover' sporting events, public meetings and theatrical performances, and to follow up information about recent happenings in which the paper's readers are likely to be interested. This news pours into the newspaper office all day and far into the night by telephone, by telegraph, by post or direct from the Press Agencies by means of the teleprinter machine which produces a typewritten report without the assistance of either a telephonist or a typist.

All this material cannot go into the paper just as it arrives; it must be selected, checked, cut or expanded, paragraphed, and supplied with headlines. The selected material or 'copy' must then be arranged in columns and pages. This is the work of the sub-editors. When the contents have been approved by the Editor or his assistant, the material is sent downstairs to be processed into the newspaper we shall find on our breakfast-table the following morning.

The 'copy' goes first to the composing-room to be set up in type. The operator taps out the words on a keyboard similar to that of a typewriter, and the type is set automatically in lines, each metal 'slug' carrying one complete line of type. These lines of type are then moved to a flat metal table called the 'stone', where they are arranged inside a shallow iron frame to form a page. Curved metal plates are then made in the foundry, each carrying an impression of a page of type. All is now ready for the actual printing process.

The giant rotary press is one of the wonders of modern engineering—powerful, yet delicate. The printing process is difficult to describe in simple language, but what happens is this. Two of the metal plates are locked together in the machine to form a cylinder. Ink is then spread over the plates by roller pads. Through the machine passes a continuous sheet, coming off a reel containing five miles of paper and weighing over half a ton. When the paper has passed backwards and forwards through the 'printer' part of the machine, where it has been printed on both sides, it goes on to be automatically cut into pages, the pages arranged into complete copies, the copies folded and counted into bundles of two dozen at a time and all this at a speed of up to sixty thousand copies an hour, one thousand copies a mintue, nearly twenty printed, folded, counted copies of a complete daily newspaper every second.

The printed papers go direct from the press to the packing department where they are tied with string in previously addressed packets and rushed by van to railway stations, and post offices, to newsagents and to street-sellers and book-stalls. The essence of the whole process is time, for a news-paper takes pride in delivering copies punctually to its customers. But although everyone must work strictly to time if the papers are to be ready to catch each train or mail, there is no feverish haste or confusion as zero hour draws near. Everyone knows his job so well, and the time it takes has been so exactly calculated that the whole combined operation runs smoothly and without a pause. And each night as the great expresses are about to pull out of the main London stations the fast-moving newspaper vans arrive on the instant to unload those bundles of copies, which are the result of the most extraordinary piece of team-work in the world.

CONVERSATION

(*In an Editor's Room in Fleet Street*)

EDITOR: Come in, Mr Brown. Nice to see you. Your father tells me you want to become a journalist.

DAVID: I'm not sure about that, sir. I'm certainly interested in journalism. At the moment I'm at Oxford, but I'm working on one of the university newspapers in my spare time. Would you recommend journalism as a career?

EDITOR: I don't know whether I can answer that one. It depends on what you want. If you are looking for a quiet life with regular hours and no risk this is not your job. But if you want excitement and variety and the opportunity to influence your fellow-men and perhaps do something to improve the world around you, journalism has much to offer. But it's not an easy life and the rewards are by no means certain. I wouldn't change my job for any other—but, of course, I tend to be prejudiced. Go and look at everything there is to see here, and try to find your own answer to the question. Now you must pardon me; I can't give you any more time now or else there'll be no newspaper on your breakfast table tomorrow morning! But come along and see me again before you go.

(The News Editor's desk)

NEWS EDITOR: What is news? The answer is simple—any happenings you think your readers will want to read about. Into this room comes information about happenings all over the universe. Battles, murders, train and air crashes, storms, wrecks and sea rescues, the resignation of governments, the birth of a republic, weddings and shootings, the finding of a new star, the launching of a new space ship—it is my job to decide which of all these my readers will want to know about, and among them, which they will think are most important. This understanding of the value of news comes only with experience —we call it 'a nose for news'.

DAVID: Do you try to influence your readers—about politics for instance?

NEWS EDITOR: Of course we do. That is part of the duty of a newspaper—'to form public opinion', as it is called. But that isn't my job. We try, as far as we can, to separate 'news' from 'views', to distinguish facts from opinions based on those facts. And my business, as News Editor, is with the facts.

DAVID: Do you try to make sure that the information you come by is correct?

NEWS EDITOR: We do, wherever we can. We have our own representatives in all the big towns in Great Britain and in most countries in the world. There are also British and foreign Press Agencies that send us news. All reporters are taught to check information very carefully before they send it in. It sometimes comes about that we make a mistake, but not often, I'm glad to say. The whole business of collecting news has grown immensely in scale since the days when messages reached a newspaper office under the wing of a carrier pigeon.

· · · ·

(David is talking to Mr Sawyer, a Leader-writer)

DAVID: What is a Leader-writer, Mr Sawyer?

MR SAWYER: He writes one or more of the leading articles for the paper each day. It's called a 'leading article' not because it's the most important article in the paper (although we Leader-writers like to boast that it is) but because it tries to 'lead' or guide public opinion.

DAVID: And does the Leader-writer express his own views and opinions or those of his paper?

MR SAWYER: If the matter is one on which the paper has a policy, the views expressed will be those of the paper; Otherwise the Leader-writer may express his own views.

DAVID: When you speak of the policy of the paper, do you mean the owner of the paper?

MR SAWYER: No—although the views of the owner tend to be more closely followed in some papers than in others. The policy of a newspaper is built up slowly over many years. It is decided partly by the views of the owner, partly by the opinions and character of the Editor but more by the outlook of the people who read the paper.

• • • •

(In the Features Editor's Room)

MR DOUGLAS: My name's Douglas—Bernard Douglas. I'm the Features Editor. We believe that besides informing and influencing readers, a newspaper should entertain. 'Features' are articles, often with pictures, which deal with all matters, other than reports of the happenings of the day, in which readers are likely to be interested.

DAVID: What sort of matters?

MR DOUGLAS: There are regular features such as the woman's page which has articles about fashion, the home and children. Then there are articles about motoring, gardening and other hobbies. Dramatic criticisms and book reviews are dealt with by the Literary Editor.

DAVID: What about special features?

MR DOUGLAS: These are usually connected with the news. When something interesting happens in a faraway country and there is a report in the news pages, we often include an interesting article on that country, its people and their way of life. These articles are not usually written by staff reporters but by men or women who have special knowledge or experience of the matter they are writing about.

DAVID: And sport?

MR DOUGLAS: Ah, sport. Yes, sports reporting takes a big share of newspaper space these days. Some of us think *too* big a share. But you must talk to the Sports Editor about this.

(*Back in the Editor's Room later that evening*)

EDITOR: Well, have you discovered the answer to your question? Are you going to make journalism your career?

DAVID: I've certainly learnt what an interesting and responsible job working for a newspaper must be—especially if you are the Editor.

EDITOR: Yes, an Editor is rather like the captain of a ship—he can't escape from his responsibility. He must, of course, depend much on the skill and loyalty of his staff, and interfere with them as little as possible but in the end he is responsible for everything that appears in his newspaper. And if his paper breaks the law he may even find himself in prison—although I'm glad to say that doesn't happen very often! I don't worry about it, anyway; I should make myself ill if I did.

DAVID: How important is advertising?

EDITOR: Very important indeed—it is the life-blood of a

newspaper, for without the large sums we get from advertising we couldn't pay our way. Newspapers get no money from the government and they certainly couldn't live on the few pence each reader pays for his daily paper.

DAVID: Do you check the truth of what advertisers say in their advertisements?

EDITOR: We try to. And if a reader complained and we found that an advertisement contained a statement that was false, or that the goods advertised did not come up to what the buyers had been led to expect, we should not hesitate to refuse advertisements from that firm in the future.

DAVID: Now I must thank you for answering all my questions so patiently and allowing me to take up so much of everyone's time. I'm afraid I have been a nuisance to you all.

EDITOR: It always makes us happy to show interested people how the machine works. Is there any last question you would like to ask?

DAVID: Well, yes there is. What is the one thing in your job that you enjoy most of all?

EDITOR: That's easy. The answer's just coming through the door now. Here's Mr East, the Chief Sub-Editor, with the first copy of tomorrow morning's paper. Everything in order, Mr East? Right, now I can go home to bed!

COMPREHENSION QUESTIONS

1. Why was David interested in journalism as a possible career?
2. Why is Fleet Street sometimes called 'The Street of Adventure'?
3. What is meant by the term 'big business'?
4. What is a Press Agency?

5. What are the duties of:

    (*a*) a newspaper reporter; (*b*) a sub-editor; (*c*) a compositor?

6. Explain these terms as used in a newspaper office:

    (*a*) copy; (*b*) headline; (*c*) teleprinter; (*d*) column; (*e*) slug; (*f*) the stone.

7. What is the meaning of the word 'automatically'?
8. Explain the phrase 'the essence of the whole process is time'.
9. Explain these terms as used in the conversation passage:

    (*a*) prejudice; (*b*) public opinion; (*c*) a feature article.

10. What was the one thing in his job that the Editor enjoyed most of all?

SENTENCE PATTERNS

16.   The Structure of the Sentence—1

The simplest pattern of sentence-structure in English is:

    subject + verb (+ object):
    Birds fly.   Fish swim.   The boy met his friend.

Adjectives, adjective phrases and adjective clauses can be added to the subject and object:

    Young children play.
    The careless boy lost his new bicycle.
    We saw a book lying on the table.
    Everyone reads the newspaper which suits him best.

Adverbs, adverb phrases and adverb clauses can be added to the verb:

    David visited Fleet Street yesterday.
    Finish this exercise as quickly as possible.
    The editor would not print the article because it was badly written.

A clause can take the place of the object.

I think (that) she has gone away.
He asked us where we were going.
They did not know what would happen next.

We have met all these patterns of sentence-structure already in *Present Day English*. Here is a new pattern:

subject + verb + (pro)noun + adjective.

In this kind of sentence the adjectives show what effect the subject has on the object; it describes the object after the subject has acted on it.

Hot weather will turn the milk sour.
Walking makes me tired.
She made herself ill.
The warm coat will keep the cold out.
Too much walking will make your feet sore.
The sea washes the sand clean.

Early to bed and early to rise,
Makes a man healthy, wealthy and wise.

17. The Indefinite Article *A—An*

A (*an* before a vowel or silent *h*) is the unemphatic form of the numeral *one*. It is used, therefore, with countable nouns, but not with uncountable nouns.

He had a book in his hand.
She has been in England for a month.

Because it is an unemphatic form it usually has the unstressed sound ǝ. When we wish to draw attention to the singular idea we use *one* and the word is stressed.

There is a vacant seat in this row.
ðer iz ǝ 'veikǝnt 'siːt in ðis 'rou.

There is one vacant seat in this row.
ðer iz 'wʌn 'veikǝnt 'siːt in ðis 'rou.

To express the 'singleness' of an uncountable noun we put a countable noun in front of it, so that the uncountable noun shows either what the countable noun is made of:

a loaf of bread,   a piece of cake,

or what it contains:

a bottle of milk,   a glass of wine.

In addition to this numerical use of *a, an* there is an indefinite or general use:

> Susan gave David an orange. (numerical)
> An orange can be very refreshing on a hot day. (general)
> Mrs Brown went to meet a friend at the station. (numerical)
> A friend in need is a friend indeed. (general)

In the plural, *a, an*, when used numerically, are replaced by *some*:

> She has a lettuce in her shopping basket.
> She has some lettuces in her basket.

but when used in a general sense, *a, an* disappear in the plural:

> A horse can be a good friend.
> Horses are friendly animals.
> A camera is useful on a holiday.
> Good cameras are expensive in England.

18.   Phrasal Verbs—*Come*

Come about

> How did this come about?
> How did it come about that you were there at the time?

Come along

> Come along! We musn't be late for lunch.
> Come along at about three o'clock and the picture will be finished.
> He's coming along well with his English.

Come by

> We stood in the street to watch the Queen come by.
> How did she come by those beautiful diamonds?

Come in

> Those presents will come in useful when they have a house of their own.
>
> Don't throw that away; it might come in useful.

Come into

> He will come into a lot of money one day.

Come to

> How much does that come to?
>
> An idea suddenly came to her, but she didn't tell us what it was.

Come up to

> The party did not come up to what we had expected.
>
> The riding boots came nearly up to his knees.

19.   How to express Ability

We can often express the same general idea or concept in a number of different ways. In each of the remaining Lessons of this book, we shall take one of these general ideas or concepts and consider the different ways in which it can be expressed in English. We begin with ability, the idea of being able to do something.

The main verbs for expressing ability are *can* and *could*.

Can is used in the present tense to express two kinds of ability:

(*a*) ability which depends on someone's physical or mental powers, or his knowledge or skill.

> He can walk twenty miles without getting tried.
>
> He can learn languages very easily.
>
> He can tell you the name of every Derby winner since 1900.
>
> He can add up three rows of figures at the same time.

(*b*) ability which depends on circumstances.

> She can come to the dance this evening.
>
> Can you let me have a room for the night?
>
> You can buy clothes cheaply in England.
>
> One can travel from London to Brighton in an hour.

Inability is expressed by *cannot (can't)*.

Is able to

This is used instead of *can* and is rather more formal.
The negative forms are *is not (isn't) able to, is unable to*.

We are able to agree to your request.

We regret that we are not able to agree to your request.

Could is used to express ability in past time.

When he was a boy he could sing beautifully.

He was driving so fast I could see there would be a crash.

The negative form is *could not (couldn't)*, and *was (was not) able to* may be used instead.

Although *could* expresses ability or capacity to do something in the past, it is not used in the affirmative to express an achievement or attainment that resulted from that ability. This is expressed by *was able to* or *managed to*.

He could read before he was three. (ability)

but

He was able (managed to) finish reading the book before he went to bed. (achievement)

In the negative, however, *could* is used.

He could not (couldn't) finish reading the book before he went to bed.

20.   Abstract Nouns

We use adjectives to describe people and things: we say that a person is *happy* or *kind*, that a ball is *round* and a knife is *sharp*. But sometimes we want to speak of the quality itself, without linking it to a particular person or thing. To do this we use the nouns of quality *happiness, kindness, roundness, sharpness*. These are often called abstract nouns. Many of them end in *-ness* but not all. Below is a list of abstract nouns that we have met so far in *Present Day English*:

ability, ambition, anger, beauty, care, charm, courage, danger,

*darkness, fear, friendship, gaiety, happiness, joy, kindness, length,
love, pity, possibility, progress, sadness, safety, shame, size,
success, truth, warmth.*

NEW WORDS

ability (ə'biliti)

adventure (əd'ventʃə)

ambition (am'biʃn)

article ('aːtikl)

base (beis)

battle ('batl)

blood (blʌd)

book-stall ('bukstoːl)

bundle ('bʌndl)

captain ('kaptin)

career (kə'riə)

column ('koləm)

combination (kombi'neiʃn)

copy ('kopi)

correspondent (kori'spondənt)

courage ('kʌridʒ)

critic ('kritik)

cylinder ('silində)

description (dis'kripʃn)

duty ('djuːti)

editor ('editə)

essence ('esəns)

fear (fiə)

feature ('fiːtʃə)

fellow ('felou)

fever ('fiːvə)

form (foːm)

foundry ('faundri)

giant ('dʒaiənt)

harm (haːm)

haste (heist)

headline ('hedlain)

hobby ('hobi)

impression (im'preʃn)

ink (iŋk)

instant ('instənt)

interest ('intrəst)

journalism ('dʒəːnəlizm)

journalist ('dʒəːnəlist)

keyboard ('kiːboːd)

leader ('liːdə)

literature ('litritʃə)

lock (lok)

loyalty ('loiəlti)

magazine (magə'ziːn)

mail (meil)

metal ('metl)

murder ('məːdə)

nose (nouz)

nuisance ('njuːsəns)

operation (opə'reiʃn)

outlook ('autluk)

pad (pad)

pigeon ('pidʒn)

policy ('polisi)

prejudice ('predʒudis)

press (pres)
pride (praid)
prison (prizn)
process ('prouses)
reporter (ri'poːtə)
republic (ri'pʌblik)
resignation (rezig'neiʃn)
ribbon ('ribn)
risk (risk)
scale (skeil)
skill (skil)
star (staː)
storm (stoːm)
string (striŋ)
telegraph ('teligraf, 'teligraːf)
teleprinter ('teliprintə)
ton (tʌn)
truth (truːθ)
universe ('juːnivəːs)
value ('valjuː)
variety (və'raiəti)
weight (weit)
width (witθ)
wing (wiŋ)
wreck (rek)
zero ('ziərou)
appear (ə'piə)
approve (ə'pruːv)
boast (boust)
calculate ('kalkjuleit)
combine (kəm'bain)
complain (kəm'plein)
compose (kəm'pouz)
confuse (kən'fjuːz)
connect (kə'nekt)
contain (kən'tein)
continue (kən'tinjuː)

crash (kraʃ)
curve (noun and verb) (kəːv)
describe (dis'kraib)
discover (dis'kʌvə)
distinguish (dis'tiŋgwiʃ)
escape (is'keip)
expand (iks'pand)
fold (fould)
hesitate ('heziteit)
impress (im'pres)
improve (im'pruːv)
influence (noun and verb)
    ('influəns)
inform (in'foːm)
interest ('intrəst)
interfere (intə'fiə)
launch (loːntʃ)
lead, led, led (liːd, led, led)
load (noun and verb) (loud)
pardon (noun and verb)
    ('paːdn)
pause (poːz)
print (print)
report (ri'poːt)
rescue ('reskjuː)
resign (ri'zain)
review (ri'vjuː)
select (si'lekt)
shoot, shot, shot (ʃuːt, ʃot, ʃot)
tap, tapped, tapped (tap, tapt,
    tapt)
tend (tend)
unload (ʌn'loud)
weigh (wei)
able ('eibl)
automatic (oːtə'matik)
chief (tʃiːf)

continuous (kən'tinjuəs)
delicate ('delikət)
essential (i'senʃl)
extraordinary (iks'trɔːdənri)
false (fɔːls)
faraway ('fɑːrəwei)
fierce (fiəs)
harmful ('hɑːmful)
independent (indi'pendənt)
literary ('litərəri)

loyal ('loiəl)
political (pə'litikl)
provincial (prə'vinʃl)
punctual ('pʌŋktʃl)
recent ('riːsənt)
rotary ('routəri)
shallow ('ʃalou)
spare (speə)
strict (strikt)
various ('veəriəs)

Idioms

from all over the world (frəm 'ɔːl 'ouvə ðə 'wəːld)
to follow up (tə 'folou 'ʌp)
far into the night ('fɑː intə ðə 'nait)
by means of (bai 'miːnz əv)
backwards and forwards ('bakwədz ənd 'fɔːwədz)
to work to time (tə 'wəːk tə 'taim)
at the moment (at ðə 'moumənt)
in my spare time (in mai 'speə 'taim)
by no means certain (bai 'nou miːnz 'səːtn)
to make sure that (tə meik 'ʃuə ðət)
to pay one's way (tə 'pei wʌnz 'wei)

EXERCISES

A. *Add a, an, one or some where necessary:*

   1. Mrs Brown bought oranges and cabbage from the green-
      grocer.
   2. Susan gave her dog piece of chocolate.
   3. Children should be seen and not heard.
   4. There is only biscuit left in the tin.

5. I have aunt in Brighton who owns restaurant.
6. Mr Brown enjoys holiday after year's work.
7. Boys can usually run faster than girls.
8. Only engineer can really understand how rotary press works.
9. Susan and Tom always enjoy evening at the theatre.
10. There are two packets of cigarettes on the table in the sitting-room. Take packet yourself and give the other to Tom.

B. *Reword these sentences using a phrasal verb with* come *instead of the words in italics:*

1. She is *making good progress* with her typing.
2. We do not know how it *happened.*
3. *She suddenly remembered* his name, but she did not know where he lived.
4. As they were crossing the flooded road the water nearly *reached* the tops of their boots.
5. *Hurry up,* or we'll be late.
6. They are planning to get married this summer, but I don't think it will *happen.*
7. This magazine *is produced* once a month.
8. At what time will he *arrive to fetch* you?
9. The bus you want, *passes* here every half hour.
10. How did you *receive* that cut on your face?

C. *Use the following words in sentences to express ability:*

can (knowledge or skill); can (circumstances); cannot; can't; is able to; is not able to; is unable to; could; could not; manage to.

D. *Put the word* yet, still *or* already *into the correct place in these sentences:*

1. I had finished my work when he arrived.
2. When we got up this morning it was dark.

3. I haven't met the Browns for years. Are they living in Bishopton?
4. Has the postman come?
5. I have spoken to him twice about his habit of arriving late.
6. It is half past nine and we haven't started work.
7. The sun had not risen and it was very cold.
8. David, have you finished in the bathroom?
9. David meets some of his old school-friends although he has left school.
10. I have called at his house three times but I haven't seen him.

E. *Use these abstract nouns in sentences. Try to make your sentences interesting:*

   charm; danger; darkness; friendship; kindness; length; love; success; truth; warmth.

F. *Rewrite these sentences, replacing the main verb by the verb* have. *After each sentence, state the particular use of* have *(see Sentence Pattern 3):*

   1. You must work harder next term.
   2. Mr Brown will arrange for his house to be painted in the spring.
   3. There is a dog and a cat in our house.
   4. Mr Brown smokes a cigar after dinner each evening.
   5. I'm going to ask the driver to remove that car from in front of my house.
   6. We were made to answer a lot of questions before the police would let us go.
   7. David plays a game of football on most Saturday mornings.
   8. Can you give me a match, please?
   9. It was necessary for him to get to London before ten o'clock.
   10. Mrs Brown often invites friends to tea on a Thursday afternoon.

G. *Give the collective noun for each of the following:*

1. a group of people who are related to each other.
2. a group of people with one or more interests in common who meet regularly.
3. a number of trees planted close together.
4. the men and women elected to govern England.
5. a collection of books.
6. a group of students studying together.
7. a group of people playing musical instruments at a concert.
8. a large group of people gathered in the street.
9. the people listening to a play or concert.
10. a group of people playing a game against a group of opponents.

H. *Write sentences using each of the following words, first as a noun, then as a verb (Book Two, Sentence Pattern 61):*

ache; act; bat; bet; comb; dance; drink; dust; fall; fight; guide; judge; kick; laugh; lift; oil; paint; place; plant; polish.

I. *Write sentences using each of the following words, first as an adjective, then as a verb:*

determined; disappointed; free; frozen; hurt; married; mixed; separate; twisted; used.

J. *Put the correct form of the verb (infinitive with or without to or the gerund in -ing) in place of the words in brackets in these sentences:*

1. Do you expect (reach) home before dark?
2. I advise you (think) before you speak.
3. Tom showed David how (mend) a bicycle tyre.
4. Help me (lift) this box into the car, please.
5. Susan enjoys (swim).
6. Mr Brown has finished (cut) the grass in the garden.

7. He changed his shoes before (come) into the house.
8. Please forgive my (arrive) so late for the lecture.
9. Mr Brown told David (drive) more carefully.
10. The policeman made the children (cross) the road at the right place.

COMPOSITION
Gathering and Arranging Material

You cannot always choose the subject on which you have to write a composition either in class or in an examination. When faced with a subject about which you cannot think of any ideas, you may at first feel helpless. But there is no need for this. You have spent your life in a busy world with many interesting things happening around you; you have friends and a family whose lives you have shared; you have learned much from teachers at school; you have read books and seen films about happenings far away from your home in place and time. All this will provide material for compositions.

The material is there, but how are you to bring it to the front of your mind so that it will be ready for use? If you have a day or two to prepare, you can look up the topic in books; you can ask others for ideas and opinions; you can think the matter over in your mind, until you have all the material you need. But if you have to write the composition there and then you must work in a different way. Do not allow yourself to become afraid that the ideas will never come and that the time will be gone before you have written a word. To stop this happening, *begin writing*—not the composition itself, but any ideas on the subject that come into your mind. It is surprising how one thing will suggest another, until you have a large enough collection of material for your composition.

But the material will not be in the right order, and you cannot make it into a composition until the ideas have been arranged into sections or groups, so that everything that belongs together has been placed together. These groups of ideas will form the paragraphs of the finished composition. Some of the ideas may have to be left out, for we cannot include in a composition everything about the subject. You must make up your mind what you will try to *do* in your composition, and on this will depend what you put in and what you leave out. If, for example, you are writing on 'England' you will not tell the reader all that you know about England—where it is, how big it is, and so on—but only the things about England that you have noticed yourself, or that make England different from other countries, or that you think your readers will be interested to hear.

When you have gathered plenty of ideas, either from books and other people, or from your own mind and memory, and when you have arranged these in a sensible order, then—and not until then—are you ready to start writing the composition. No one but a very foolish person would sit down and begin writing before he had thought out carefully what he was going to say.

EXERCISES

1. Write a composition on 'The Responsibility of the Press'.
2. Write a composition on 'My Favourite Newspaper'.
3. Describe in your own words what happens to the news from the time it arrives at the newspaper office to the time it reaches the reader.

LESSON 5

A Motoring Tour of England—2

TOM and Susan spent the next morning of their holiday visiting the places of interest in Bath—the Roman baths, the abbey, the eighteenth-century squares and terraces They imagined themselves back in that age of elegance, riding in a fine carriage drawn by six horses over the beautiful Pulteney Bridge, or dancing gracefully in the splendid Assembly Rooms.

In the afternoon they drove out to the Cheddar Valley. Here, deep in the heart of the hillside, in the famous Cheddar Caves they saw the many coloured pieces of stone like huge fingers, formed by water dripping slowly through the rocks for millions of years. The place shone in the bright flood-lighting like a fairy palace.

After leaving the caves they ate strawberries and cream in one of the cottages nearby, and finished the day by a visit to the small country town of Wells. Here they wondered at the finely ornamented west front of the cathedral, one of the finest examples of church building from the middle ages. They saw, also, the ancient Bishop's Palace, its grey stone walls rising from the peaceful waters of a lake on which swans moved gracefully towards them in the warm light of a lovely summer evening while a soft breeze whispered gently among the leaves—a scene they would never forget.

．　．　．　．

On the following morning they continued their journey towards the Welsh border, crossing the River Severn at Gloucester. The ancient city of Gloucester is not only the market town for a wide agricultural district but it is also attracting an increasing number of light industries. Its cathedral was built all in one style right at the end of the middle ages. It is much lighter than most cathedrals, for by this time architects had learnt how to carry the weight of the roof on masses of stone at intervals along the wall, so that the rest of the wall could be cut away to make large windows. These window spaces were then filled with stained glass—purple and red, blue and green, pink and yellow. Much of this stained glass was destroyed in the seventeenth century, but some beautiful examples remain at Fairford in Gloucester-shire, in York Minster and in Canterbury Cathedral.

Just after leaving Gloucester they picked up a young airman who was 'thumbing a lift' on his way home to Cardiff on leave. For several miles here the road to South Wales runs beside the broad, slow-moving waters of the Severn. A little farther along they came to a steep hill, at the bottom of which flowed the River Wye with the road rising upward again to the square Norman tower of Chepstow Castle on the opposite hill. They had come to the end of England; beyond lay the 'no man's land' of Monmouthshire, which is neither English nor Welsh, and beyond that again the land of Wales.

At the bottom of the hill, where the road curves sharply at right angles to cross the bridge over the Wye, a lorry had run into a car coming in the opposite direction. Luckily no one was badly hurt, but it was a reminder to Tom that it is necessary to drive with caution and patience and not to exceed the speed limit if you are to avoid accidents on the roads.

A long stretch of main road through Newport brought them at last to Cardiff, the capital of Wales. Tom and Susan had expected to find a dirty sea-port, covered in coal-dust, but as they drove through the wide, clean streets they soon realised that Cardiff was one of the finest cities they had seen. It was a Saturday afternoon and the streets were full of busy shoppers, for Cardiff is the administrative and shopping centre for the important industrial district of South Wales. Susan was delighted with the fine shops and surprised at the large number of smartly dressed women who were to be seen in the streets.

The airman to whom they had given a lift had told them that they ought to see the famous Civic Centre. Here they found a magnificent collection of public buildings, all in shining white stone, set in a beautiful park, its green lawns and bright flower-beds crossed by wide, tree-lined avenues. Here were the City Hall, the Law Courts, the University, the College of Technology and many government offices. Nearby—linking the past with the present—stood the ancient castle, built first by the Romans and again by the Normans, rebuilt during the nineteenth century with the profits from the coal and iron industries of South Wales, and now presented to the City by its former owners. As a College of Music and Drama, however, it plays a more useful part in the life of the city than it ever did before. Cardiff was made the official capital city of Wales some years ago.

After a meal at the 'Angel Hotel' they took the road north towards the mining valleys. They were going to stay for the week-end with a friend of Tom's who was the manager of a factory making electrical instruments—for South Wales is now developing other industries than coal, iron and steel. As one drives farther into the heart of the mining country, the mountains close in and the valleys, once green with trees and grass and watered by clear streams, have become blackened with coal-dust and filled with railway-lines, roads and crowded villages whose ugly little houses crawl in grey terraces up the side of the mountains. The clear streams have been almost choked with dirt and oil. South Wales has paid a heavy price for industrial progress.

CONVERSATION

(Tom and Susan see an airman by the roadside 'thumbing a lift'. His name is Owen Morgan)

TOM (*stopping beside him*): Can we give you a lift? How far are you going?
MORGAN: Cardiff.
TOM: So are we. Jump in.
MORGAN: Thanks a lot. Shall I put my pack in the boot?
TOM: No, it's full of luggage. Put it on the seat beside you. Going on leave?

MORGAN: Yes, I've got forty-eight hours. Do you know Cardiff?

TOM: No, we've never been to South Wales before. What sort of a place is it?

MORGAN: Cardiff's not at all the sort of place you'd expect. To begin with, it's very clean. The nearest coal-mines are twenty miles from the city and very little coal is exported from Cardiff these days; most of it goes into the home market.

SUSAN: Are you Welsh?

MORGAN: Certainly I am—and proud of it.

TOM: What are the things about Wales and the Welsh that you're most proud of?

MORGAN: That's easy. Singing and Rugby football.

SUSAN: Can you sing?

MORGAN: Every Welshman can sing. I've never been in a choir, myself, but yes—I can sing a bit, you know.

TOM: Wales has its own National Anthem, hasn't it?

MORGAN: Oh, yes. We call it 'Land of my Fathers' in English.

SUSAN: Do most people in Wales speak Welsh?

MORGAN: Not in South Wales, I'm afraid. When Wales was joined to England, English became the official language, and children were even forbidden to speak Welsh in the schools. The Welsh language nearly died out, but now it's coming back to life. All children must learn Welsh in school and there are programmes in Welsh on radio and television. There are still some people in North Wales who speak only Welsh, but not many. Most Welsh-speaking people can speak English as well.

SUSAN: Oh, look at that! What a wonderful view.

MORGAN: That's the River Wye with Chepstow Castle beyond and the Welsh hills on the horizon—your first sight of Wales.

TOM: But that's Monmouthshire ahead of us—I thought that was an English county.

MORGAN: Not any longer. We Welsh have taken it over—as well as the castle your King Edward I built to keep us in order. And now we've got them, we're going to stick to them—"Cymru am byth!"

SUSAN: And what does that mean?

MORGAN: It means 'Wales for ever'.

(As they reach the bottom of the hill the road is partly blocked by a lorry that has run into a car)

SUSAN: Look out, Tom. There's been an accident.

TOM *(as they drive slowly past)*: It doesn't look as though anyone's been hurt. It's a nasty crash, though. That car must have been well on the wrong side of the road.

MORGAN: You can't be too careful, can you? But even then, you never know what will happen. The other day a cat ran under the wheels of the Air Force car I was driving; I swerved to avoid it and finished up in the ditch with the steering twisted. The officer in the back wasn't too pleased, I can tell you.

SUSAN: Do you live in Cardiff?

MORGAN: My family do now. My father was a miner, and we used to live in the Rhondda valley. But he had a disease of the lungs that miners often get, and so we came to Cardiff where he could find other work. I can still remember the miner's cottage we lived in, although I was only eight when we left.

SUSAN: I've read about the Welsh mining villages in Richard Llewellyn's *How Green was my Valley*.

MORGAN: They're not very pleasant places to look at—rows of dull little houses, one above the other on the sides of the valley, with the coal-mine, the black 'slag-tips' and the railway at the bottom. The people are happy enough though. They have their family-life, their religion, their love of education—and above all, their singing. But many young people find the life too narrow and they move to the big towns like Cardiff and Swansea or go off into England. It's sad, but you can't blame them.

TOM: We have the same problem in many country districts in England. Today, most people who live in the country want to live in the town, and most townspeople wish they lived in the country.

MORGAN: Well, here we are in Cardiff. If you'll put me down by the next traffic-lights, I shall be only a few yards from my home. Don't forget to see the Civic Centre while you're here.

SUSAN: Make sure you haven't left anything.

MORGAN: I think I've got everything. Many thanks for the lift, and good luck for the rest of your holiday.

COMPREHENSION QUESTIONS

1. What were the Assembly Rooms at Bath?
2. What can be seen in the Cheddar Caves?
3. What is a 'market town'?
4. What do you understand by the sentence 'The cathedral was built all in one style'?
5. What are 'light industries'? Give examples.
6. What is the meaning of the expression 'thumbing a lift'? Give another name for this way of travelling.
7. Why is Monmouthshire called a 'no man's land'? How did the expression first come into use?
8. How did the appearance of Cardiff differ from what Tom and Susan had expected?
9. Mention some of the problems likely to exist in a country where two different languages are spoken.
10. What effect has industrial development had on the valleys of South Wales?

SENTENCE PATTERNS

21.   The Structure of the Sentence—2

In the simple sentence pattern of subject + verb + object

> Tom met his friend.

the object is a different person or thing from the subject. Now
consider this structure:

> Tom was appointed manager.

Here *Tom* and *manager* refer to the same person. Similar examples
are:

Elizabeth II was crowned Queen.
London has long been the largest city in Britain.
The Prime Minister is a very important person.
She seems an intelligent girl.
David was chosen captain of his football team.
He was elected Chairman of the Company.
She was called 'The Prisoner's Friend'.

There is a related structure in which the object noun or pronoun
is followed by another noun referring to the same person or thing
as the object.

They chose him captain.
The firm made Tom manager.
We found him a most interesting person.
The people called Wellington 'The Iron Duke'.
The Board appointed him Chairman.
His father left him a very rich man.

22.   How to express Permission

May and *can* are the most usual words for expressing permission.
Of these, *may* is the more formal and is required in written
English, but *can* is more common in speech.

Readers may change books at any time when the library is open.
In this country anyone may vote in an election if he or she is
  over twenty-one.

"You may leave now, if you wish," said the teacher.

"Can I come in?" "Yes, please do."

"Can I carry your bag for you?" David asked his mother.

"Can I have a little more sugar in my tea, please?"

May not and *cannot* (*can't*) are used in the same way to express denial of permission. The shortened form *mayn't* exists, but is seldom used as *can't* almost always replaces it in conversation. If the denial of permission is strong enough to become a prohibition, then *must not* is used.

Passengers must not cross the line except by the bridge.

(See Sentence Pattern 32, p. 137)

Might expresses a more polite or hesitant request for permission than *may*:

Might I ask you to close the window?

Might I have a little more coffee, please?

Might I borrow your programme for a moment?

Permission can also be expressed by the words *permit, give permission, allow, let*:

No one is permitted to smoke in the theatre.

He gave them permission to go home early.

No smoking allowed.

The teacher will not allow his students to eat sweets in class.

I can't let you waste your time in this way.

Once the policeman had caught them, he would not let them go.

23.   How to express Possibility

Permission and possibility are linked together by the common use of *may*. *May* (and to a greater extent *might*) suggests doubt as well as possibility:

He may reach the station in time to catch the train.

(But there is some doubt.)

He might reach the station in time to catch the train.

(Here the doubt is even more marked.)

Possibility can also be expressed by forms of the word *possible* itself:

Possibly he has already arrived.

It is possible that he has already arrived.

and by the word *perhaps*:

Perhaps he has already left.

Perhaps they will come tomorrow.

24. Non-conclusive Verbs

There are some verbs which are seldom found in the continuous tenses. The actions or states they describe are not under the control of the persons about whom they are used.

I know he has arrived.

I think he is a clever boy.

Although they refer to a particular moment of time, they are not thought of as having a beginning and an end as are such verbs of action as

I am drinking a cup of tea.

Because they have no end or conclusion, they are sometimes called Non-conclusive Verbs. Here are the chief verbs of this kind:

(*a*) *The verb 'to be'.* When this verb describes a state it is non-conclusive and is not used in the continuous tenses:

He is clever. (Not *He is being clever.*)
He was tired. (Not *He was being tired.*)

When, however, the verb *to be* is used to express an action and not a state, it is used in the continuous tenses in the usual way:

He is being clever   (i.e. behaving cleverly).
He was being noisy   (i.e. making a noise).

(*b*) *Verbs of Perception*

see, hear, smell, taste, feel, recognise, notice:

I see you have bought a new car.

I hear they are coming to England next summer.

Don't those roses smell sweet!

This cake tastes good. Did you make it yourself?

I notice you aren't wearing your new watch.

Notice that *to see* (which does not depend on our will) is non-conclusive, but *to look*, an action which we control, is an ordinary verb. The same distinction applies to *hear* and *listen*:

She sees much better with her new glasses.

She is looking for the book she left on the table.

I hear you are leaving London.

Susan is listening to her favourite piece of music.

(c) *Verbs of Liking and Disliking*

like, dislike, love, hate, prefer, mind, care, forgive.

I like a lot of sugar in my coffee.

We dislike sitting in a room that is untidy.

Susan loves going to the theatre.

Mrs Brown hates cold, rainy weather.

Mr Brown prefers the country to the seaside.

He doesn't mind how much he spends on cigarettes.

(d) *Verbs of Wanting or Wishing*

want, wish, desire, refuse.

He wants to catch the next train to Manchester.

I wish I had enough money to buy that gold watch.

We cannot have everything we desire.

I refuse to move one step further until you apologise.

(e) *Verbs of Knowing and Thinking*

know, understand, think, remember, forget, believe, hope, doubt, suppose, seem, mean.

I know where the ring is hidden.

He understands everything you say.

I think we have lost our way.

Do you remember where we left the car?

I believe she has fallen asleep.

David hopes to do well at his university.

I doubt if we shall arrive in time.

(f) Verbs of Having

have, possess, own, belong to

She has a new hair style which is very smart.
He possesses a house in London and a castle in Scotland.
Does Mr Brown own the house he is living in?
Blenheim Palace belongs to the Duke of Marlborough.

25.   The Definite Article

The definite article is so called because it is used when nouns have a definite or particular and not a general sense. In the sentence

> We wish we had a house of our own.

no particular house is referred to: but in the sentence

> The house next door is for sale.

we are referring to a particular house.

The definite article is also used when we refer to a person or thing for the second time: the noun has become definite because it is the one we have already mentioned.

> Tom and Susan are planning a holiday. The holiday must be interesting and unusual, but not too expensive.

Here the first *holiday* is general, and has the indefinite article *a*: by the time we come to the second usage, the idea of *holiday* has become familiar and special enough to require *the*. These are the general rules, but there are many idiomatic uses of *the*. Here are some of the most common:

(a) The with adjectives

    (i) with *next* and *last*, except when these refer to the period immediately before or after the present:

> During the last term at school David was busy with examinations.

but

> David was in Switzerland with his friends last summer.

> Tom and Susan are getting married next month.

but

This coming week-end we shall be away, but the next is free, so will you spend a day or two with us then?

(ii) with superlatives:

These are the best watches you can buy.
He is the kindest man I know.

(iii) with ordinal numbers:

The first place they visited was Windsor.
You will find the third chapter more interesting than the first.

(iv) with adjectives used as nouns:

He was always ready to help the poor and the hungry.
It is the duty of a doctor to care for the sick.

(b) *The* with names

(i) Groups of islands and mountains:

The West Indies, the Alps, the Pennines.

(ii) Names of seas and rivers:

The English Channel, the Atlantic, the Thames, the Severn.

(iii) Some names of countries, particularly if they include the word State, Kingdom, Union, etc.

The United States, the Irish Republic,
the United Kingdom, the U.S.S.R.,
the Netherlands.

(iv) Names of newspapers:

The Times, The Daily Mail, The Guardian.

(v) Family names in the plural:

The Browns live in Bishopton.
We have invited the Brays to dinner.

(vi) Some names of things of which there is only one in existence:

the sun, the moon, the Strand, the Tower of London, the Leaning Tower of Pisa.

(c) *The* is used with some nouns when the objects named are not being spoken of as used for their proper purpose.

They go to church every Sunday.
They visited the church to look at the pictures.

Mr Stansbury, the farmer, has taken his pigs to market.
The police went to the market to look for pickpockets.

(d) *The* and *a*

Notice the difference between:

The horse is a useful animal.
A horse is a useful animal.

The is followed by *horse* in a general sense; it represents the idea of horse.

A is followed by horse in a more definite sense; someone is thought of as possessing a horse and finding it useful.

26.   Phrasal Verbs—*Go*

Go about

She would like to become an air hostess, but she doesn't know how to go about it.

You can usually get what you want if you go about it in the right way.

Go along

If you go along about seven-thirty this evening you'll probably see him.

He's going along nicely. He'll soon be quite better.

Go by

As you get older, the time seems to go by more quickly.

I saw her go by the window just now.
You can usually go by the church clock; it's never wrong.

Go over

I've told you all about it once. I can't go over it again.
I hear he's changed his views and gone over to the opposition.

Go through with

I think we should go through with it, now we've started.
I never thought he would go through with it.

Go together

Bacon and eggs go well together, and so do bread and cheese.

27.   *Leave*

Leave has many uses, particularly in colloquial English.

(a) *Not to take away*
   Leave the book on the table.
   You can leave the dog with us; we will look after it.
   They drank all the wine, but left half the food.

(b) *To go away, depart*
   She is leaving school at Christmas.
   Our train leaves at five-thirty.
   We had to leave the party early.
   She left the room without a word.

(c) *To pass on to someone else*
   When she died she left all her money to her brother.
   He left a wife and three children.
   They left the carpets and curtains for the new tenants.

(d) *To pass the responsibility or choice to someone else*
   You can choose which book you like; I leave it to you.
   He left me to carry all the luggage.

(e) *A sum remaining* (in arithmetic)
   Four from ten leaves six.

Fifteen shillings from a pound leaves five shillings.
If I buy three books at five shillings each and give the shop-keeper a pound, how much have I left?

NEW WORDS

accident (ˈaksidənt)
administration (ədminisˈtreiʃn)
agriculture (ˈagrikʌltʃə)
airman (ˈeəmən)
angle (ˈaŋgl)
anthem (ˈanθəm)
architect (ˈaːkitekt)
assembly (əˈsembli)
avenue (ˈavinjuː)
berry (ˈberi)
bishop (ˈbiʃəp)
boot (of a car) (buːt)
border (ˈboːdə)
bottom (ˈbotəm)
breeze (briːz)
case (keis)
cat (kat)
caution (ˈkoːʃn)
cave (keiv)
choir (kwaiə)
cottage (ˈkotidʒ)
cream (kriːm)
delight (diˈlait)
development (diˈveləpmənt)
direction (diˈrekʃn)
disease (diˈziːz)
district (ˈdistrikt)
ditch (ditʃ)
education (edjuˈkeiʃn, edʒuˈkeiʃn)

fairy (ˈfeəri)
grace (greis)
hill (hil)
horizon (həˈraizn)
instrument (ˈinstrəmənt)
interval (ˈintəvl)
lawn (loːn)
leave (liːv)
limit (ˈlimit)
lorry (ˈlori)
lung (lʌŋ)
miner (ˈmainə)
mining (ˈmainiŋ)
ornament (ˈoːnəmənt)
problem (ˈprobləm)
profit (ˈprofit)
religion (riˈlidʒn)
sea-port (ˈsiːpoːt)
scene (siːn)
speed (spiːd)
stick (stik)
strawberry (ˈstroːbri)
style (stail)
swan (swon)
tax (taks)
technology (tekˈnolədʒi)
thumb (θʌm)
traffic (ˈtrafik)
valley (ˈvali)
attract (əˈtrakt)

block (blok)
choke (tʃouk)
develop (di'veləp)
educate ('edjukeit, 'edʒukeit)
exceed (ik'siːd)
floodlight ('flʌdlait)
flow (flou)
forbid, forbade, forbidden
(fə'bid, fə'bad, fə'bidn)
increase (verb) (in'kriːs)
link (noun and verb) (liŋk)
rise, rose, risen (raiz, rouz,
rizn)
scatter ('skatə)
stain (noun and verb) (stein)
steer (stiə)
stretch (stretʃ)
swerve (swəːv)
whisper ('wispə)
administrative (əd'ministrətiv)
broad (broːd)

civic ('sivik)
deep (diːp)
delighted (di'laitid)
direct (di'rekt)
graceful ('greisfl)
main (mein)
nasty ('naːsti)
necessary ('nesisri, 'nesəsri)
opposite ('opəzit)
patient ('peiʃnt)
pink (piŋk)
sharp (ʃaːp)
steep (stiːp)
technical ('teknikl)
ugly ('ʌgli)
ahead (ə'hed)
further ('fəːðə)
sharply ('ʃaːpli)
towards (tə'woːdz)
upward(s) ('ʌpwəd(z))

Idioms

by this time (bai 'ðis taim)
thumbing a lift ('θʌmiŋ ə 'lift)
on leave (on 'liːv)
no man's land ('nou 'manz 'land)
to give a lift (tə 'giv ə 'lift)
Thanks a lot! ('θaŋks ə 'lot)
To begin with (tə bi'gin wið)
to die out (tə 'dai 'aut)
coming back to life ('kʌmiŋ bak tə 'laif)
to take it over (tə 'teik it 'ouvə)
to keep us in order (tə 'kiːp ʌs in 'oːdə)
we're going to stick to them (wiə gouiŋ tə 'stik tə ðəm)
I can tell you ('ai kən 'tel ju)

EXERCISES

A   *Complete these sentences by adding a noun or pronoun which refers to the same person or thing as the noun or pronoun in italics:*

1. *Tom* was chosen . . .
2. *George Washington* was . . .
3. Mr Carter found *Tom* . . .
4. *Mr Brown* was appointed . . .
5. *Rome* was once . . .
6. *This boy* seems . . .
7. Her friends chose *her* . . .
8. *The cleverest man among them* was elected . . .

B.   *Write sentences expressing the following ideas and using the word given in brackets:*

Example: Idea: A possibility of rain. (may)
          Sentence: It may rain tomorrow.

1. A request for permission to leave the room. (may)
2. A prohibition against bringing books into an examination room. (must)
3. The possibility that someone has lost his way. (may)
4. An order against smoking in a theatre. (permit)
5. A refusal of permission to come in. (let)
6. A refusal of permission to stay out late at night. (allow)
7. The possibility that someone's car has broken down. (perhaps)
8. A polite request for another cup of tea. (might)
9. A request to see someone's driving licence. (can)
10. The possibility of spending a holiday abroad. (possible)

C.   *Write sentences using the following verbs in the present tense:*

notice; forgive; refuse; forget; own; see; dislike; wish; understand; belong to.

D. *Write sentences using the following phrasal verbs:*

put by; put up with; take over; take down; come about; come on; go along; go over; go on; go out.

E. *Put* a, an *or* the *into the blank spaces in the following passage as required:*

David and . . . friend had decided to spend . . . day or two in Rome during . . . summer. They went by . . . train, because they wanted to see more of . . . countries through which they passed than if they had gone by . . . air. When they arrived in . . . Eternal City, they bought . . . guide-book and decided on . . . places they wanted to visit. At . . . beginning of each day they made . . . list of . . . places to be seen during . . . day. It was . . . difficult task to choose among . . . many places of interest as they could only stay for . . . short time. But at . . . end of . . . holiday they decided their first visit to Rome would be . . . memory which would stay with them for . . . rest of their lives.

F. *Here is a report of a speech. Write down the words you think the speaker actually used:*

The Chairman declared it was no easy task to introduce a speaker to an audience especially when he was such a well-known public figure as Mr X. It was rather like introducing a man to his own family. He would, however, be on safe ground, he thought, if he contented himself by thanking Mr X on their behalf for coming along to their meeting that day, and asking him to address them.

G. *Re-write these sentences, using a sentence pattern with* too *instead of the sentence pattern with* enough.

Example: He is not old enough to go to school.
He is too young to go to school.

1. He is not tall enough to reach that high shelf.

2. This coat is not big enough for you.
3. This village is not far enough from London to be really in the country.
4. This exercise is not difficult enough for you.
5. This train is not fast enough to be called an express.
6. This shirt is not clean enough to wear.
7. He did not arrive early enough for dinner.
8. The hats Mrs Brown buys are not cheap enough for Susan.
9. That case is not light enough for you to carry.
10. She was not well enough to come to the party.

COMPOSITION
Expressing Ideas

In Lesson 4 we discussed the gathering of material for a composition and its arrangement under paragraph-headings. Let us suppose that you have chosen your subject with care, have decided how you are going to deal with the subject, and have collected and arranged all the material. You are now ready to set your ideas down in written English, and as you have done the thinking first, you can give all your attention to the way in which you are going to express your ideas.

What you write will not be clear to the reader unless every sentence actually says what you meant to say; that is, unless you have chosen the right words and put them in the right order. Think out each sentence carefully before you begin to write it down.

Besides being clear, you should try to make your writing *interesting*. Statements of what everyone knows are seldom interesting to read. We prefer to be given a lively word-picture or a true story to make the truth real to us. It will help to gain your reader's interest, too, if he feels you are giving your own opinions or knowledge about something gained from your own experience.

Take care in choosing the words you use. Do not be satisfied with the first word that comes into your mind but search until you find the one that exactly expresses what you wish to say. This applies specially to adjectives and adverbs, for it is these 'describing words' that build up vivid pictures.

Your writing will seem more interesting if you do not make all your sentences alike. Consider this example:

It was a beautiful day. We decided to go out into the country. We got out our bicycles and set off. We took our lunch with us. But after a while it began to rain. We took shelter in an old barn.

A story that went on much longer like this would become very dull. All the sentences are constructed in the same way, and they sound as if they were being fired one after another from a gun. Try to smooth out your writing by linking two or more sentences together in different ways.

When you have finished your composition, read it through carefully. Watch particularly for mistakes in spelling, punctuation and the use of words. Be sure that every sentence is properly constructed and says exactly what you meant to say.

EXERCISES

1. Write a composition on 'My Favourite Relative'.
2. Write a letter to an English friend whom you have invited to visit your home town or village, giving a description of the place and the surrounding district.
3. Write the letter of thanks that David might send to the Editor after his visit to Fleet Street.

LESSON 6

Election Day at Bishopton

ONE morning in late summer David found a letter waiting for him on the breakfast-table with the heading: House of Commons, London, S.W.1. It was from his father's old friend Stephen Turner, Member of Parliament for Bishopton. Here is the letter.

House of Commons,
London, S.W.1
1st September, 19—

Dear David,

When we met during your visit to Westminster last year
you expressed some interest in making politics your career.
I thought perhaps you might like to see one very important
part of a politician's life 'from inside'.

As you know, there is to be a General Election next month,
and I am organising a small group of young people to help
my agent and his committee in Bishopton during the election
campaign. Would you care to join us?

You would be expected to make yourself generally useful
at meetings, in the committee-rooms, driving speakers about
and so on. There is a great deal to be done, as you can
imagine, and I can promise you a lively and interesting three
weeks. Polling Day is on the 6th October. So it will be all
over before your term begins at Oxford.

You will not be expected to make speeches, and it doesn't
matter whether you know all about our policy—or even
whether you entirely agree with it!

Please give my good wishes to your father and mother.

Yours sincerely,
Stephen Turner

David readily accepted this invitation and soon found
himself in the thick of the political battle. As the sitting
Member, there was no need for Mr Turner to be 'adopted'
by the local committee of his party, so the first step was to
hand in his nomination papers to the Mayor at the Town
Hall. David went with him to this little ceremony, and saw
him hand in the nomination paper together with the sum of

£150 as a deposit. A candidate who does not gain one eighth of the total number of votes loses his deposit.

For the next three weeks everyone connected with the election was kept very busy indeed. Thousands of envelopes had to be addressed so that a copy of the candidate's election address, in which he set out the good deeds he proposed to do if elected, could go out to all voters. Mr Turner and his supporters visited as many houses as possible, trying to persuade people to vote for him. David spent a good deal of time driving Mr Turner round the streets of Bishopton in a car with a loud-speaker so that he could reach even more of the voters and whip up interest in the election.

The public meetings were interesting but not as lively as David had expected. He had read stories of elections years ago when it was common for the candidates to make violent attacks on each other's reputation as well as policy, and where things were thrown at the speakers. Indeed, he wondered whether election meetings had much effect today. Most of the people in the hall were supporters who had already decided to vote for the candidate holding the meeting. The others were supporters of the other party, who had made up their minds to vote for his opponent and had come to interrupt. On the whole, the meetings were very orderly. The best-attended was that at which the Prime Minister spoke. It was most impressive to see the skilful manner in which he presented his party's policy and handled interrupters.

At last Polling Day arrived. The time for discussion and argument about the rival policies of the Conservative, Liberal and Labour Parties was over—and the time for decision had come. From the time the polling stations opened at eight in the morning until they closed at nine in the evening David was kept busy fetching elderly or invalid voters from their homes to the polling stations in an attempt to see that no one who could vote omitted to do so. In the old days candidates would bribe voters to support them on polling day by gifts of money as well as of food and drink. But the introduction of secret voting during the nineteenth century put an end to this. Now it is illegal for a candidate to spend more than a fixed sum on an election campaign.

Although David was too young to vote himself—he would have to wait for this until he was twenty-one—he was allowed to see how the voting was done. Each voter's name was checked on the list of those with the right to vote and he or she was then given a piece of paper containing the names of the candidates. This he took to a desk shut off from other voters and put a cross against the name of the candidate he wished to vote for. He then dropped the paper into a large box.

At the end of the day, all these boxes were collected from the polling stations and taken to the Town Hall. And then the counting of the votes began. Excitement grew as the piles of voting papers mounted up. Who would be the winner?

Just before midnight the last paper was counted, the candidates were asked if they were satisfied with the way the counting had been done, and the Mayor was handed a piece of paper showing the result. In a little procession His Worship the Mayor walked out on to a balcony overlooking Bishopton Market Place, followed by the candidates. Even at this late hour, there was quite a large crowd waiting below to watch the ceremony, and a cheer greeted them as they appeared. Slowly the Mayor read out the names of the candidates in the same order in which they had appeared on the ballot papers.

> "Alan Nicholson   16,324
> Stephen Turner   23,196
> Herbert Williams   10,569

I therefore declare Stephen Turner duly elected as Member of Parliament for Bishopton."

There was a cheer from the crowd as Mr Turner stepped forward to thank all who had voted for him and in particular all those who had helped in the election campaign. The defeated candidates then each spoke in turn, thanking their supporters and congratulating the winner—and Election Day was over, perhaps for another five years.

CONVERSATION

(*It is the end of a busy day. David has driven Mr Turner home, for as a good Member of Parliament should, Mr Turner lives in the town. He has invited David in for a chat*)

MR TURNER: Well, that's the end of another day! Only three more days now. Are you enjoying it?

DAVID: Immensely. It was good of you to ask me to help. I've learnt a lot, too.

MR TURNER: Good. About what, in particular?

DAVID: About the way we are governed mainly. Take the party system, for example. This seems terribly important in day to day affairs and at election time, but no notice is taken of it officially. Anyone can become a candidate for Parliament so long as he or she is willing to risk £150 and can get the support of ten voters, whether he belongs to a political party or not. Again, the list of names on the voting paper does not say which party each supports, and when the result is declared, the candidates' parties are still not mentioned. The Ministers who form the Government are not chosen by a party but by the Prime Minister, who is sent for by the Queen as the man who can command a majority of supporters in the House of Commons. He usually chooses his Ministers from his own party, but he need not do so, and in times of difficulty or danger—during a war, for example—a government may be formed from all parties.

MR TURNER: Yes, it's all very peculiar, isn't it? The answer is, of course, that we have had a parliament very like our present one with an Upper and a Lower House since the end of the thirteenth century, while the party system dates only from the end of the seventeenth century. And in this country we don't like to get rid of the ancient ways to which we have become accustomed; instead we change the old ways to meet new conditions, leaving as much of the old as we can.

DAVID: I've been impressed, too, by the friendly way in which everyone behaves. Each side wants to win, but no one gets angry or really excited. Even those who come to meetings to interrupt seem to do it more for fun than anything else. I don't think I've heard a really insulting remark during the whole campaign.

MR TURNER: I think this is because on many matters the three parties are largely agreed—they differ chiefly on the way in which changes should be made and the speed at which the government should move. Knowing this, the majority of voters, who do not belong actively to any political party, are not much worried about which party wins the election: moreover, any government which loses the support of the mass of the people can be changed after four or five years when there is another General Election. And now I think that's enough for tonight; it's time you went to bed. We've got another very long day tomorrow and my throat's quite sore with making speeches. Good-night, David, and many thanks for your help.

COMPREHENSION QUESTIONS

1. What is the chief difference between the House of Commons and the House of Lords?
2. What is 'an election campaign'?
3. What were David's duties during the campaign?
4. What are 'nomination papers'?
5. Which are the three main political parties in England?
6. How is voting at an election kept secret?
7. What are the duties and powers of the Prime Minister?
8. What were the two things that surprised David most about the election?
9. What is 'the party system'?
10. What happens to a candidate who receives less than one-eighth of the total number of votes at an election?

SENTENCE PATTERNS

28.   How to express Obligation and Necessity

Obligation and necessity are expressed by *must, have to, have got to, should, ought to, need to.*

(a) *Must* is used to express obligation in the present and future:

I must go home now.
We must visit him when we are in London next week.

The negative of *must*, that is an absence of obligation, is *need not (needn't)*:

Must we go home now. No, we needn't.

Must not (mustn't) is not the negative of *must*, but is used for a positive prohibition:

Passengers must not cross the line.
You mustn't do that again.

Notice that in the question form of *need* to express necessity

    Need he go?

the verb does not have the usual *s* of the third person singular.

(*b*) *Have to* is used to express obligation and necessity in the present, past and future. In conversation *have got to* is often used.

    I have to do my homework now.
    We have got to be in London by six o'clock.
    We had to do the work all over again.

Notice these question forms:

    (i) Do I have to . . . ?   Do I need to . . . ?
    (ii) Have I (got) to . . . ?   Need I . . . ?

The (i) forms are used for customary actions, the (ii) forms for a single occasion:

    Do we have to hand our books in each week? Do we need to . . . ?
    Do we have to speak English all the time? Do we need to . . . ?
    Have we (got) to finish this exercise today? Need we finish . . . ?
    Have we (got) to go now? Need we go now . . . ?

The same difference is seen in the negative forms:

    (i) I don't have to . . .   I don't need to . . .
    (ii) I haven't (got) to . . .   I need not (needn't) . . .

    He doesn't have to drive to London every day. He doesn't need to . . .
    We haven't (got) to drink all this wine if we don't want to. We needn't . . .

In the past tense *had to* has two negative forms with *need*: *didn't need to* and *needn't have* with slightly different meanings. Thus

    He didn't need to run. (There was plenty of time to catch the train without running, so he probably didn't run.)

He needn't have run. (He ran, but there was no need for him to do so as there was plenty of time.)

Other examples showing this difference are:

Tom didn't need to buy a new car. (His old one was still in good condition, so he probably didn't buy one.)

Tom needn't have bought a new car. (But he did, even though his old one was in good condition.)

The students didn't need to read all the books on the list.

He needn't have read all the books on the list.

(c) *Must* and *Have to* in the Present. Usually if the obligation depends on the speaker, we use *must*. If the obligation comes from someone or something other than the speaker, we use *have to*. Consider these examples:

I must buy myself a new suit. (Because I want one.)

I have to be at work by nine o'clock. (The time is fixed by someone else.)

I must eat less bread and potatoes. (Because I don't want to get fat.)

I have to stay in bed for a week. (The doctor has ordered me to.)

Notice that *must* is used in straightforward questions seeking information, *need* is used in questions in which the speaker hopes for a negative answer. Thus if the speaker says

Must we go to school at nine o'clock?

he is merely asking for information, but if he says

Need we get to school at nine o'clock?

he is hoping the reply will be

No.　or　No, you needn't.

(d) *Ought to, should* express duty or advisability.

You ought to be more careful.

David ought to speak more politely to his sister.

Children should be seen and not heard.

You should always look both ways before crossing the street.

The negative of *ought to* and *should* (an absence of duty) is *have not to* or *need not*.

You haven't to read all the books on this list.
We haven't to be home until next Saturday.
You needn't go if you don't want to.
You needn't pay until you are ready to leave.

The forms *ought not to* and *should not* are used to express a duty or an advisability *not* to do something.

You ought not to waste so much time.
Tom ought not to drive so fast.
He shouldn't get up so late in the morning.
One shouldn't believe everything one sees in newspapers.

All the forms expressing obligation, necessity or duty have a Fulfilled and an Unfulfilled Past, depending on whether the action concerned was or was not carried out.
The Fulfilled Past is always formed with *had* and a to-infinitive.

I had to finish my work (and I did actually finish it).

The Unfulfilled Past is formed with *should* or *ought to* with a Perfect Infinitive.

I ought to (should) have finished my work (but I didn't).

29. The Structure of the Sentence—3

In this sentence structure the verb is followed by a noun or pronoun as object and a past participle closely linked with it. Sometimes there is an adverb also. The pattern is:

subject + verb + (pro)noun + past participle (+ adverb)

I saw him killed.
I want this work done carefully.
I like my shoes well polished.
The wicked king made himself feared and hated.

The causative use of *have, get* (see Lesson 1, Sentence Pattern 3) is found in this pattern:

They have had their house painted.
I'm going to have my watch mended.
You should get your garden gate repaired.

Verbs used thus are:

find, get, have, like, make, see, want, wish.

30.   Phrasal Verbs—*Look*

Look about

He looked about him for some time, but could not see his friend.
They were looking about for somewhere to stay for the night.

Look down on

You should not look down on people less fortunate than yourself.
I'm afraid they rather look down on their old friends now they
   have moved into a bigger house.

Look forward to

We are looking forward to our holiday in Italy.
I think we may look forward to better weather now we have
   moved farther south.

Look into

I must look into this a little more carefully before reaching a
   decision.

Look through

I have looked through these homework exercises and they seem
   satisfactory.
He looked through several books in the library, but he could not
   find the information he wanted.

31.   Manage

Manage has two meanings:

(*a*) To control.

   Bobby eats with a spoon because he is too young to manage
      a knife and fork.
   This boat is easy to sail; a crew of two could manage her.

Tom hopes to manage a factory of his own one day.
David is now old enough to manage his own affairs.

(b) To succeed in achieving an aim.

I managed to find an empty seat.
I hoped to catch the train, but I didn't quite manage it.
She generally manages to get her own way.

NEW WORDS

balcony ('balkəni)
behaviour (bi'heivjə)
campaign (kam'pein)
candidate ('kandideit)
ceremony ('seriməni)
condition (kən'diʃn)
Conservative (kən'səːvətiv)
cross (kros)
danger ('deindʒə)
deed (diːd)
deposit (di'pozit)
difficulty ('difikəlti)
effect (i'fekt)
election (i'lekʃn)
envelope ('envəloup)
hall (hoːl)
heading ('hediŋ)
insult (noun) ('insʌlt)
invalid ('invəlid)
Labour ('leibə)
Liberal ('libərəl)
majority (mə'dʒorəti)
minister ('ministə)
nature ('neitʃə)
nomination (nomi'neiʃn)
notice ('noutis)

opponent (ə'pounənt)
organisation ('oːgənai'zeiʃn)
pile (pail)
procession (prə'seʃn)
reputation (repju'teiʃn)
result (ri'zʌlt)
rival (raivl)
supporter (sə'poːtə)
system ('sistəm)
throat (θrout)
total ('toutl)
war (woː)
whip (wip)
accustom (ə'kʌstəm)
act (akt)
adopt (ə'dopt)
attack (ə'tak)
behave (bi'heiv)
bribe (noun and verb) (braib)
chat (tʃat)
command (kə'maːnd)
congratulate (kən'gratjuleit)
declare (di'kleə)
defeat (di'fiːt)
elect (i'lekt)
fix (fiks)

greet (griːt)
insult (verb) (inˈsʌlt)
interrupt (intəˈrʌpt)
mount (maunt)
notice (ˈnoutis)
omit (əˈmit)
organise (ˈoːgənaiz)
support (səˈpoːt)
worship (ˈwəːʃip)
active (ˈaktiv)
common (ˈkomən)
difficult (ˈdifiklt)
elder (ˈeldə)
elderly (ˈeldəli)
entire (enˈtaiə, inˈtaiə)
general (ˈdʒenərəl)
illegal (iˈliːgl)
impressive (imˈpresiv)
legal (ˈliːgl)

local (ˈloukl)
natural (ˈnatrəl)
official (əˈfiʃl)
peculiar (piˈkjuːljə)
rid (rid)
secret (ˈsiːkrit)
sincere (sinˈsiə)
sore (soː)
thick (θik)
upper (ˈʌpə)
violent (ˈvaiələnt)
whole (houl)
duly (ˈdjuːli)
entirely (inˈtaiəli)
officially (əˈfiʃəli)
sincerely (sinˈsiəli)
inside (inˈsaid)
moreover (moːˈrouvə)

Idioms

in the thick of (in ðə ˈθik əv)
on the whole (ˈon ðə ˈhoul)
in the old days (in ði ˈould deiz)
day to day affairs (ˈdei tə ˈdei əˈfeəz)
to get rid of (tə get ˈrid əv)

EXERCISES

A. *Put these sentences into the past tense:*

1. I must be home by nine o'clock.
2. I shall have to spend more time on my work.
3. Each candidate must hand in his nomination papers by a certain day.
4. I've got to finish my work before I go out.
5. Every polling station must close at eight o'clock.

6. He needn't go if he doesn't want to.
7. David needn't accept Mr Turner's invitation to help with the election.
8. We shan't need to be there until three o'clock.
9. He won't need to take an overcoat.
10. He must have a bath every day.

B. *Make these sentences negative, so that the obligation is removed:*

1. You must speak English all the time while you are in this class.
2. You have to believe all you see in the newspapers.
3. We must brush our teeth after every meal.
4. David will have to make some political speeches during the election.
5. They had to hurry to catch the plane.
6. Everyone must be there before the show starts.
7. You'll have to finish this work before you go home.
8. A Member of Parliament must be present whenever the House is sitting.
9. The Mayor had to count all the votes himself.
10. Mr Turner will have to address a meeting every evening during the election.

C. *Use the following verbs in the sentence pattern:*

subject + verb + object + past participle (Sentence Pattern 29).

Example: I want this work done carefully.

make; find; see; want; wish; like; have; get.

D. *Put the indirect object in brackets into the correct place in these sentences, adding* to *or* for *where required:*

1. Mr Turner gave a small present. (David)
2. The teacher offered a prize. (all those who had passed the examination)
3. Can you lend half a crown? (me)

4. Mr Thompson teaches geography. (the boys)
5. He wrote long letters. (all his friends)
6. She buys nice Christmas presents. (her younger brothers and sisters)
7. David owes a pound already. (Susan)
8. She sold her house. (the first person who would buy it)
9. Fetch some flowers from the garden, please Susan. (me)
10. Susan chose a book. (a friend in hospital)

E. *Use a part of the verb* to be *in place of the words in italics in each of these sentences:*

1. Mr Turner *seemed* a very friendly person.
2. *Don't* do that again.
3. This work *must* be finished before you go home.
4. She *appeared* very unhappy.
5. She *had* to be home before midnight.
6. We *had planned* to visit some friends before leaving Rome.
7. He *stood* waiting for a taxi.
8. David *seemed* pleased to hear from Mr Turner.
9. *Don't* waste all your money on buying sweets.
10. Tom and Susan *intend* to get married later this year.

F. *Put* a, an, some, any *into these sentences as required:*

1. Boys are usually stronger than girls.
2. The cook gave him piece of cake and slice of bread.
3. She put oranges in basket to carry them home.
4. Wise man has hobby as well as his work.
5. Holiday is not very pleasant without sunshine.
6. She had milk in bottle and sugar in paper bag.
7. Glass of lemonade is very refreshing but chocolates make one thirsty.
8. Journey by train is quicker than journey by bus.
9. Election is busy time for candidate and his helpers.
10. Napoleon said the English were nation of shopkeepers.

G. *Express the idea of* ability *or* inability *in each of these sentences in another way:*

1. He can add up three columns of figures at the same time.
2. It is possible to see five counties from the top of this hill.
3. I can't come to the party this evening.
4. He did not jump into the water because he could not swim.
5. He could speak four languages before he was ten.
6. We are not able to deliver these goods in less than three months.
7. It is not possible for us to stay for more than a week.
8. Although he could swim only a short distance he was able to reach the bank of the river in safety.
9. He managed to make himself heard above the noise because he had a strong voice.
10. In most great cities of the world you can usually find someone who speaks English.

H. *Write sentences using the following verbs in the present tense:*

hear; smell; recognise; like; love; hate; prefer; mind; care; want.

I. *Put the correct prepositions into the blank spaces in this passage:*

I climbed . . . bed and rolled myself . . . my blankets, first putting . . . the light that burned steadily . . . the door. I lay still, trying to get . . . sleep, but my fears made that impossible and soon I sat . . . . . . bed peering . . . the darkness and occasionally looking . . . the round window . . . the side . . . the ship which seemed like a plate hanging . . . the blackness. . . . an hour I must have sat like this, and then I was suddenly roused . . . a draught . . . cold air. I jumped . . . . . . bed but, not having allowed . . . the motion . . . the ship, I was instantly thrown violently . . . the room. . . . difficulty I got . . . and felt my way . . . the window, which . . . my surprise I found wide open for I was certain that I had fastened it securely before I went . . . bed.

J. *Use the following phrasal verbs in sentences:*

take out; put in for; come across; go in for; look down on; look after; look forward to; look up to; look out for; look round.

COMPOSITION

Beginning and Ending a Composition

Students would produce better compositions if they thought of themselves as journalists writing articles which they hoped to be able to sell. They would then consider their readers and their work would be more interesting.

If you are looking through the pages of a magazine on a station bookstall, which are the articles that catch your eye and make you want to buy the magazine? They are those that begin in an interesting way, for a dull opening does not win the reader's attention. This, then, is the first thing to remember about the beginning of a composition: you must seize and hold the reader's attention from the start.

There are various ways of doing this. You can begin with a little story taken from your reading or from a personal experience. This, of course, is how most discussions begin in real life: something rather out of the ordinary happens, and people begin talking about the problem it raises. For example, we see an accident in the street and we begin to discuss the need for 'safety first' on the roads. Another interesting way of opening an essay is to make some brief and striking statement of fact or opinion. A quotation, too, can sometimes make an effective opening. But whatever method you use, the first few sentences must hold the reader's attention, so that he wishes to read on.

Now for the ending. If you have tried, as you should, to *do* something in your composition—to persuade the reader, to express your views, to give him a clear picture of what happened or what some person or place was like, then the last few sentences should leave the main thought or impression clearly in the reader's mind. It is quite a good plan to take up again the thought or story or quotation with which you began; this gives a roundness or completeness to the composition. Or you can look back over the way that you have come, stating the arguments again briefly. Or you can look forward into the future, suggesting what later years will bring.

There are many ways of ending as well as beginning a composition. But as you must begin by gaining and holding the reader's interest, so you must end firmly with a sense of completeness. No one should be left in any doubt that you have reached the end.

EXERCISES

1. Write a composition beginning 'I shall never forget that day as long as I live'.
2. Write a composition on 'Younger Brothers and Sisters'.
3. Write the speech you think Mr Turner might have made when the Mayor announced that he had been re-elected Member of Parliament for Bishopton.

LESSON 7

A Motoring Tour of England—3

AFTER spending a pleasant week-end with their friends in South Wales, Tom and Susan began their return journey. Again they reached the English border at Chepstow, but this time they turned north and followed the west bank of the River Wye as far as Monmouth. On their way they passed the grey ruins of Tintern Abbey, with dark green woods rising behind them on the farther bank. The air was very still in the noon heat, and they saw rabbits running about in the sacred places where once the priests had prayed and the monks had sung the praises of 'the God who made the hills'. They remembered the verses written by the poet Wordsworth as he stood here, drinking in the scene so that he would remember it in the future:

'Here I stand,' he wrote, 'not only with the sense
Of present pleasure, but with pleasing thoughts
That in this moment there is life and food
For future years.'

They stopped for lunch at an old roadside inn where brass lamps hung from dark oak beams, lines of shining copper jugs and kettles stood on shelves, and the beer was drawn from barrels in the bar. It was cool indoors after the hot sunlight, and they enjoyed a long refreshing drink before sitting down to a meal of cold Wye salmon with salad and new potatoes. They spent a pleasant hour after lunch chatting to the landlord, who was not quite the sort of man they had expected to find in the heart of the country.

They crossed the River Wye at Monmouth and the Severn at Tewkesbury. In Tewkesbury they saw, in the abbey church, the graves of the brave young Prince of Wales who was killed in battle here during the Wars of the Roses and of the Prince who was drowned in a barrel of wine by order of his brother, the wicked King Richard III. Susan and David had tea at an inn, called the 'Hop-Pole' mentioned by the writer Charles Dickens in the *Pickwick Papers*.

Late in the evening they came to the red brick and green trees of Stratford-on-Avon. Down by the river, the swans were floating gently on the still water, as they did in Shakespeare's time, and the bells were ringing from the tower of Holy Trinity Church, where Shakespeare himself lies buried. Here, Susan felt, was the heart of England—the England that Shakespeare knew and loved. And she remembered what he had written about 'this England':

'This royal throne of Kings, this sceptred isle,
This earth of majesty, this seat of Mars,
This other Eden, demi-paradise;
This happy breed of men, this little world;
This precious stone set in the silver sea,
Which serves it in the office of a wall
Or as a moat defensive to a house,
Against the envy of less happier lands;
This blessed plot, this earth, this realm, this England.'

In most parts of England it is easy to find a hotel in which to spend the night without booking, but in places like Stratford, which are crowded with visitors in the summer, you may find all the hotels full. So Tom had written in advance to book rooms. This is the letter he wrote:

86, Hilltop Road,
Bishopton,
Surrey

25th May, 19—

The Manager,
The Red Lion Hotel,
Stratford-on-Avon

Dear Sir,

I wish to book two single rooms for myself and a friend for the two nights of Sunday and Monday, 17th and 18th June. We shall arrive before dinner on Sunday evening and shall leave after breakfast on the Tuesday.

Yours truly,
Thomas Smith

This is the letter he received in reply:

> The Red Lion Hotel,
> Stratford-on-Avon
> 27th May, 19—

Thomas Smith, Esq.,
86, Hilltop Road,
Bishopton,
Surrey

Dear Sir,

Thank you for your letter of 25th May. I have pleasure in reserving two single rooms for you for the nights of Sunday and Monday, 17th and 18th June.

Will you kindly confirm this booking?

> Yours faithfully,
> Henry Dyson
> Manager

Susan and Tom spent two days in Stratford, visiting the house where Shakespeare was born, the Grammar School and the cottage near Stratford where his wife, Anne Hathaway, lived as a girl. Both Tom and Susan enjoy the theatre and they saw a performance of one of Shakespeare's plays at the Royal Shakespeare Theatre. On the morning they were due to leave, they got up early and went rowing on the river. In the early sunlight, before the crowds of visitors were out, the river and the little town looked very peaceful. As Tom dipped his oars into the water he thought that this must have been how Stratford looked when Shakespeare came back here to escape from the noise of London.

It had been arranged that they should pass the last two or three days of their holiday with a school-friend of Susan's who lived with her family in Cambridge. As they had plenty of time, they took a roundabout route from Stratford across the breadth of England so that they could visit places of interest on the way.

Their first stop was at Warwick Castle. They found here no ruined shell of broken stones, but a solid and complete building from the middle ages, changed and added to through the centuries, and still the home of the Earls of Warwick. The present Earl has won fame and wealth as a film actor and producer. When he drives through the arched gateway of his ancient castle he must feel as though he is acting in an historical film, ready to take a flying arrow on his shield, or strike down an enemy with his good sword and battle-axe.

From Warwick they drove through leafy by-roads to Northampton, an old market town which has now become a busy industrial centre where most of the working population are engaged in making boots and shoes. They spent the afternoon at the Whipsnade Zoo—a beautiful stretch of open parkland on the side of Dunstable Downs, where a fine collection of animals can be seen under natural conditions.

The next day they visited Woburn Abbey, the home of the Duke of Bedford. They were amused to find not only some splendid furniture and pictures in the house itself, but 'all the fun of the fair' in the grounds, with souvenir-shops, sports and games for the children, and the Duke in person receiving visitors and thoroughly enjoying himself as host to the general public.

They arrived in Cambridge towards evening, and spent the next few days with Susan's friend at the little riverside village of Grantchester, made famous by Rupert Brooke in a poem which ends:

> 'Stands the church clock at ten to three—
> And is there honey still for tea?'

It was a pleasant ending to a wholly delightful holiday.

CONVERSATION

(*Susan and Tom have stopped for lunch at a wayside inn on the banks of the River Wye*)

LANDLORD: Good morning. Lovely day!

TOM: Yes, isn't it? Can we get lunch here?

LANDLORD: Certainly. What would you like?

TOM: What do you recommend?

LANDLORD: Well, we think the fresh salmon is rather good. It came out of the river yesterday—not out of a tin! I expect you'd like it cold with salad on a warm day like this?

SUSAN: That sounds wonderful. I'm so thirsty, I think I'd like a long, cool drink first.

(*The Landlord gives them their beer and, at Tom's suggestion, draws one for himself*)

LANDLORD: How far have you come today?

TOM: Only from outside Cardiff. This part of the country is new to us, so we're not hurrying. You're not a native here, are you?

LANDLORD: No, I'm not. My wife and I have wandered about the world so much we're natives of nowhere. When I retired from the Regular Army three years ago we decided we'd settle down in the country to enjoy some of the peace and quiet we've never had before. I didn't want to sit about doing nothing, so we took over this little place and we run it between us.

SUSAN: And *are* you enjoying it?

LANDLORD: Immensely. After commanding a regiment in India and being responsible for keeping law and order in a district of Africa nearly as big as the whole of England, running a country inn is a complete change. We like the people we meet, too—both the visitors like yourselves and the people who live round about. Couldn't have done this at one time, you know, but times have changed—and for the better, too, I think. But you'll be wanting your lunch. The dining-room's through there on the right. Ask my wife to see that you have a cut off one of the salmon I caught yesterday.

(*After lunch*)

LANDLORD: Well, did you enjoy your lunch?

SUSAN: It was excellent. Quite the best salmon I have ever tasted, and a wonderful apple pie to follow. I feel as though I shan't want to eat again for a week.

LANDLORD: Good. Do you ever do any fishing?

TOM: A little. But Susan's father is the great fisherman in the family.

LANDLORD: You should get him to bring his rods down here for a holiday. We have some of the finest salmon-fishing in the country here. The flavour of Wye salmon is as good as anything you'll find even in Canada—and I know, because I fished most of their salmon streams when I was attached to the Governor-General's staff at Ottawa.

SUSAN: Don't you sometimes miss all the moving about from place to place?

LANDLORD: Not a bit. When you've lived without a permanent home for thirty-four years you're quite content to begin putting down some roots.

SUSAN: Which did you like best of all the places you lived in?

LANDLORD: That's hard to say. Every place has its advantages—and its disadvantages. But I think we enjoyed India most. It's a wonderful country—full of colour and life and interest. Kipling said,

'East is East, and West is West
And never the twain shall meet,'

but I found the Indians in many ways very much like ourselves. And what amazing steps forward they have taken since independence. We saw the beginning of this before we left. The British may be proud to think that they helped to lay the foundations for much of this progress.

SUSAN: And now you have come to settle down in this little corner of the English countryside.

LANDLORD: Yes, and here we intend to stay. Only those who have lived away from home for a long time really appreciate England. And now I expect you'll be wanting to get on your way. I hope you enjoy the rest of your tour—although my wife and I still find it hard to get used to the idea that in England people spend two or three days over a journey that in Africa or Canada or Australia would be an afternoon's drive.

SUSAN: Good-bye—and thank you for our excellent lunch. I shall certainly tell my father he must come here when he wants some good fishing.

COMPREHENSION QUESTIONS

1. What did Wordsworth mean by the words quoted in the reading passage?
2. In which year was Shakespeare born, and when did he die?
3. Why was the landlord of the inn 'not quite the sort of man they had expected to find in the heart of the countryside'?
4. Why had he settled down in this English village?
5. Which of the countries he had visited did he enjoy most, and why?
6. What did he find strange about life in England?
7. What is meant by the 'British Commonwealth of Nations'?
8. In what ways do you think the Stratford of today differs from the town that Shakespeare knew?

9. Why do many people enjoy visiting places of historic interest ?
10. What other places in the south of England would Tom and Susan find interesting, and why?

SENTENCE PATTERNS

32. How to express Commands, Requests and Prohibitions

Commands vary from a direct imperative to the politest request. The difference in tone and intention is expressed partly by the form of words used and partly by intonation. The tone in which a command is given is often more important than the words that are used.

(*a*) *Direct Commands*

Shut the window! Be quiet! Let me go!

(*b*) *Polite Commands*

You must be more careful.
Shut the door, please.
Pass me the sugar, will you?
Keep this seat for me, please.
Please be quiet.

(*c*) *Requests*

Will you be quiet?
Will you close the door, please?
Would you lend me your pen for a moment?
Would you mind holding my umbrella while I find my ticket, please?
I wish you would talk more quietly.
Could you speak a little more loudly, please? I can't hear very well.
May I close the window, please?

(d) *Prohibitions*

Don't swim too far out.

Don't be so rude!

Don't let him do it.

No smoking!

No talking in class, please.

Books must not be taken from the library.

Passengers must not cross the line except by the bridge.

You can't come in here.

He can't do just as he likes, you know.

Please don't make so much noise.

Will you please not walk through the house in those dirty boots?

33. Phrasal Verbs—*Get*

(See Book Two, page 240)

Get about

It's nice to see old Mr Jones getting about again.

It got about that his business was doing badly.

Get along

I don't know how he'll get along without his partner.

Get away with

The thieves got away with over a thousand pounds.

You won't be able to get away with that story; no one will believe you.

Get through

The young man's father left him a lot of money; but he got through it in no time.

When I get through my work I'll call round to see you.

Mr and Mrs Brown will be pleased if David gets through his examination.

34. *Now that . . .*

This conjunction is used to join two parts of a sentence, one half of which states a present situation and the other half states the result that follows from that situation. The part introduced by *Now that* . . . may come before or after the other. *That* is often omitted in conversation.

Now (that) summer has come, we can wear lighter clothes.
Now (that) you have started work, you will have to get up earlier in the morning.
Tom has a good deal more money to spend, now (that) he has become a manager.
David no longer plays football every Saturday now (that) he has left school.

NEW WORDS

advantage (əd'vaːntidʒ)
air (eə)
arch (aːtʃ)
army ('aːmi)
arrow ('arou)
axe (aks)
bar (baː)
barrel ('barəl)
beer (biə)
brass (braːs)
breadth (bretθ)
copper ('kopə)
earth (əːθ)
flavour ('fleivə)
foundation (faun'deiʃn)
God (god)
grave (greiv)
heat (hiːt)
inn (in)
jug (dʒʌg)
lamp (lamp)
landlord ('landloːd)

noon (nuːn)
oak (ouk)
oar (oː)
population (popju'leiʃn)
priest (priːst)
prince (prins)
rabbit ('rabit)
regiment ('redʒəmənt)
rod (rod)
root (ruːt)
route (ruːt)
ruin(s) ('ruːin(z))
salmon ('samən)
sense (sens)
shell (ʃel)
shield (ʃiːld)
song (soŋ)
souvenir (suːvə'niə)
sword (soːd)
thought (θoːt)
tin (tin)
verse (vəːs)

advance (əd'vaːns)

confirm (kən'fəːm)

dip (dip)

drown (draun)

envy (noun and verb) ('envi)

praise (preiz)

pray (prei)

refresh (ri'freʃ)

row (rou)

wander ('wondə)

amazing (ə'meiziŋ)

brave (breiv)

content (kən'tent)

cool (kuːl)

holy ('houli)

native ('neitiv)

permanent ('pəːmənənt)

precious ('preʃəs)

regular ('regjulə)

sacred ('seikrid)

solid ('solid)

wayside ('weisaid)

wicked ('wikid)

farther ('faːðə)

indoors (in'doːz)

nowhere ('nouweə)

quite (kwait)

roundabout ('raundəbaut)

Idioms

in the heart of the country (in ðə 'haːt əv ðə 'kʌntri)

to confirm a booking (tə kən'fəːm ə 'bukiŋ)

to take a roundabout route (tə 'teik ə 'raundəbaut 'ruːt)

all the fun of the fair ('oːl ðə 'fʌn əv ðə 'feə)

times have changed ('taimz həv 'tʃeindʒd)

to settle down (tə 'setl 'daun)

EXERCISES

A. *Tell someone to do each of the following, first as a request, then as a polite command, and finally as a direct order:*

1. to pass you a pencil
2. to speak more quietly
3. to read the next sentence
4. to close the window
5. to fetch a book from the cupboard
6. to leave the room
7. to work more carefully
8. to hurry for fear of being late

      9. to give you a match
    10. to tell you his name

B. *Rewrite these sentences, using a phrasal verb with* get *instead of the words in italics:*

1. *People were saying* that the police were looking for him to arrest him.
2. When Mrs Brown *has finished* her housework she is going shopping with Susan.
3. He could not *do his work successfully* without his secretary.
4. Mr Brown asked David a lot of questions in order to *discover* the truth.
5. She had *dressed herself* to look like a boy.
6. Mr Brook fell and broke his leg. He will take a long time *to recover*.
7. I had to lend him the money. I couldn't *avoid it*.
8. They had *developed* the habit of going to the theatre once a week.
9. We were very late home last night. We didn't *arrive home* till after midnight.
10. I have lent him five pounds, but I don't expect *to recover it*.

C. *Complete these sentences, using a* to-*infinitive (Sentence Pattern 8):*

1. You were very kind . . .
2. It was nice . . .
3. They seemed pleased . . .
4. Mr Brown was quite right . . .
5. It is always rude . . .
6. You were silly . . .
7. Susan was sorry . . .
8. It was stupid of you not . . .
9. The doctor appeared surprised . . .
10. David is sure . . .

D. *Add a phrase with* now that . . . *to these sentences. Omit* that *where not required.*

1. . . . I no longer need to take lessons.
2. . . . we can go swimming again.
3. . . . we can start lunch.
4. . . . she will need some new clothes.
5. . . . we wish you joy.
6. You must stop being so childish . . .
7. Tom will be earning more money . . .
8. Mr Carter has become an important man in the town . . .
9. We must put on warmer clothes . . .
10. We should have some finer weather . . .

E. *Rewrite these sentences, replacing the main verb by the verb* have. *After each sentence, state the particular use of* have *(Sentence Pattern 3).*

1. They own a beautiful house in the country.
2. It was necessary for her to stay up all night because her husband was ill.
3. He told someone at the garage to clean his car.
4. I must stay at home tomorrow because some friends are coming to see me.
5. We eat our breakfast at eight o'clock each morning.
6. David is suffering from a very bad cold.
7. She made the servants bring her meals up to her bedroom.
8. I was made to stand outside in the cold for half an hour.
9. We always take a holiday in the early part of the summer.
10. You should be very careful when crossing a busy street.

F. *Write ten sentences each containing a* self-*pronoun used with the verb given, and say whether the pronoun is reflexive or intensive (Book Two, Sentence Pattern 10).*

Example: He killed himself with a knife (reflexive).

1. find 2. cut 3. do 4. ask 5 wash 6. go 7. make 8. shoot 9. cook 10. lose.

G. *Add the correct expressions of time to these sentences:*

1. How long is it . . . you last saw him?
2. Nothing more happened . . . the night, so . . . the morning they sent for the police.
3. I have been here . . . two days, and . . . that time I have spoken to no one.
4. We first met three weeks . . . and I have not seen him . . . .
5. The library is closed . . . Christmas Day and . . . the three days . . . Christmas.
6. I have been in England . . . the beginning of September and I am staying . . . another three months.
7. He did not say a word . . . dinner, but . . . the meal was over he chatted to me . . . more than an hour.
8. Next summer I hope to visit Italy and stay there . . . about a month.
9. It must be at least a month . . . I lent him the book.
10. No one called . . . the morning, so . . . twelve o'clock I decided to go home.

H. *Add the definite article* the *where required in these sentences:*

1. London is capital city of England.
2. When he was chosen captain everyone in team was pleased.
3. This is first time Susan has visited Stratford.
4. Will last boy close door?
5. They crossed Atlantic in *Queen Mary*.
6. Sun is not shining today although weather is warm.
7. When David came home ill from school Mrs Brown sent for doctor.
8. On her way to market each Wednesday Mrs Stansbury gets off bus at church.
9. Browns have friends staying with them at week-end.
10. People who read *Times* are usually well informed.

I. *Express in two different ways an obligation to do the following:*

1. going to Manchester tomorrow
2. meeting a friend in London last Thursday
3. finishing some work before bedtime
4. attending English classes every day
5. cutting the grass in the garden this week-end
6. eating breakfast hurriedly yesterday
7. running to catch a bus
8. always speaking politely
9. being careful not to get lost
10. getting up earlier in the morning

COMPOSITION

Discussion and Argument

An essay is a written composition in which the writer expresses his own personal views or feelings about some topic or problem. The essence of the essay is its individuality, its personal quality. It is this that distinguishes it from other forms of written composition such, for example, as the examination answer. For where an examination answer gives the generally accepted facts and opinions on a topic, the essay attempts to reflect the writer's own thoughts and feelings about it.

Many essay subjects require the discussion of some matter on which there can be more than one opinion. The writer's first task is to decide what exactly is the problem to be discussed. Sometimes the topic of discussion is clearly stated in the title: 'Are the British too interested in sport?' for example. More often the title is general—e.g. 'International Sport' or 'The Responsibility of the Press', and the writer must make up his mind what aspect of the matter he is going to discuss. Sometimes the title is even less helpful, e.g.

'Railways' or 'Coal', and then the choice of treatment is left entirely to the writer.

Having decided what is the topic he intends to discuss, the writer must next choose the way he is going to treat the topic. He can either give both sides of an argument and then 'sum up' like a judge at the end, or he can take the side he believes is right and present this, giving arguments on the other side in order to show that they are wrong. This second method is usually more interesting because the writer has entered the battle and is fighting for what he believes to be right.

Particular care must be taken in the discussion essay with the selection and arrangement of material. Only what will help to make the argument clear should be included, but there should be plenty of examples and illustrations drawn from the writer's experience and reading to add interest and variety. So that the 'train of thought' may be clear, the material should be arranged in paragraphs, each dealing with one part of the argument and following each other in a sensible order (see Composition Note in Lesson 4). The first paragraph of the essay should be lively and interesting to catch and hold the reader's attention, and the last paragraph should bring the essay to a firm and effective end (see Composition Note in Lesson 6).

EXERCISES

1. Write an essay giving your views on whether it is better to live in the country or in the town.
2. Write an essay on 'The Good Old Days—were they really so good?'
3. You have booked a room at a hotel in Cambridge and then find that you will not need it. Write a letter to the manager cancelling the booking.

LESSON 8

His Worship the Mayor

MR HENRY CARTER, the manager of the factory where Tom Smith works, has been a Town Councillor of Bishopton for many years, and this year he has been chosen Mayor.

In most towns in Britain the Councillors are closely linked with one or other of the political parties, but in some towns there are Councillors who are concerned only with local affairs. It is to a group of this kind that Mr Carter belongs.

To be elected Mayor is the greatest honour a man can receive from his fellow-citizens, and the Carter family and their friends were very pleased about it. During his year of office, the Mayor is the Chairman of the Town Council. It is not an honour only, for the Mayor has considerable power and influence. He can propose ideas for the improvement of the town, and he can encourage any good cause which he thinks deserves help. Mr Carter will make a good Mayor, for he is honest and sincere, eager to help others, respected and trusted by all who know him.

Mr and Mrs Brown, David and Susan were invited to be present at the ceremony when Mr Carter was installed as Mayor. It was held in the Town Hall. All the Councillors were there in their red and blue robes trimmed with fur, and the chain of office was placed solemnly round the neck of the new Mayor as he took his seat as Chairman of the Council. After the ceremony, the Mayor invited his friends into the Mayor's Parlour, a delightful room overlooking Bishopton Park, and there they drank the health of the new Mayor, wished him well and signed the Vistors' Book.

When it was all over, Mr Carter asked David and Susan if they would like to come with him on a tour of the Town Hall, so that they could see something of the work being done there. They went first to the Town Clerk's Department. Mr Bennett, the Town Clerk, explained that he was responsible for all the legal business of the corporation. He also arranged Council and committee meetings, saw that they were properly reported and kept track of all their decisions. Mr Ward, the Treasurer, told them that it was his job to collect the rates,* to see that they were spent according to the wishes of the Council, and to keep the town's accounts. He always attempted to reduce the amount of rates that people had to

* Rates: the money collected from the citizens of a town and used to pay for local services such as education, the police, etc.

pay, but this was not easy now that the cost of everything was going up, while the services being provided for the citizens tended to increase rather than decrease.

This became clear when they reached the Department of Education. The Chief Education Officer explained that providing schools and technical colleges, paying teachers and supporting the large numbers of students now at universities would be too much for a small town like Bishopton. On the other hand, in Britain we like to manage as many of our affairs locally as we can. So primary schools in Bishopton for children up to the age of eleven were controlled by him on behalf of the Council, while secondary education for children from eleven to fifteen or older, and further education for those who had left school, were provided and paid for by the county and controlled by the county Education Committee. It all seemed a little complicated, but the system became clearer when he showed them a plan.

Susan found the Public Health Department particularly interesting. Dr Anderson, the Medical Officer of Health, told them that his department was a good example of how work is shared between the central government officials in London, who are responsible to Parliament, and the local government officials, who are responsible to the Town Council. Both groups of officials worked closely together to see that the sick, the blind, the deaf and all who needed medical care were looked after, that the town was clean and healthy and that disease was not allowed to spread. Under the National Health Service all medical care is free, either in hospital or in the patient's own home, and only a small charge is made for medicine.

Before completing their tour, Susan and David met the Engineer, who is responsible for streets, roads, drainage and the upkeep of corporation houses, the Water Engineer (electricity and gas are now nationalised industries, and are not controlled locally) and the Chief Constable who commands the Police Force and is responsible for law and order. In thanking the Mayor for his kindness in showing them round, both agreed that they had not realised quite how big a job it is to run even a small town like Bishopton. Now that they knew more about the work of the Town Hall they would think more highly of the Councillors and their officers. There was one more pleasant surprise still in store for Tom and Susan. As they descended the steps of the Town Hall, they found the Mayor's official car with the town's coat of arms on the door, and a smart driver in uniform waiting to take them home. It had been a most interesting day.

CONVERSATION

(*A meeting of the Bishopton Town Council at the Town Hall. The Mayor, Alderman Henry Carter, is in the Chair*)

THE MAYOR: Item five on the agenda—the proposed new library building. Councillor Collins, Chairman of the Library Committee.

COUNCILLOR COLLINS: Mr Chairman, for a long time now it has been the desire of this Council to fill a gap in the provision made for our citizens by building a Public Library worthy of this town. The present library in the High Street, with its modest stock of books, is too small to meet the needs of a population which has nearly doubled over the last ten years. I fear it must come as a shock to newcomers to Bishopton to find how poorly we are provided for in our town library. From other parts of the country we hear reports of more and more people reading more and more books, while in Bishopton we cannot meet the needs either of the general reader who requires books for pleasure or of the pupils of our schools who need books to help them qualify for the careers they wish to follow. We now have the opportunity to wipe this stain from our town. We have found a suitable piece of land and plans have been very carefully prepared. I urge the Council most strongly to act boldly and give this proposal their approval today.

COUNCILLOR PARSONS: Mr Chairman, Councillor Collins has drawn for us a sad picture of the miserable state of this town without a Public Library. In my humble opinion, much of what he has said is nonsense. We already possess a Public Library—perhaps not as grand a one as Councillor Collins would like, but quite large enough for a town of moderate size such as Bishopton. Those of us who oppose this scheme, Mr Chairman, are, believe me, as patriotic as Mr Collins and his friends; we have no wish to be mean or to keep from our citizens what they have a right to expect. But we have a duty to see that the money paid in rates is spent wisely, and that we make plans within the limits of what we can afford. Councillor Collins may refer to me with scorn as un-civilised and a man without a soul if he wishes, but I declare most earnestly that the need for this new and expensive library building has not been proved and that we should be mad if we permitted ourselves to be rushed into something which, on reflection, we may regret.

COUNCILLOR SAUNDERS: Mr Chairman, I have listened to the previous speaker with some surprise and a good deal of sadness. I must confess that I am doubtful whether we can afford quite so fine and up-to-date a building as the Library Committee have proposed, but it comes as a shock to me that, in spite of all the evidence that has been laid before the Council at previous meetings, anyone should suggest that there is no need for a new library building at all. Perhaps the Library Committee are themselves a little to blame. They might have overcome the objections of those who think we should not owe more than we can pay, if they had put forward a rather simpler plan which could, if necessary, be added to later. I suggest, Mr Chairman, that this scheme should be referred back to the Library Committee for further consideration.

COUNCILLOR COLLINS: Mr Chairman, I do not intend to pour scorn on Councillor Parsons and those who share his views, nor to preach at length on the value of education and culture. Their objections are, if I understand them, merely about expense: the new building, they say, would cost more than we can afford. May I point out to them that the present library building in the High Street, though too small for our needs, is a most valuable property and could be sold for a very considerable sum; this, with the government help for which we could apply, would go a long way towards meeting the cost of the proposed new building. This new Library, Mr Chairman, must not be regarded as just another public expense, one more charge on the rates. It is an act of faith in the future, a declaration that we as a Council believe that there are other things in life besides eating and sleeping and earning one's living. I propose that we accept the architect's plans as they stand and that we go ahead with the new building at the earliest possible moment.

THE MAYOR: You have heard the motion. I now put it to the vote. Those in favour? Those against? I declare the motion carried by 28 votes to 12. The next item on the agenda . . .

COMPREHENSION QUESTIONS

1. By whom are Town Councillors chosen, and for how long do they serve?
2. What are the duties of a Mayor?
3. Why will Mr Carter make a good Mayor?
4. What public services are paid for from the rates?
5. How do the Central and Local Government share the responsibility for education in a small town like Bishopton?
6. How does the education system in England differ from that in your own country?
7. What is meant by 'the National Health Service'?
8. What is a 'nationalised industry'?
9. What is the agenda of a meeting?
10. What is the difference between an Alderman and a Councillor?

SENTENCE PATTERNS

35.   How to express Condition
                    (See Book Two, page 122)

Condition in English is expressed partly by the conjunction with which the conditional part of the sentence begins and partly by the tenses used in the conditional and in the main parts of the sentences.

The conditional conjunctions are:

if, unless, even if, as if, if only, suppose, supposing, so/as long as, provided, providing, on condition that.

The tenses to be used in any conditional sentence will depend (as always with tense in English) partly on time and partly on the idea or intention in the speaker's mind.

Types of Conditional Sentence

(*a*) The result of a stated event. The event may or may not happen, but if it does then the stated result follows. The speaker is thinking in terms of plain fact. The main clause verb may be in any tense of the Indicative, the conditional clause verb may be in any tense of the Indicative except the Future.

> He came if they called him.
> He is on his way to school unless he has been stopped.
> He is a good child if only people leave him alone.
> They will build the new library if the Council agree.
> David will play football tomorrow if his cold is better.

Notice that *will* and *would* are sometimes found in *if*-clauses when they are used as ordinary verbs meaning *willing to* or *determined to* and not as auxiliaries to express the future.

> If you will climb trees, you are likely to fall and hurt yourself.
> I shall be obliged if you will do this as soon as possible.
> I should be glad if you would lend me some money.

(*b*) The probable result of an imagined event. This imagined event may be either possible or impossible. The speaker is thinking in terms of a situation he has created in his mind. In sentences of this kind, the verb in the main clause contains one of the auxiliaries *should, would, could* or *might* and the verb in the conditional clause will be in the Past Tense if the condition refers to the present or future, and in the Past Perfect Tense if the condition refers to the past. If the condition refers to the past, the main verb will have the form *would* (*should, could, might*) *have done*, instead of *would* (*should, could, might*) *do*.

> I should go to London tomorrow if I had the time.
> They would be in Cardiff by mid-day if they left Oxford by nine.
> He could work much harder if he tried.
> You might enjoy yourself there if you went.

They might have avoided the accident if they had been more careful.

They would have gone to the party if they had been invited.

They could have caught the train if they had hurried.

We should have spoken to him if we had recognised him.

If he had taken his coat, he would not have got wet.

If she had worked harder, she might have passed her examination.

If they had set off earlier, they would not have been late.

'If I'd known you were coming, I'd have baked a cake.'

Notice the form 'if I were you' instead of 'if I was you';

You don't look well. I should take a long holiday, if I were you.

I should get rid of that old car, if I were you, and buy a new one.

(c) A statement of general truth or custom, or of cause and effect. In these sentences, the same tense (either Present or Past according to the time) is used in the main and conditional clauses.

If the Romans needed a new road, they built one.

If he travels by train he is always sick.

If the weather is frosty, roads are dangerous.

Centuries ago, if a man had fever he usually died.

If water is heated for long enough, it boils.

If you tease dogs they bite.

Plants usually grow well so long as you give them enough water.

36.   Short Responses—1

When answering a question or making a comment on something which has just been said we can generally use a short form of response in English; this saves us from having to repeat all the other speaker's words. Thus if someone asks *Is Tom going to London tomorrow?* the answer would be *Yes, he is.* (not *Yes, he is going to London tomorrow*). In conversation we use these short responses a great deal, and they are worth careful study. Some of the most commonly used short responses are given here and in Lesson 9. Notice that in all these, the response is made by using one of the special verbs. In the first two kinds of short response the speaker is answering a straightforward question.

(*a*) *Short answers to* Yes/No *Questions*

Did you hear that noise? Yes, I did.
Can you come with us tomorrow? Yes, I can.
Has she finished her work yet? Yes, she has.
Will he be late for his appointment? No, he won't.

A simple answer 'Yes' or 'No' is, of course, also possible here.

Notice that the negative of *must* is *needn't* (Sentence Pattern 28).

Must we go home now? Yes, we must.
Must I answer all the questions? No, you needn't.

(*b*) *Answering questions beginning with question words*

Which of you can drive a car? We all can.
Which of you have been to Edinburgh? Three of us have.
Who gave you that book? Tom did.
Which train goes to Manchester, please? That one does.

In the next two kinds of response, the speaker is agreeing or disagreeing with what has been said.

(*c*) *Agreeing with an affirmative statement*

(i) *Simple agreement*

It's a lovely day today. Yes, it is.
He works hard every day. Yes, he does.

A question-tag is sometimes added here.

David is a very clever boy. Yes, he is, isn't he?
Tom swims very well. Yes, he does, doesn't he?

(ii) *Agreement showing surprise*

You've left your hat in the train. So I have.
Look at the time; it's after five o'clock. So it is.
Look! He has learnt to drive. So he has.

(iii) *Agreement with what is obvious*

I expect it will rain tomorrow. Of course it will.
That clever boy has passed his examination. Of course he has.
He can speak French very well. Of course he can. He has lived in France for years.

(d) *Agreement with a negative statement*

It's not very warm today. No, it's not. *or* No, it isn't.

Very often a question-tag is added here:

He hasn't done very well at school. No, he hasn't, has he?
He's not very polite to his mother. No, he isn't, is he?

(e) *Disagreeing with an affirmative statement:*

His name is John Brown. No, it isn't.
He travels to Manchester very day. No, he doesn't.

Sometimes *But* is used instead of *No*, especially after questions:

Why did you say you would come? But I didn't.
Why have you taken my book without asking? But I haven't.

(f) *Disagreement with a negative statement*

It won't rain today. (Oh) yes, it *will*.
David hasn't won the prize. Yes, he *has*.
You can't swim across that river. Oh yes, I *can*.

Sometimes *But* is used instead of *Yes*, especially after questions:

Why haven't you brought the book back? But I *have*.
Why didn't you write and tell us you were coming? But I *did*.

37.   Possessive of Nouns
(Book Two, Sentence Pattern 35, page 124)

(*a*) To form the possessive of a group of words expressing a single idea, the '*s* is added to the last word of the possessor.

> The Duke of Edinburgh's horse
> My son John's bicycle.
> John and Mary's house.

(*b*) Whatever is alive and can move forms the possessive with '*s*; other nouns form the possessive with *of*:

> John's arm
> the dog's leg
> the leg of the chair.

There are exceptions to this rule, in particular some expressions of time, value and measure:

> a fortnight's holiday
> a shilling's worth of oranges
> two pounds' worth of sixpences
> A stone's throw
> to be at one's wits' end.

38.   Phrasal Verbs—*Do, Make*
(See Book Two, page 256)

Do for

This bicycle's done for; I'll have to buy a new one.
Is it quite done for, or could you use it a bit longer?

Do in

At the end of the long journey he was quite done in.

Make

Make into

They have made this into quite a pleasant town since I was here last.
He is going to make this wood into bookshelves.

Make of

What do you make of this story?

When we heard that she had run away to get married, we didn't know what to make of it.

NEW WORDS

agenda (ə'dʒendə)
alderman ('oːldəmən)
amount (ə'maunt)
chairman ('tʃeəmən)
citizen ('sitizn)
concern (kən'səːn)
constable ('kʌnstəbl)
council ('kaunsl)
councillor ('kaunsələ)
county ('kaunti)
drain (drein)
drainage ('dreinidʒ)
faith (feiθ)
favour ('feivə)
force (foːs)
gap (gap)
honour ('onə)
item ('aitəm)
motion ('mouʃn)
neck (nek)
nonsense ('nonsəns)
objection (əb'dʒekʃn)
parlour ('paːlə)
power ('pauə)
property ('propəti)
provision (prə'viʒn)
pupil ('pjuːpl)
rate (reit)

scorn (skoːn)
shock (ʃok)
soul (soul)
spite (spait)
stock (stok)
track (trak)
treasure ('treʒə)
treasurer ('treʒərə)
upkeep ('ʌpkiːp)
apply (ə'plai)
attempt (ə'tempt)
civilise ('sivilaiz)
confess (kən'fes)
consider (kən'sidə)
control (kən'troul)
decrease (di'kriːs)
descend (di'send)
deserve (di'zəːv)
desire (di'zaiə)
encourage (in'kʌridʒ)
install (in'stoːl)
mean, meant (miːn, ment)
nationalise ('naʃnəlaiz)
object (verb) (əb'dʒekt)
offend (ə'fend)
overcome (ouvə'kʌm)
owe (ou)
permit (verb) (pə'mit)

possess (pə'zes)
preach (priːtʃ)
propose (prə'pouz)
prove (pruːv)
provide (prə'vaid)
qualify ('kwolifai)
realise ('riəlaiz)
reduce (ri'djuːs)
refer (ri'fəː)
reflect (ri'flekt)
regard (ri'gaːd)
regret (ri'gret)
respect (ri'spekt)
trim (trim)
trust (noun and verb) (trʌst)
urge (əːdʒ)
wipe (waip)
according (ə'koːdiŋ)
blind (blaind)
bold (bould)
complicated ('kompli'keitid)
considerable (kən'sidərəbl)

deaf (def)
double ('dʌbl)
eager ('iːgə)
earnest ('əːnist)
grand (grand)
humble ('hʌmbl)
mad (mad)
medical ('medikl)
mere (miə)
miserable ('mizrəbl)
moderate ('modərət)
modest ('modist)
patriotic (patri'otik)
primary ('praiməri)
secondary ('sekəndri)
sick (sik)
simple ('simpl)
solemn ('soləm)
wise (waiz)
worthy ('wəːði)
accordingly (ə'koːdiŋli)
merely ('miəli)

Idioms

his year of office (hiz 'jiər əv 'ofis)
to be present at (tə bi 'prezənt ət)
when it was all over ('wen it wəz 'oːl 'ouvə)
to keep accounts (tə 'kiːp ə'kaunts)
to manage one's affairs (tə 'manidʒ wʌnz ə'feəz)
on behalf of (on bi'haːf əv)
a surprise in store for (ə sə'praiz in 'stoː fə)
a coat of arms (ə 'kout əv 'aːmz)
to meet the needs of (tə 'miːt ðə 'niːdz əv)
to come as a shock to (tə 'kʌm əz ə 'ʃok tə)

in my humble opinion (in mai 'hʌmbl ə'pinjən)
a good deal of (ə 'gud 'diːl əv)
I must confess (ai məst kən'fes)
up-to-date ('ʌp tə 'deit)

EXERCISES

A. *Put the given verb into the right tense in these sentences:*

1. They went to the seaside every week-end if it (be) fine.
2. I should finish this work before going to bed if I (not be) so tired.
3. If ice is placed in a warm room it (melt).
4. They would have visited her if they (know) she was ill.
5. Most children behave well provided they (give) plenty to do.
6. We shall go for a long walk tomorrow unless it (rain).
7. You might enjoy playing tennis if you (try) it.
8. Most people enjoy going to the theatre so long as the acting (be) good.
9. We shall be glad if you (reply) as soon as possible.
10. You look ill. I should see a doctor if I (be) you.

B. *Give negative short answers to these questions:*

1. Have you been in England for long?
2. Will you be at home all day tomorrow?
3. Must we speak English all the time in class?
4. Need we come to school tomorrow?
5. Could he have got there in time?
6. Must everyone be here by nine o'clock?
7. Did you see the Queen while you were in London?
8. Has he ever been here before?
9. Will you and your family spend many weeks in France?
10. Ought those children to be playing in the road?

C. *Give short answers agreeing with these statements:*

1. He has a very charming wife.
2. Susan likes going shopping with her mother.
3. He isn't very good at his work, is he?
4. We have had a lot of rain this summer, haven't we?
5. This cat likes fish.
6. Wait a minute. You've dropped your glove.
7. The Mayor acts as Chairman of the Council.
8. Look! They've scored a goal at last.
9. Susan mustn't be late at the office again.
10. Mrs Brown is very fond of her son, David.

D. *Give short responses, disagreeing with the following:*

1. Mr Brown will be the next Mayor of Bishopton.
2. Why have you left me to do all the work?
3. You can't go for a walk in this rain.
4. Why didn't you bring your book with you.
5. Cardiff is the capital of England.
6. Susan hasn't any friends of her own age.
7. Why hasn't he paid you what he owes you?
8. Why did she go without saying good-bye?
9. There are some chocolates on a table in the sitting-room.
10. He won't be in time to catch the bus.

E. *Give the possessive form of:*

1. the wedding of Susan and Tom
2. the shoes of the children
3. the church of St James
4. John, the son of the butcher
5. the house of Mr Brown the bank manager
6. a school for boys
7. leave of absence of two months
8. apples worth two shillings
9. the store of Marks and Spencer
10. the book of Charles

F. *Rewrite these sentences, using a phrasal verb with* do *or* make *instead of the words in italics:*

1. Read this letter, and tell me what you *think it means.*
2. After entertaining so many guests at Christmas, she was quite *tired and ready for a rest.*
3. This old coat is *worn out*, so throw it away.
4. If you can't get any more cigarettes, you'll have to *be content without* them.
5. That adventure didn't really happen to her; she *invented it.*
6. We *no longer use* steam trains on many of our railway lines, and have introduced diesel trains instead.
7. The letter was old and stained, so that we could hardly *read* what it said.
8. I *should like* a little more sugar in this tea.
9. The thieves *escaped* with the diamonds from the jeweller's shop.
10. As soon as the curtain came down most of the audience *hurried to* the bar for a drink.

G. *Put these sentences into the reported form:*

1. "Will you play football on Saturday?" the captain asked David.
2. The teacher said, "Be quiet, boys".
3. "What are you doing?" their mother asked the children.
4. "We always go abroad for our holidays."
5. "What have you got in your hand?" the policeman wanted to know.
6. "Please don't be so unkind," she begged.
7. "Can we afford such an expensive holiday?" she asked her husband.
8. "Don't be so stupid," said the manager to the two young workers.
9. "Shall we catch the train, do you think?" she asked me.
10. "You may find the roads blocked with snow," he warned them.

H. *Rewrite these sentences, using* too *or* enough *followed by an infinitive or* for:

1. It is dark; I cannot see to read.
2. You are not clever; you will not pass this examination.
3. The cost of education is high; a small town cannot pay it all.
4. It is so cold today that we may have snow.
5. It is early in the year; roses will not flower yet.
6. This is a small book; it would go into my pocket.
7. We have been very busy; we haven't sent any Christmas cards this year.
8. Tom is sensible; he does not drive fast on narrow roads.
9. He is much cleverer than I am.
10. He is so much older than she is that he could be her father.

I. *Tell someone, in two different ways, not to do each of the following:*

1. run across the road without looking
2. talk so loudly
3. lean out of the window
4. believe everything someone tells him
5. smoke in the theatre
6. waste time playing cards
7. speak anything but English
8. leave the door open
9. put off till tomorrow what you can do today
10. bring books into the examination room

COMPOSITION

Speeches and Written Conversation

There is a great deal of difference between the English used in everyday speech and the English used in writing. You can learn much about these differences by writing passages of conversation for yourself similar to those given after the reading passages in *Present Day English*.

The most important difference between speech and writing is in the choice of words. English is a mixture of many languages. There are two main streams: the Germanic language spoken by the Anglo-Saxons, which had been strongly influenced before the Norman Conquest by another Germanic language spoken by the Danes; and Latin, either brought directly into English by scholars and churchmen or coming in through French, which was the official language in England for three hundred years after the Normans conquered the country in the eleventh century. To these main streams the English have added many words, which they have picked up on their travels, from countries all over the world. So English is a very rich language, often with several different words for the same idea. It has been easy, therefore, to keep some words for use in homely, everyday speech and others for use in serious writing and on formal occasions. It is the Germanic words that are usually the homely ones used in speech; the Latin and French words are usually more formal. Here are some examples:

Germanic	Latin
hurt	injure
clever	intelligent
at once	immediately
often	frequently
lucky	fortunate
show	exhibit
large	enormous, extensive
grow	increase, expand
used to	accustomed to
take	accept, receive

English speakers are usually lazy in their choice of words in everyday speech. Instead of making use of the large number of words they have to choose from, they prefer to use a few common words over and over again, giving them a slightly different meaning according to the subject they are talking about or altering the meaning by adding an adverbial. Thus the word *pipe* may be a noun meaning a drain, a tube, a musical instrument or an article used for smoking tobacco, or it may be a verb meaning to play a musical instrument, or to bring a liquid such as oil from one place to another. The many meanings which can be given to a common word such as *go, come, put* and *take* by adding adverbials we have seen in our study of the phrasal verb.

Another difference between the English of speech and of writing is the use in speech of shortened forms, such as the shortened forms of *not* (*don't, can't, won't,* etc.), short responses such as *Yes, I can, No, he doesn't* (see Sentence Pattern 36), and 'question tags' (*It's a lovely day, isn't it?*). English speakers often drop out all but the key words in a sentence, leaving the hearer to fill in the gaps from his own common sense and knowledge of the situation. Thus a man, meeting a friend in the street, might say,

"Nice day." And his friend will reply, "Bit cold for May, though."

Apart from the differences between spoken and written English, there are two other points to keep in mind in writing conversation, particularly if it is to be read or acted in the form of a play. In ordinary conversation we 'run on' without thinking too carefully what we say; but in dramatic dialogue each speech, although sounding natural, must take the thought or the story a step forward, it must tell the hearers something about the people who are speaking or the subject they are discussing. Secondly, the dialogue must be 'in character', that is, each person must use the kind of language he or she would use in real life. Thus a farm worker or a fisherman will not talk in the same way as a schoolmaster or a doctor or priest. You may be interested to look through the conversation passages in *Present Day English* and notice the ways in which Mr Brown's way of speaking differs from that of his son and daughter.

EXERCISES

1. Imagine you are entertaining an English friend in your home town or village. Write the conversation that might take place as you show your visitor round.

2. You have been asked to give a short talk in English to the members of your class on your favourite hobby or leisure-time occupation. Write out the talk you would give.

3. Imagine you are a member of the Bishopton Town Council and that you think they should spend money on some other improvement than a new library: for example, a town theatre. Write the speech you would make to the Council.

LESSON 9
Tom Smith in Lancashire

TOM SMITH is training to be a Manager, and in order to gain wider experience he is spending some months working in a factory in Lancashire. He chose Lancashire because he wanted to go to a part of the country where working conditions are very different from those he knew in the small factories in the South of England. On one day a week his employer allows him to attend a course in Management Studies at a College of Technology.

He and a companion from Bishopton named Geoffrey
Foster have spent a great deal of their spare time exploring
industrial Lancashire. In the wide, level plain on either side
of a line between Manchester and Liverpool the beauty of
nature has been almost entirely sacrificed for the sake of
industrial progress. Only here and there have a few green
fields or the park round a big house been preserved to show
what the valleys of the Mersey and the Irwell once looked
like. In the big towns they found that many of the houses
were small, ugly and overcrowded, but they saw few signs
of poverty, for wages are high and there is plenty of employment for almost everyone. They were told that gradually the
old houses are being pulled down and the workers are moving
out to new houses which are being built by the Councils on
the edge of the towns.

One day they visited a coal-mine near Wigan. At the pit-
head they were each given a helmet and lamp and were taken
down in the cage to the underground workings. For more
than a mile they travelled by a small electric train to the
coal-face, where they saw miners stripped to the waist and
streaming with sweat cutting the coal which provides the
power to keep the wheels of industrial Britain turning. They
heard something about the long struggles by the miners'
trade union for higher wages and improved working conditions and they were told that miners are now among the best
paid workers in the country. Tom was greatly impressed by
the care that is taken to guard against the risk of fire, explosion
and falls of rock. By the time he came out once more into the
sunlight he was sure that the coal-miner more than earns his
wages.

On another day they went for a trip down the famous Ship
Canal which has turned Manchester from an inland city into
a port for ocean-going ships. At one point the Canal crosses
the River Irwell, so that boats can be seen moving one above

the other. At Liverpool they visited the docks, which handle so much of Britain's trade with America, and travelled through the Mersey Tunnel, one of the finest underground motorways in the world.

Tom found the Lancashire people different from those among whom he had grown up in the South. On the whole they took life more seriously, were more outspoken and were less ready to spend their money unless they got good value for it. But there was no doubt that the Lancastrians knew how to enjoy themselves. While Tom was there, the town where he was staying had its yearly holiday, known as 'Wakes Week', when all the factories in the town were closed and everyone went off to the seaside at Blackpool or Morecambe. Tom Smith and Geoffrey Foster went too, and they were amazed at the gaiety and high spirits they saw everywhere. On the beach, in the cafés, restaurants and dance-halls, in the 'fun-fairs', public houses and hotels they found the same laughing, joking crowds. It was difficult to believe that these were the same people who walked or cycled to work, with their coat collars turned up round their ears, through the early morning fog of the grey industrial towns from which most of them had come.

The factory to which Tom had been sent worked three 'shifts', so that he was sometimes on duty at night. As he walked to work he could see the sky lit up by the huge flames from the foundry, and he knew that a flood of white-hot liquid metal, melted in the extreme heat of the furnace, was being poured into hollow moulds that would shape it into a hundred and one useful articles to be sold at home and overseas. He thought sometimes of the century and a half of industrial development since the invention of the steam engine, which had changed this distant corner of England into one of the workshops of the world. Coal-mines, iron foundries, cotton mills and textile factories, and the large and small towns that had grown up around them, now stood where once wheat ripened in the sunshine and pure air, and cattle and sheep ate the short grass on the bare slopes of the Pennines. Where men once ploughed and sowed the good earth and ground their grain into flour, industry has now conquered, and the earth trembles with the thunder of machines.

At the week-ends, when the weather was fine, Tom and Geoffrey would hire a car and get away from the smoke and dirt of Manchester and drive up to the Lake District. Leaving the car they would spend long days climbing mountains, sailing on Lake Windermere or exploring the quiet green valleys of this lovely part of England. On one occasion they saw, as the poet Wordsworth had seen before them, the breath-taking beauty of a field of daffodils

> 'Beside the lake, beneath the trees,
>   Fluttering and dancing in the breeze.'

Tom remembered that Wordsworth had said that the sight had always been a treasured memory for him; he would think of the flowers in times of sadness

> 'And then my heart with pleasure fills,
>   And dances with the daffodils.'

He remembered, too, Shakespeare's lines:

> '. . . the daffodils
>   That come before the swallow dares, and take
>   The winds of March with beauty.'

Tom had much to think about and remember as the train carried him back to London after his stay in the North.

CONVERSATION

(Tom Smith and Geoffrey Foster are attending lectures at a College of Technology during their stay in Lancashire. A lecture on the industrial history of Lancashire has just ended, and the students are asking questions)

STUDENT: Why did Lancashire become the main centre for the British cotton industry?

LECTURER: There were a number of causes for this. Raw cotton has to be imported, and Liverpool was a convenient port for trade with America, from where most of the cotton came. The new machines for spinning and weaving which were invented during the eighteenth century needed power to drive them: at first water power was provided by rushing streams which flow down from the Pennines, then, after the invention of the steam engine, steam power depended on coal, in which Lancashire is very rich.

STUDENT: Had the climate of Lancashire anything to do with it?

LECTURER: Yes, that was another reason. Cotton thread breaks easily when it is stretched tight during weaving unless it is kept damp. Thus the damp climate of Lancashire was particularly suitable for this industry. This is not so important today because 'air conditioning' can be used in factories to produce a damp air artificially.

STUDENT: Is there any reason, therefore, why Lancashire should go on being the centre of the industry?

LECTURER: No, not really. Cotton weaving and experiments with artificial silk, nylon and other man-made fibres are going on in other parts of the country. But it is said that the cotton workers of Lancashire have developed through years of experience a special skill, which is passed down from parents to children, by which they can produce the highest standard of work.

STUDENT: Had Liverpool's share in the slave trade any connection with the cotton industry?

LECTURER: Very much so. This evil trade grew up largely to supply cheap workers for the cotton plantations in the Southern States of America. The slave traders took cotton cloth and other cheap goods to the West Coast of Africa and used these to buy slaves. These miserable slaves were then shipped across to America to be sold, the vessels completing their round voyage by returning to Bristol and Liverpool with sugar, tobacco and raw cotton. The whole operation was very profitable indeed.

STUDENT: Have Liverpool and Manchester always been large trading centres?

LECTURER: No. The rapid growth of Liverpool as a sea-port and Manchester as a commercial city happened during the eighteenth century. Now the cotton industry extends from one end of South Lancashire to the other, and as you know it is difficult to say where one town begins and another ends. Trade is, of course, very much a matter of 'supply and demand': as the British Empire overseas extended, particularly in tropical countries, so the demand for light cotton goods increased, and this demand was supplied by the growing cotton industry in Lancashire. Today many of these countries, now independent, are manufacturing cotton goods for themselves, and other countries such as Japan and India are in competition with Britain in world markets, particularly in the cheaper lines; but Lancashire still continues to turn out some of the finest high-quality cotton goods in the world.

COMPREHENSION QUESTIONS

1. In what ways did Tom Smith find that life in the North of England differed from life in the South?
2. What are the main industries of Lancashire?
3. How does the appearance of Lancashire today differ from what it was two hundred years ago?
4. What are the chief dangers a coal-miner has to face? What is done to guard him against these dangers?
5. What has been the effect on Manchester of the opening of the Manchester Ship Canal?
6. How did the Lancashire people seem to Tom to differ from those he knew in the South?
7. Explain the phrase 'the factory worked three shifts'.
8. Why did Lancashire become the main centre for the British cotton industry?
9. How did the Slave Trade begin, and how was it organised?
10. What changes have taken place in the cotton trade in recent years?

SENTENCE PATTERNS

39. How to express Willingness, Determination and Intention

Will is used for both willingness and determination, the difference being a matter of stress or emphasis.

(a) Willingness

I will come, if you want me to.
I will do as you ask.
He will let you have it, if you ask him.
Will she let us stay to tea?
Do you think Mr and Mrs Brown will allow Susan to marry Tom before she is twenty-one?

(b) Determination

I *will* go, whatever he may say.

He *will* have his own way; he has only himself to blame if things go wrong.

I'm sure he'll have an accident: he *will* drive so fast.

Shall is used with the second and third persons to show determination on the part of the speaker.

You *shall* do as you are told.

He *shall* finish his work before he goes out, no matter what he says.

Determination can also be expressed by:

determine, decide, make up one's mind.

David is determined to pass his examination.

We have decided to stay in England for another three months.

They have made up their minds to get married this summer.

Willingness can also be expressed by:

to be willing, to agree to.

I am willing to forgive you this time, but it must not happen again.

His father agreed to letting him have the car on condition that he promised to drive carefully.

Intention The commonest way of expressing intention is with the *going to* + infinitive construction.

I am going to start learning Italian next year.

Are you going to wait until he comes back?

The Present Continuous is also used to express intention when the arrangements for carrying it out have already been made.

We're staying with the Browns next week.

Mr and Mrs Brown are going to Rome for their holiday next month.

Intention can also be expressed by *intend* and *mean to*.

She intends to stay in England until she can speak the language well.

I mean to work really hard at my studies next term.

40.　　　　　　　Relative Pronouns

(a) *Kinds of Relative Pronoun*

Relatives (*who, which, that, when, where*) are used to introduce adjectival clauses. These clauses are either defining or commenting. Defining clauses are necessary to complete the meaning of the sentence; they are not marked off by commas. Commenting clauses are additions not necessary to the meaning, and are marked off by commas. Examples are:

(i) *Defining Clauses*

The friends (whom) we met in London are staying with us next week-end.

The things (that) one likes best are usually the most expensive.

This is the factory where (in which) Tom works.

They have bought the house that has been empty for three months.

People who live in glass houses should not throw stones.

They have got rid of the dog which used to bark all night.

Notice that if these defining clauses were taken away, the sentence would have no complete meaning. When the relatives *who, which* or *that* are the object of the clause, they are often omitted, especially in conversation.

(ii) *Commenting Clauses*

The people of Lancashire, who like good food, are often excellent cooks.

This house, which has been empty for some time, has now been sold.

My son, who has been learning to drive, has now passed his driving test.

Notice that if these commenting clauses were taken away the sentence would still make sense. The relatives are never omitted from commenting clauses.

(b) *Defining Clauses*

    (i) *Relative as Subject* to the verb in the defining clause

        For persons: who, that. The relative is never omitted.

> The person who has taken this book from the library must return it at once.
>
> The people who used to live in that house were friends of ours.
>
> Anyone who wants to leave early must get permission from the Principal.
>
> I have written to the friends who went on holiday with us last summer.
>
> I have written to all those who answered our advertisement.

        Who is almost always used for persons after *those* and *people*. *For things: that, which. That* is used much more often than *which*. The relative is never omitted.

> Have you seen the books that were on the table?
>
> All exercises which (that) are finished should be handed in to the teacher.
>
> We have been looking at the photographs that were taken while we were on holiday.
>
> They killed the goose that laid the golden eggs.

    (ii) *Relative as Object* to the verb in the defining clause

        For persons: that (occasionally *whom*, but not in conversation). The relative is usually omitted.

> These are the people (that) we like best.
>
> The Andersons are the family (that) the Browns met at Bournemouth.
>
> The Prime Minister is the man whom the Queen invites to form a government.
>
> I was introduced to the boy Susan is going to marry.

For things: that, which
The relative is usually omitted, particularly in conversation.

> You can't have everything you want.
> This is the house that Jack built.
> They took all the money they could find.
> The ring (that) Susan wanted was too expensive.

(iii) *Relative as Object to a Preposition* in its clause

For persons: whom
In speech the relative is almost always omitted and the preposition is placed after the verb or its object, usually at the end of the clause.

> Tickets will be issued only to those from whom we have received written application.
> Do I know the man you were talking about?
> She is one of the girls Susan is going on holiday with.
> The boy I was speaking to is a student at the college.

For things: which
In speech *which* is almost always omitted or replaced by *that*, and the preposition is placed after the verb or its object, usually at the end of the clause.

> The book to which he referred is not in the library.
> Is this the book you are speaking about?
> The town in which he was born is situated about twelve miles from London.
> There's the house I was born in.
> The road along which they were now driving was almost clear of traffic.
> The road (that) we were now driving along was quite new to me.

(iv) *Relative as Possessive*

For persons: whose. The relative is never omitted.

> The prize will be given to the student whose composition has fewest mistakes.

Anyone whose home is near a river is likely to be interested in fishing.

People whose television licences have run out can be fined.

For things: There is no possessive form for *which*.

The possessive can be expressed by using *whose*, by a phrase with *of which*, or by a preposition phrase.

This is the house which had its roof blown off in the storm last night.

This regiment, of which the first commander was the Duke of Wellington, is one of the most famous in the British army.

The book the binding of which is torn (*or* of which the binding is torn) belongs to me.

This last would be better expressed:

The book with the torn binding belongs to me.

(v) *Relatives after Place and Time words*

Where and *when* are often used instead of *in which*, *on which*, etc.

She went back to the seat where (on which) she had left her handbag.

The bed where (in which) we slept was damp.

I shall never forget the day when (on which) I first arrived in England.

(c) *Commenting Clauses.* These are far less common than defining clauses. They are found in formal writing, but very seldom in speech.

(i) *For persons: who* is used for the subject, *whom* for the object to a verb and following a preposition, and *whose* for the possessive. The relative is never omitted in commenting clauses.

Napoleon, who had already won a high reputation as a general, was now placed in command of the whole army.

Jane Austen, whom the English regard as one of their greatest novelists, seldom moved far from her native village.

The Prime Minister, to whom the question was addressed, did not reply.

Shakespeare, whose father was a butcher in Stratford, was educated at the local Grammar School.

(ii) *For things: which* for subject, object and following a preposition. The possessive form is usually *of which.*

Rome, which is built on seven hills, is known as the Eternal City.

Gulliver's Travels, which Swift wrote as a fierce attack on his political opponents, is now read as a children's story.

The 'Hop-Pole Hotel', to which Dickens refers in *Pickwick Papers*, is in Tewkesbury.

This novel, the author of which is unknown, was very popular a century ago.

(iii) *When* and *where* are used in commenting clauses following nouns of *time* and *place.*

The summer of 1939, when the world was on the edge of war, seemed to us like any other summer.

Waterloo, where Wellington defeated Napoleon, is a small village near Brussels.

(iv) The relative introducing a commenting clause sometimes refers not to a single noun or pronoun but to the whole of the statement that comes before it. Here it has the meaning *and this.*

We have lived here now for twenty years, which makes us very sorry to move.

Our train leaves London at seven-thirty, which means that we shall have to set off from home soon after six.

41.   Position of Adverbs

In discussing the position of adverbs in the sentence, there are two groups of adverbs to be considered: (*a*) ordinary adverbs and (*b*) frequency adverbs.

(*a*) *Ordinary Adverbs*

These are usually placed at the end of a sentence or clause.

> She came to see us yesterday.
> You can do this quite easily, if you work carefully.

Where more than one adverb is used to modify the same verb, they are usually placed in this order: manner, place, time.

> He spoke to me rudely yesterday.
> They go off happily to the nearby town every Saturday evening.
> We expect him here tomorrow.

Sometimes a time adverb, adverb phrase or adverb clause is placed at the beginning of the sentence; especially where a number of adverbs coming at the end would produce a too loosely constructed sentence.

> Tomorrow we set off for London by car.
> After the funeral, they all went away sadly to their homes.

(*b*) *Frequency Adverbs*

These are adverbs that tell how often something happens or is done. They are placed immediately before the main verb, but after an auxiliary.

> We often come to England for our holidays.
> I sometimes meet him at a restaurant for lunch.
> We have generally finished dinner by eight o'clock.
> He has always been fond of gardening.

The commonest of these frequency adverbs are: *already, always, nearly always, ever, frequently, generally, hardly* (*scarcely*) *ever, never, occasionally, often, seldom, sometimes, usually.*
Notice that the frequency adverb is sometimes placed before

the auxiliary, and this has the effect of emphasising the auxiliary.

"I've broken a plate, Mother."
"You generally *do* manage to break something when you wash up."

> "My mother said I never should,
> Play with the gypsies in the wood."

Particular care must be taken not to place an adverb between the verb and the object in a sentence. Sentences such as:

I met yesterday my friend.
I left here my umbrella.

are common errors.

42.   Short Responses—2

In Lesson 8 we considered some short responses answering questions and agreeing or disagreeing with affirmative and negative statements. Here are some short responses which add something further to what has been said.

(a) *Additions to affirmative statements*

Tom can swim well. So can I.
David has finished his work. So has Henry.
Bob likes going to the theatre. So does Susan.
Mr Brown is fond of gardening. So is Mrs Brown.

Notice the inversion after *so*. This distinguishes this response from the agreement showing surprise (Sentence Pattern 36*c*).

(b) *Additions to negative statements*

Mr Brown doesn't enjoy walking in the rain. Nor do I.
Mrs Brown isn't fond of playing cards. Nor is her husband.
Tom wouldn't like to live in the North. Nor would Susan.
David has not been to Spain. Neither has Susan.

Notice the inversion after *neither, nor* here.

(c) Additions offering a contrast

He likes sugar in his tea. But I don't.

Tom can swim a mile. But Susan can't.

Mr Brown has a good memory. But Mrs Brown hasn't.

"I want to go to the theatre this evening," says Tom. "But I don't," Susan replies.

I must get up early tomorrow, but you needn't.

Mr Brown doesn't like onions, but Mrs Brown does.

Susan can't sing very well, but her mother can.

You needn't hurry, but I must.

Notice that as usual in these Short Responses, special verbs are repeated in the response; other verbs are replaced by *do*.

NEW WORDS

cage (keidʒ)

canal (kəˈnal)

cattle (ˈkatl)

climate (ˈklaimit)

collar (ˈkolə)

commerce (ˈkoməːs)

companion (kəmˈpanjən)

convenience (kənˈviːnjəns)

daffodil (ˈdafədil)

dock (dok)

empire (ˈempaiə)

employer (imˈploiə)

employment (imˈploimənt)

evil (ˈiːvil, ˈiːvl)

extent (iksˈtent)

fibre (ˈfaibə)

flame (fleim)

flood (flʌd)

flour (flauə)

fog (fog)

furnace (ˈfəːnis)

grain (grein)

growth (grouθ)

helmet (ˈhelmit)

invention (inˈvenʃn)

joke (dʒouk)

lecture (noun and verb) (ˈlektʃə)

lecturer (ˈlektʃərə)

liquid (ˈlikwid)

management (ˈmanidʒmənt)

memory (ˈmeməri)

mill (mil)

mould (mould)

nylon (ˈnailən)

occasion (əˈkeiʒn)

ocean (ˈouʃn)

pit (pit)

pit-head (ˈpithed)

plantation (planˈteiʃn)

plough (noun and verb) (plau)
port (poːt)
poverty (ˈpovəti)
quality (ˈkwoliti)
sacrifice (noun and verb)
    (ˈsakrifais)
sail (seil)
sake (seik)
shape (ʃeip)
shift (ʃift)
ship (ʃip)
sign (sain)
slave (sleiv)
steam (stiːm)
sweat (noun and verb) (swet)
textiles (ˈtekstailz)
thread (θred)
thunder (ˈθʌndə)
trip (trip)
tunnel (ˈtʌnl)
union (ˈjuːnjən)
vessel (ˈvesl)
voyage (ˈvoiidʒ)
wage(s) (weidʒ(iz))
waist (weist)
wheat (wiːt)
attend (əˈtend)
cause (noun and verb) (koːz)
conquer (ˈkoŋkə)
demand (noun and verb)
    (diˈmaːnd)
employ (imˈploi)
experiment (noun and verb)
    (iksˈperimənt)
explode (iksˈploud)
explore (iksˈploː)
extend (iksˈtend)

flutter (ˈflʌtə)
grind, ground (graind,
    graund)
guard (gaːd)
invent (inˈvent)
melt (melt)
preserve (priˈzəːv)
ripen (ˈraipən)
sail (seil)
shape (ʃeip)
sow, sowed, sown (sou, soud,
    soun)
strip (strip)
struggle (noun and verb)
    (ˈstrʌgl)
train (trein)
tremble (ˈtrembl)
weave, wove, woven (wiːv,
    wouv, ˈwouvn)
artificial (aːtiˈfiʃl)
bare (beə)
convenient (kənˈviːnjənt)
evil (ˈiːvil, ˈiːvl)
extreme (iksˈtriːm)
hollow (ˈholou)
level (ˈlevl)
outspoken (autˈspoukn)
plain (plein)
rapid (ˈrapid)
raw (roː)
ripe (raip)
tight (tait)
tropical (ˈtropikl)
beneath (biˈniːθ)
inland (ˈinland)
therefore (ˈðeəfoː)
thus (ðʌs)

Idioms

here and there ('hiə ənd 'ðeə)
to keep the wheels turning (tə 'kiːp ðə 'wiːlz 'təːniŋ)
working conditions ('wəːkiŋ kən'diʃnz)
to guard against (tə 'gaːd ə'geinst)
ocean-going ships ('ouʃn gouiŋ 'ʃips)
one above the other ('wʌn əbʌv ði 'ʌðə)
to grow up (tə 'grou 'ʌp)
to get good value (tə 'get gud 'valjuː)
there's no doubt that (ðeəz 'nou 'daut ðət)
to work shifts (tə 'wəːk 'ʃifts)
on duty (on 'djuːti)
to get away from (tə get ə'wei frəm)
on one occasion (on 'wʌn ə'keiʒn)
anything to do with ('eniθiŋ tə 'duː wið)
air conditioning ('eə kən'diʃəniŋ)
to go on being (tə 'gou on 'biːiŋ)
very much so ('veri 'mʌtʃ sou)
a matter of supply and demand (ə 'matər əv sə'plai ənd
    di'maːnd)

EXERCISES

A. *Write sentences expressing (a) a willingness, and (b) a determination to do each of the following:*

1. buy a new car
2. get up early tomorrow morning
3. stop smoking cigarettes
4. visit Scotland next summer
5. get home before midnight
6. finish the work before going to bed
7. go to the football match next Saturday
8. stay at home this evening to watch a television programme
9. make friends with the people next door
10. be elected captain of the cricket team

B. *Add relative pronouns to these sentences where required:*

1. This is the street . . . we used to live.
2. The dog . . . barks all night belongs to our next-door neighbour.
3. Tom Smith, . . . is training to be a Manager, works in a factory in Bishopton.
4. Tom and Susan, . . . enjoy the theatre, are now visiting Stratford.
5. The customer . . . you gave the money to has now left the shop.
6. Let me see all the letters . . . you have written.
7. The book . . . you borrowed from the library should now be returned.
8. The King thanked the soldiers . . . had fought bravely in the battle.
9. They lived by the seaside, . . . is very pleasant in summer.
10. Whitehall, . . . many of the government offices are, is near Westminster Abbey.
11. The house . . . we used to live has been pulled down.
12. King James II was the Duke of York from . . . New York took its name.

C. *Link these pairs of sentences by means of relative pronouns. Put the relative in brackets if you think it could be left out.*

1. Mr Brown is a friend of ours. He lives next door.
2. My closest friend is a bank manager. This is very useful when I need advice.
3. Stratford is in Warwickshire. Shakespeare was born in this town.
4. Wordsworth lived in the Lake District. Many people consider him a great poet.
5. I put the money in a box. The box has now disappeared.
6. This coat has a red lining. It belongs to me.
7. Wellington beat Napoleon at the Battle of Waterloo. It was fought in 1815.
8. The park has a lake in it. The park is near our house.

9. The station is Paddington. Our train leaves from here.
10. Many people sent me good wishes on my birthday. I have replied to them all.

D. *Put the given adverbs in the correct position in these sentences*

1. They played (all the afternoon) (happily) (in the garden).
2. The Browns have guests for dinner (sometimes).
3. It *is* certain that this train will be on time (never).
4. I went (on Monday) (to the seaside).
5. I have met him several times (already).
6. He is asked where he learnt English (often).
7. Mr Brown is travelling (by train) (tomorrow) (to Bristol).
8. Our cousins spend Christmas with us (nearly always).
9. I have seen anyone so beautiful (seldom).
10. He *was* a silly boy (always).
11. We know what he will say next (never).
12. Robert has worked (this term) (hard).

E. *Make additions to these statements, beginning with* so, neither/ nor, *or* but

1. Tom enjoys spending a day in the country.
2. Mr Brown can drive a car.
3. Mrs Brown is a good cook.
4. Susan doesn't like getting up early in the morning.
5. Tom Smith is very interested in engineering.
6. David enjoys listening to modern dance music.
7. I must go home at once.
8. You needn't go to work this morning.
9. Mrs Brown isn't good at adding up accounts.
10. Tom works a five day week.

F. *Write sentences using the following verbs in the present tense:*

taste; feel; desire; know; think; remember; believe; hope; doubt; suppose; seem; mean; possess.

G. *How is the verb* to be *used in each of these sentences? (Sentence Pattern* 11.)

1. Tom is working in Lancashire at present.
2. Do be kind to her.
3. She is to finish those letters before she leaves the office.
4. David will be a university student for another three years.
5. The gates are closed at midnight.
6. The building is to have a tower two hundred feet high.
7. He is one of the kindest men I know.
8. We are leaving for Poland on Monday.
9. You are not to speak to him again.
10. She is to stay with us for another fortnight.

H. *Write sentences in which these adjectives are followed by a* to-*infinitive (Sentence Pattern* 8):

certain; likely; wicked; wise; wrong; sad; delighted; disappointed; excited; willing; ready; quick.

I. *Put the correct prepositions into the blank spaces in this passage:*

While Tom was . . . Lancashire, he and his friend hired a car . . . a garage . . . Manchester and drove . . . the road . . . the North until they came . . . the Lake District. . . . Lake Windermere they spent the night . . . a hotel, and . . . the following morning, leaving the car . . . the hotel garage, they set . . . . . . foot . . . the lake. Hiring a boat, they sailed . . . the lake. . . . the other side they climbed . . . the steep slopes . . . a mountain. . . . the top they could see . . . miles . . . the lakes and hills . . . the sea. They got . . . . . . the hotel . . . time . . . dinner, and . . . dinner they sat . . . . a blazing fire . . . a glass . . . beer . . . their hands talking . . . the events . . . the day.

J. *Write sentences, other than those given in the Sentence Patterns, containing the following phrasal verbs:*

put by; put forward; take for; take over; come about; come by; go by; go over; look down on; look forward to.

COMPOSITION

Summarising

The best way to make sure you have understood what you have read or heard is to reproduce it briefly in your own words. This is called summarising.

At the heart of every piece of writing there is a central idea that the writer is trying to express. To summarise a passage you must first find this central idea: the *subject* of the passage and what the writer says about the subject. You may have to read a passage more than once, but when you are quite sure of this, note it down in a few words.

The next task is to follow the writer's line of thought step by step through the passage. If he has been careful, the paragraphing will help, for each main step will be marked by a fresh paragraph. When the line of thought is clear to you, note down the main point in each paragraph. In this way, you will have made an outline or plan of the whole passage. Before writing your summary, read the passage again, deciding what is necessary if the writer's meaning is to be understood, and what can be safely left out.

The summary should be written in continuous prose, and not in note-form. Sentences should not be copied from the passage itself, but the main ideas should be reproduced briefly in your own words. When the original passage is a speech, or the expression of a writer's views or opinions, the summary should be in the past tense and in reported speech. (See Book Two, pp. 94–6.) For the summary of a story or description, reported speech is not necessary. The finished summary should be checked carefully against the original to see that nothing of importance has been left out and nothing unimportant has been put in. See that you have added no ideas of your own.

EXERCISES

1. Write a summary of the debate by the Bishopton Town Council given on pages 148–150.
2. Write a summary of the information given in answer to the students' questions on pages 170–1.
3. Write one of the letters Tom might have sent to Susan telling about some of his experiences in Lancashire.
4. Write a summary of the letters in Lesson 2, pages 32–35.

A Good Example

A wise old owl sat in an oak;
The more he saw, the less he spoke;
The less he spoke, the more he heard—
Why don't you copy that wise old bird?

LESSON 10

A Day at the Zoo

MR BROWN's cousin Tony Mason and his wife Brenda have two small children, so it is not easy for them to get away for a holiday on their own. But this year Mrs Brown said she would take the children for a week. Jackie is eight and Sheila is six. They are lively children and Mrs Brown did not find it easy to keep them amused. One day she decided to take them to London to visit the Zoological Gardens, which are always called the Zoo.

They set off early so as to have a good long day, and arrived at Regent's Park about eleven. As they reached the gates they could hear the lions roaring and the tropical birds shrieking—it was all very exciting.

The first thing the children wanted to do was to ride on the elephant. They were a little frightened as they climbed the ladder to take their seats on the swaying back of the huge beast. Elephants seem awkward creatures as they move heavily along, their legs covered in loose folds of tough skin, and their trunks swinging from side to side in search of food or drink. And yet the elephant is an intelligent animal with a very long memory. It can move carefully, too, and balance its immense weight on quite a small surface. An elephant has great strength in its trunk and can drag heavy loads with ropes, but it can also use its trunk to pick up small articles such as coins or nuts from the ground.

After their ride on the elephant, the children went to see the lions and tigers fed. Crowds of people stood watching, protected from the cruel hungry beasts by the strong metal bars that formed the cages. Presently a keeper arrived with great pieces of raw flesh, which he pushed into the cages at the end of an iron hook. The lions seized the meat in their powerful jaws, shook it and walked off into a corner of the cage to enjoy their meal. Some people think it is a little sad to see these noble animals shut up in captivity when they should be free to wander in the forests of Asia or Africa.

From here they went on to see the monkeys—a whole colony of them. These merry creatures were jumping about the rocks or swinging on the wire of their cages, or begging for nuts and ripe fruit from the passers-by. If anyone annoyed them they would chatter and scold angrily and shake the wire of their cage or beat their chests with their hairy hands.

As one watches the more intelligent monkeys it is not hard to believe that man and monkey have developed from a common origin.

The children enjoyed their visit to the parrot-house. They spent a long time talking to one particular bird which could imitate the human voice remarkably well. It would stretch its neck, put its head on one side, tap the cage with its beak, move along with a dancing motion and then repeat what they said to it. Mrs Brown liked looking at the tropical birds with their brightly coloured feathers, the male birds always so much finer than the female.

They saw the snakes, too, but this they did not enjoy. They watched these deadly creatures curling and uncurling, tying themselves into knots, their black tongues flashing in and out as they crept along. There were large snakes, too, that could hold a man or an animal so tightly that he would be crushed to death. The bear-pit was more amusing. Here they saw the white (or polar) bears, diving into their pool, and black and brown bears begging for bread and cakes, or lying only half awake in the sunshine.

Mrs Brown showed the children many other creatures. Some of them looked like the familiar animals: the horse, the donkey, the dog, the rat, the mouse, the goat, but were either much bigger or smaller, or a different colour. Others, like the giraffe with its long neck, reaching a height of 18 feet, or the camel with its hump and short beard, were curious creatures, very different from anything to be found in England.

But what they enjoyed most of all was the Pets' Corner— a collection of quiet, mild animals that would not bite or kick, but were so tame that children could stroke them or ride on their backs. While the children were playing in the Pets' Corner, Mrs Brown met a friend who is a member of the Zoological Society, to whom the Zoological Gardens belong.

When at last the time came for them to go home, Jackie and Sheila agreed that it had been one of the nicest days of their holiday.

CONVERSATION

(Mrs Brown is talking to Dr Reynolds while the children are playing in the Pets' Corner)

DR REYNOLDS: Hello, Mrs Brown. What brings you to the Gardens? I didn't know you were particularly interested in animals.

MRS BROWN: I've brought some children. They're playing over there in the Pets' Corner. But you're wrong in thinking I'm not interested myself. You're a member of the Zoological Society, aren't you?

DR REYNOLDS: Yes, I am. Is there anything I can tell you about our work here?

MRS BROWN: Do you get all your animals from abroad, or are some born in the Zoo?

DR REYNOLDS: Most still come from abroad. Not all animals will breed in captivity, but some—lions and monkeys, for example—reproduce themselves readily enough; and a few multiply too quickly for us to keep them all. The birth of an animal that has not bred in captivity before is always an exciting event here and everyone does his best to see that the young one survives.

MRS BROWN: Some people say it's cruel to keep animals in captivity. Is it?

DR REYNOLDS: No—so long as the animals are well looked after and given suitable food. Most of the animals we have were either trapped when very young or born in captivity and so don't feel the lack of liberty they've never known. The life of the wild animal is cruel, short and without mercy, a hard struggle to survive where instant death is the fate of those who make one false step. In comparison with this, animals in a well-run Zoo enjoy a long, comfortable and easy life where all their wants are cared for. I don't think we need have a bad conscience about them or think it is immoral to keep them here. As a matter of fact the chief danger to our Zoo animals comes from man himself. To begin with, it takes some of them a long time to get used to the visitors crowding round their cages, and many of them are made ill or even killed by foolish and thoughtless people who give them unsuitable food. Some animals are more sensible than human beings in refusing to eat what will do them harm, but others aren't and will swallow almost anything that's given to them.

MRS BROWN: How do you treat the dangerous animals when they are injured or ill?

DR REYNOLDS: We have a special cage with a net inside which can be lowered over the animal to hold it still. There is a special floor which slides back so that the animal's paws rest on bars with its toes between the bars. In this way we can cut their nails or claws and heal any sores or swellings or other injuries on their limbs. We have made some progress in medical science since the days when the standard treatment for an injury was to rub salt into the wound. When teeth decay and have to be pulled out, or an operation has to be performed, the animal is put in another special cage and an anaesthetic is pumped in. If a wild animal is injured in the jungle it may live on in pain for months or even years with no one to care for it.

MRS BROWN: We always think of Zoos as a good place to take

the children to keep them amused. Do Zoos serve any other useful purpose?

DR REYNOLDS: Yes, indeed they do. Men of science like myself can observe the habits and behaviour of animals here and learn far more about them than we could in museums or libraries or even by watching wild animals in the jungle or desert. And even for those who are not scholars, a first-hand knowledge of the animal kingdom is a necessary part of everyone's education. For most people, this can only be gained by visits to a Zoo. Looking at pictures or even films can never be the same as watching the animals themselves. Zoos also serve another useful purpose. If it were not for these places some animals would have disappeared entirely from the world and others would be in danger of disappearing. The demand for ivory, and certain kinds of horn, bone, fur and eggs is so great that some animals have been, or are being, hunted out of existence until only those kept in captivity remain alive.

MRS BROWN: All this is most interesting—you've given me quite a new view of the Zoo, Dr Reynolds. Next time I come I must leave the children at home and then perhaps I shall have a little more time to look at the animals. Now I must run or I'll never get them back to Bishopton in time for bed.

COMPREHENSION QUESTIONS

1. In what ways are elephants different from other animals?
2. In what ways are monkeys similar to human beings?
3. Relate one or more examples to show that animals are intelligent.
4. What is meant by the term 'Pets' Corner'?
5. Who maintains the Zoological Gardens in London?

6. Where does the Zoo obtain its animals?
7. How does the life of an animal in captivity differ from that of an animal in its natural state?
8. What is the chief danger to animals in a Zoo, and why?
9. How are dangerous animals dealt with when they are injured or ill?
10. What useful purposes does a Zoo serve?

SENTENCE PATTERNS

43. How to express Comparison

We compare objects or actions to show that they are either similar or dissimilar.

(a) The comparative forms of adjectives and adverbs are used to compare things and actions which are dissimilar or unequal.

> David is taller than Susan.
> David works harder than his friend Bob.
> Mary's hat was more expensive than Joan's.
> This book is less interesting than the one I read last week.

(b) *As . . . as* is used to compare things or actions that are equal or similar.

> David is as tall as Bob.
> He was as hungry as a hunter.
> She sang as sweetly as a nightingale.
> Susan types as quickly as her friend Anne.

(c) *Not as . . . as. Not so . . . as.* These are used for negative comparisons. Notice that the verb in the comparative clause is often omitted.

> Susan isn't as tall as her brother (is).
> He has not worked so hard this year as (he did) last.
> This is not so easy as it looks.
> You can't come to work as late as you please.

(d) *The . . . the* is used with comparative adjectives and adverbs to show that two things or actions become lesser or greater at the same rate.

> The sooner you finish your work, the sooner you can go home.
>
> The more he ate, the fatter he became.
>
> "The more I see of men, the more I like my dog."
>
> The more, the merrier.
>
> The bigger, the better.
>
> The longer he listened, the angrier he became.
>
> The nearer the bone, the sweeter the meat.

44.   Uses of the Verb *Do*

Do can be used both as a special verb and as an ordinary verb. It has particular importance because it is the verb with which we form the negative and question forms of all ordinary verbs and it is used to replace ordinary verbs in short responses.

Do as a Special Verb

(a) To form the negative and interrogative of ordinary verbs.

> Mr Brown works in London.   He doesn't work in London.
>   Does he work in London?
>
> Mrs Brown goes shopping every morning.
>   She doesn't go shopping every morning.
>   Does she go shopping every morning?

(b) To avoid repetition:

    (i) In short responses

> Did you finish your work? Yes, I did.
>
> Does he go to London every day? Yes, he does.

    (ii) In comparative sentences

> He works harder than I do.
>
> He swims better than Susan does.
>
> Mr Brown does not drive as fast as David does.

(iii) In question tags

> You came here last year, didn't you?
> They got married last July, didn't they?
> He doesn't live in Bishopton, does he?

(iv) In additions to statements, with *So, Neither, Nor, But*

> "I like strawberries." "So do I."
> "I wish I was twice as clever." "So do I."
> Tom doesn't like driving at night. Nor does Mr Brown.
> "I'm afraid I don't dance very well." "Neither do I."
> "You never work on Saturday." "But I *do*."

> (Distinguish this from:

> "You never work on Saturday, but *I* do.")

(*c*) To form the Emphatic Affirmative of ordinary verbs (that is, all verbs except the special verbs). When we wish to emphasise that what we say is really so we use a stressed form of the verb, thus:

> You *are* a naughty boy.
> I *can* come if you really want me to.

If the verb is a special verb, we stress that verb, as shown. If the verb is an ordinary verb, we add a stressed form of *do* to it, thus:

> She *does* like going to the theatre.
> I *do* want to learn English.
> I *did* go to London last week.
> We *did* enjoy your party.

Where, however, we have a compound tense of an ordinary verb which contains an auxiliary other than *do*, it is the auxiliary that is stressed.

> I *had* finished my work, although he said I hadn't.
> I *will* go if it's really necessary.

It is possible to stress an ordinary verb in a simple tense, but if we do this it has the effect of emphasising the *meaning* of the word, not the truth of what is said, thus:

> I *killed* him. (i.e. I did not just strike him or injure him— I took away his life.)
> After all these years lying in bed—she *walked!*

(*d*) In the Imperative

Do with the Imperative changes an order into a polite request.

Order	Request
Listen to me.	Do listen to me.
Be quiet.	Do be quiet.
Answer when I speak to you.	Do answer when I speak to you.

Do not (*don't*) is also used to form the negative imperative or prohibition construction.

> Don't leave the door open.
> Don't speak so sharply.
> Please don't drive so fast.

Do as an Ordinary Verb

Do is used very commonly with its own meaning of *to act, to perform a task* and also has a number of idiomatic uses.

(*a*) Act, perform a task

> Do as you are told.
> I don't know who did it.
> He did what he had to do, and then went home.
> Well done!

(*b*) Serve a purpose

> Will this do?
> This will do for now, but we must mend it properly before long.
> Coffee will do, although I should prefer tea.

(c) Progress, get on

> How is he doing?
> He is doing very well at his English.
> How do you do?
> He has done well since he went to Australia.

(d) Finish (the past participle *done* is the form here)

> You may go home as soon as you have done.

>> 'It was a summer evening,
>> Old Kaspar's work was done.'

> I've done. It's your turn now.

(e) For *Do* as a phrasal verb see Lesson 8.

Do is being increasingly used in conversation to replace other verbs of action:

> To *do* one's hair. (To *brush* one's hair)
> To *do* the vegetables. (To *clean* the vegetables)
> To *do* the garden. (To *dig* the garden)
> To *do* the bedrooms. (To *tidy* the bedrooms)
> To *do* the fires. (To *clean* the fireplaces and *light* the fires)

When *Do* is used as an ordinary verb, it forms its negative and interrogative with *do* like any other ordinary verb.

> He did his homework.
> He didn't do his homework.
> Did he do his homework?

> Mr Brown does his own income tax accounts.
> Mr Brown doesn't do his own accounts.
> Does Mr Brown do his own accounts?

45. Uses of *It*

We have already met *It* as an impersonal subject, referring to the weather, temperature, distance:

> It is cold.
> It is raining.

It is a fine day.
It is a long way to London from here.

It is also used as the subject to the verbs *be, seems, appears, happens* where the real subject is a clause usually beginning with *that*, an infinitive phrase, or a gerund in *-ing*, which would be long or clumsy if placed before the verb.

It is now certain that he has been killed.
It seems clear that something has gone wrong.
It appears that he was not told of his failure.
It happens that we shall be travelling on that train too.
It's doubtful whether we shall get there in time.
It's uncertain when he will arrive, or whether he will come at all.

It is likely to be a very exciting match.
It seems difficult to find a good hotel in this town.
It appears useless to complain to the manager.

It is no use crying over spilt milk.
It seems no good asking for better service.
It appears useless waiting any longer.

46. *Only*

Only singles out one particular word in a sentence, emphasising that what is said in the sentence applies to that and nothing else. *Only* must, therefore, be placed close to the word to which it refers, usually immediately before it. If, however, the word qualified by *only* is at the end of the clause or sentence, *only* may be placed after it.

Notice how a change in the placing of *only* alters the meaning of sentences such as this:

Only the English import wine from Italy.
The English import wine only from Italy.
The English import wine from Italy only.

47.   Phrasal Verbs—*Run*

Run away

When they saw the policeman the thieves ran away.

You should face your responsibilities, and not run away from
   them.

Run across

I hadn't seen him for years, and then I ran across him in Paris.

We had hoped to run across some of our old friends while we
   were in London.

Run after

If she runs after the boy like that she'll lose him.

Run down

His watch had run down so he wound it up.

He was feeling run down, so he decided to take a holiday.

Run for

He ran for the bus but didn't catch it.

When the boys saw they had broken a window they decided to
   run for it.

Run into

His car overturned when he ran into a tree.

The builders ran into a lot of trouble as the ground had not been
   drained.

We ran into a party of our friends and stayed with them till after
   midnight.

Run off

While he was bathing someone ran off with his clothes.

Someone has run off so much hot water that there isn't enough
   left for a bath.

Run out

Will you have lemon in your tea? We seem to have run out of
   milk.

My driving licence runs out next week, so I must renew it.

Run over

The driver ran over a dog, but he did not stop.

They ran over to see us last night, but they could not stay long.

I will run over this passage with you, and then you can write out a translation.

Run through

I'll run through the rules again, and then we'll start playing.

His father left him a large fortune, but he ran through it in no time.

Run up

The children ran up to their mother and asked for an ice-cream.

In an expensive restaurant you can run up a big bill in a very short time.

NEW WORDS

anaesthetic (anəs'θetik)
beak (biːk)
beard (biəd)
beast (biːst)
being ('biːiŋ)
birth (bəːθ)
bone (boun)
camel ('kaməl)
captive ('kaptiv)
captivity (kap'tiviti)
chest (tʃest)
claw (kloː)
coin (koin)
colony ('koləni)
conscience ('konʃns)
creature ('kriːtʃə)
death (deθ)
desert ('dezəːt)
devil ('devl)

donkey ('doŋki)
elephant ('elifənt)
fate (feit)
feather ('feðə)
flesh (fleʃ)
fool (fuːl)
forest ('forist)
goat (gout)
habit ('habit)
height (hait)
hook (huk)
horn (hoːn)
hump (hʌmp)
injury ('indʒəri)
ivory ('aivəri)
jaw (dʒoː)
jungle ('dʒʌŋgl)
kingdom ('kiŋdəm)
knot (not)

knowledge (ˈnolidʒ)
ladder (ˈladə)
leg (leg)
liberty (ˈlibəti)
limb (lim)
mercy (ˈməːsi)
monkey (ˈmʌŋki)
mouse (maus)
museum (mjuːˈziəm)
nail (neil)
net (net)
nut (nʌt)
origin (ˈoridʒin)
pain (pein)
parrot (ˈparət)
paw (poː)
pet (pet)
poison (ˈpoizn)
pool (puːl)
pump (pʌmp)
purpose (ˈpəːpəs)
rat (rat)
rope (roup)
salt (solt)
scholar (ˈskolə)
science (ˈsaiəns)
skin (skin)
snake (sneik)
strength (streŋθ)
toe (tou)
trap (noun and verb) (trap)
treatment (ˈtriːtmənt)
trunk (trʌŋk)
voice (vois)
wire (waiə)
wound (wuːnd)
annoy (əˈnoi)

balance (ˈbaləns)
beg (beg)
bite, bit, bitten (bait, bit, ˈbitn)
chatter (ˈtʃatə)
creep, crept (kriːp, krept)
crush (krʌʃ)
decay (noun and verb) (diˈkei)
dive (daiv)
drag (drag)
flash (flaʃ)
heal (hiːl)
imitate (ˈimiteit)
injure (ˈindʒə)
lack (noun and verb) (lak)
multiply (ˈmʌltiplai)
observe (əbˈzəːv)
protect (prəˈtekt)
repeat (riˈpiːt)
reproduce (riprəˈdjuːs)
roar (roː)
rub (rʌb)
scold (skould)
search (səːtʃ)
seize (siːz)
shake, shook, shaken (ʃeik, ʃuk, ˈʃeikn)
shriek (ʃriːk)
slide, slid (slaid, slid)
stroke (strouk)
sway (swei)
swell, swelled, swollen (swel, sweld, ˈswouln)
treat (triːt)
awake (əˈweik)
awkward (ˈoːkwəd)
cruel (ˈkruəl)

curious ('kjuəriəs)
familiar (fə'miljə)
female ('fiːmeil)
foolish ('fuːliʃ)
loose (luːs)
male (meil)
merry ('meri)
mild (maild)
moral ('morəl)
noble ('noubl)

polar ('poulə)
powerful ('pauəful)
remarkable (ri'maːkəbl)
sensible ('sensəbl)
tame (teim)
tough (tʌf)
zoological (zuː'lodʒikl)
absolutely (absə'luːtli)
remarkably (ri'maːkəbli)

Idioms

on their own ('on ðeər 'oun)
to keep them amused (tə 'kiːp ðəm ə'mjuːzd)
in search of (in 'səːtʃ əv)
it's hard to believe (its 'haːd tə bi'liːv)
What brings you to the Gardens (wot 'briŋz 'juː tə ðə 'gaːdnz)
over there ('ouvə 'ðeə)
everyone does his best ('evriwʌn dʌz hiz 'best)
indeed they do (in'diːd ðei 'duː)

EXERCISES

A. *Write sentences (twenty sentences in all) expressing in two different ways a comparison between the following pairs:*

1. Mrs Brown and Susan as cooks
2. The heights of David and Susan
3. The skill of Mr Brown and of Tom as fishermen
4. The distances of Oxford and Edinburgh from London
5. The life of an animal in a zoo and the life of an animal in the jungle
6. The size of an elephant and the size of a camel
7. The amount of rain in England and in Spain
8. Travelling by bicycle and travelling by car
9. The ages of Susan and David
10. The price of wine and the price of beer in England

B. *Complete the following to form sentences:*

1. It is certain . . .
2. It appears . . .
3. It seems sensible . . .
4. It is unwise . . .
5. It happens . . .
6. It is doubtful . . .
7. It is no use . . .
8. It is time . . .
9. It seems clear . . .
10. It is usual . . .

C. *Place the word* only *in the correct position in these sentences:*

1. There is one biscuit left in the tin.
2. We allow members to borrow books from the library.
3. I'm afraid I can lend you a pound.
4. I can let you have the car for one week.
5. An elephant could drag such a heavy load.
6. He had one drink before he set off.
7. If we can reach land we shall be safe.
8. I have met him once.
9. A goat could climb that steep mountain.
10. This shop closes on one day a week.

D. *Use these phrasal verbs in sentences:*

get about; get through; done for; make into; run away; run after; run down; run into; run out of; run through.

E. *Put the indirect object in brackets into the correct place in these sentences, adding* to *or* for *where required:*

1. He offered high wages (all who would take a job with his firm).
2. Mother always cooks a good meal (us).
3. He left presents (the younger members of the family).

4. He showed his beautiful garden (them).
5. He owes money (most of the shopkeepers in the town).
6. He is always ready to do a good turn (anyone).
7. He has taught French for ten years (the boys at the top of the school).
8. He never refuses anything (me).
9. I am choosing books (two of my children).
10. Mr Robinson promised an extra week's holiday (Susan).

F. *Write out in full the question or suggestion which might be expressed by the following:*

1. What about a game of cards?
2. What about the cat?
3. What about the taxi-driver?
4. What about leaving it till tomorrow?
5. What about a pair of gloves?
6. What about a drink?
7. What about your income-tax?
8. What about these old pictures?
9. What about Mr Thompson?
10. What about Paris?

G. *Write sentences expressing someone's ability or inability to do each of these actions:*

1. to speak five languages
2. to come to a party next Monday
3. to work all day, without a good meal
4. to accept a firm's offer to supply goods at an increased price
5. to find his way home in the fog last night
6. to play the piano well when she was a child
7. to make friends with animals easily
8. to put a friend up for the night
9. to grow good vegetables in a very dry summer

H. *Use these abstract nouns in interesting sentences:*

caution; development; grace; speed; danger; advantage; envy; power; respect; poverty.

I. *Link these pairs of sentences by means of relative pronouns. Put the relative in brackets if you think it could be left out.*

1. Animals are born in captivity. They have never known freedom.
2. My uncle is a sailor. He has recently come home on leave.
3. Mrs Brown was talking to the keeper. He feeds the lions.
4. Have you seen the exercise books? They were in that cupboard.
5. This is the house. Jack built it.
6. Do I know the man? You went on holiday with him.
7. That is the house. We used to live there.
8. Shakespeare lived in the time of Queen Elizabeth I. He was born at Stratford-on-Avon.
9. England is a small country with a large population. It must export or go hungry.
10. We had worked all day without stopping for a meal. This made us all hungry and bad-tempered.

J. *Complete these sentences:*

1. . . . if he goes on working hard.
2. He always lends me money if . . .
3. We shall be glad if . . .
4. . . . if he can't find a room in a hotel.
5. . . . if I could speak the language.
6. They would have missed the train if . . .
7. . . . unless you have a passport.
8. If they had taken their coats . . .
9. You have a nasty cold. I should see a doctor if . . .
10. If metal is heated . . .

COMPOSITION

Exercises

1. Discuss the arguments for and against keeping animals in captivity.
2. Imagine that you are the secretary to a firm of manufacturers in your own country which wishes to develop a trade connection in England. Write a letter to a retail store in London enclosing details of some of your products and suggesting that you are ready to send samples if the English firm is interested.
3. Write the letter of thanks you would send after spending an enjoyable week-end in the house of a friend.

On Target

"What's the matter with you?" shouted the pedestrian to the driver of the car that had just run into him. "Are you blind?"

"Blind? Certainly not. I hit you, didn't I?"

LESSON 11

Trial by Jury

ONE morning Mr Brown received a letter from the Town Clerk of Bishopton telling him that he had been appointed to serve on the jury at the next assizes to be held in the large town nearby. Mr Brown was not very pleased about this, because he would have to be absent from work for a day, or perhaps longer, but he knew that to serve on a jury when called upon is the duty of every citizen. So on the day mentioned in the letter, he attended the Law Courts and was shown into a room where he met the other men and women who had been called for jury service that day.

After a while twelve of them, ten men and two women, were taken into the court room and asked to sit in the 'jury box'—two rows of seats facing the dock. The dock was a small enclosed space where the accused person would stand. A number of lawyers in wigs and black gowns sat facing the judge's raised bench, and any members of the general public who were interested enough to come, sat on the benches at the back of the court. Presently the Judge came in to take his seat, and all present rose to their feet to show respect to him as a judge and as a representative of the Queen. He was a severe-looking old man in a red robe and full white wig, and he looked round the court with an eye that missed nothing. The court officer called for silence and the day's work began.

First the jury was 'sworn in'. The words used have been used in English courts for centuries:

"Do you swear to do justice between our Sovereign Lady the Queen and the prisoner at the bar and a true verdict give according to the evidence?"

The first person to appear in the dock was a pale, pasty-faced young man named Eric Ridley, who was accused of theft. The prosecuting lawyer explained that the accused was a factory worker living in lodgings away from home. A small radio set had been stolen from a shop in the town where he was living and the owner had said that Ridley was in the shop just before he discovered it was missing. The radio had later been found by the police when they had searched Ridley's lodgings. Ridley had been arrested, taken to the police station, charged with the crime and freed 'on bail'. Witnesses were called and were questioned by both barristers.

The lawyer defending the accused man then put his case. He said that Ridley admitted having the radio but said he had bought it from a young man he had met at a Youth

Club. He did not know it had been stolen. All he knew about
the man was that he was not from the South of England, that
he was always called 'Shorty' and he had now gone back to
his own part of the country—but he did not know where that
was.

As Mr Brown listened to the evidence he felt certain the
accused man must be guilty. But when Ridley went into the
witness box to tell his own story, Mr Brown was not so sure.
This young man may have been weak and yielded to temptation, but he did not act like a liar or a thief. It was hard to
believe such an unlikely story as he had told, but then Mr
Brown thought to himself: 'This boy is not stupid—he
speaks clearly and intelligently. If he were going to invent a
story to explain why he had the stolen radio, he would invent
a better one than this.' Next the defence barrister called his
witnesses. First the leader of the Youth Club, who said he
knew the young man named 'Shorty' and where he had
been living. Then came the woman in whose house Shorty
had had lodgings. She said she had seen a radio similar to the
stolen one in his room, but that he no longer had it when he
left to return home. She did not know where he had gone as
he had left no address.

In his 'summing up' the Judge went over the evidence
carefully step by step. He was very fair. He pointed out that,
as there was no clear proof on either side, it was for the jury
to decide whether the accused was telling the truth or not.
He warned them that if there was any reasonable doubt in
their minds about whether the prisoner was guilty or
innocent they must give him the benefit of that doubt.

The jury then returned to their room to consider their
verdict. For some time they sat round a table, discussing the
case. It soon became clear that most of the jury shared Mr
Brown's opinion that Ridley was probably telling the truth,
and that whether he was or not, there was enough doubt for a

verdict of 'Not guilty'. But two people on the jury, one man and one woman, would not agree. So the argument continued, for a jury cannot bring in their verdict until all are agreed. For nearly an hour the discussion went on, until at last the two admitted that there was just enough doubt in their minds to make a verdict of not guilty the right decision.

Back in the court, Mr Brown, who had been elected Foreman of the jury, was asked for their verdict, and the slight nod the Judge gave when Mr Brown said "Not guilty" showed that he approved. By the time the court rose at five o'clock, two more cases had been tried and when Mrs Brown asked her husband later that evening how he had got on, he replied: "A very interesting day indeed."

CONVERSATION

(*In the Assize Court. The Prisoner, Eric Ridley, stands in the dock, accused of theft. The Judge and Jury listen as the Prosecuting Counsel questions a Witness*)

PROSECUTING COUNSEL: Your name is Albert Granger and you live at 25, High Street, Bishopton?

WITNESS: That's right.

PROSECUTING COUNSEL: What is your business?

WITNESS: I'm a radio and television dealer.

PROSECUTING COUNSEL: Do you recognise the accused?

WITNESS: Yes, I've seen him in my shop several times.

PROSECUTING COUNSEL: When was the last time you saw him?

WITNESS: On the 5th of March last.

PROSECUTING COUNSEL: How can you be sure of the exact day?

WITNESS: It was the day the radio set was stolen. He'd been in the shop several times looking at sets of that kind, and saying he would like one if he could afford it. Then after he had gone out on this particular day, I noticed that the set was missing.

PROSECUTING COUNSEL: And you are sure the set produced in court is the one stolen from your shop?

WITNESS: Definitely. I made a note of the number at the time.

PROSECUTING COUNSEL: Thank you. No further questions.

DEFENCE COUNSEL: Now Mr Granger, may I ask you just one or two questions? You feel quite certain in your own mind that it was this young man who took your radio set?

WITNESS: Yes, sir. Quite.

DEFENCE COUNSEL: How was it that you didn't see him take the set? After all, it's not something he could slip into his pocket unnoticed.

WITNESS: Well I was busy serving another customer.

DEFENCE COUNSEL: Oh, there were other people in the shop at the time, were there? How many other people?

WITNESS: One or two—perhaps more.

DEFENCE COUNSEL: Perhaps more? You have quite a good business in Bishopton I believe, Mr Granger? They tell me your shop gives very good service to its customers.

WITNESS: Yes, we like to think so. We're always pretty busy, I'm glad to say.

DEFENCE COUNSEL: And you were pretty busy on this day in March, I suppose?

WITNESS: Yes, we were.

DEFENCE COUNSEL: Indeed, the shop was so crowded that you couldn't see someone walk off with a radio set he hadn't paid for?

WITNESS: Yes, there were a lot of people about.

DEFENCE COUNSEL: So you don't really know that the prisoner

was the one who took it. It might have been anyone else in the shop at the time.

WITNESS: But he'd been asking about this set and saying he couldn't afford it.

DEFENCE COUNSEL: So, Mr Granger, if I come into your shop and look at a radio set I can't afford and you later find it is missing, you will send for the police and have me arrested. Is that right?

WITNESS: No, certainly not. But this set was later found in his lodgings.

DEFENCE COUNSEL: That has nothing to do with how the set left your shop. Let's be quite clear about this, shall we, Mr Granger? There is not an ounce of evidence, as far as you know, that this young man stole anything from you. All you know is that the prisoner was in your shop on the 5th March with a crowd of other customers and that later on you found a radio set was missing.

WITNESS: Yes.

DEFENCE COUNSEL: How much later did you discover the loss, Mr Granger?

WITNESS: When I checked the stock at the end of the day.

DEFENCE COUNSEL: Oh, not till the end of the day. The 5th March was a Saturday. Bishopton's Market Day. How many customers do you think would have entered your shop during that busy Saturday, Mr Granger?

WITNESS: It's difficult to say. A hundred—perhaps more.

DEFENCE COUNSEL: Any one of whom might have stolen the missing radio set?

WITNESS: Yes, I suppose so.

DEFENCE COUNSEL: Thank you, Mr Granger. No further questions.

. . . .

THE JUDGE (*summing up*): Ladies and gentlemen of the Jury. At first sight this may appear a simple case for you to decide, but it is not quite so simple as it seems. A quantity of evidence has been produced which throws suspicion on this young man: he had shown particular interest in this radio set, which he admitted he could not afford; he was in the shop at or about the time when the set was stolen, and the shop was crowded at the time so that he could, you may think, have taken the radio away unobserved. The set was later found by the police in his lodgings. No one, however, saw him take the set and the defence have shown that at least a hundred other people had the same opportunity of taking it. The prisoner has told you in the witness box that he bought the set cheaply from this young man called 'Shorty'. You might consider this mysterious person, whom the police have failed to find, as an invention of the prisoner's if it were not for the fact that his existence has been proved by the evidence of the Leader of the Youth Club, and his landlady has told you she saw a similar radio set in this Shorty's room and that it had gone from his room before he himself left. The scales have been to some extent weighted against the defence because they have been unable to produce in court the only person who really knows the truth or falsity of the accused man's story. It is for you to decide therefore, ladies and gentlemen of the jury, what is shadow and what is sub-stance in this rather puzzling case. You have had the advantage of seeing and hearing the prisoner giving evidence in the witness box. As so often happens in a trial of this kind, your verdict will depend very largely on whether or not you consider the accused was speaking the truth. You will now retire to consider your verdict.

COURT USHER: I swear to conduct the jury to a convenient

place and not to suffer any to speak to them, nor will I speak to them myself, except to ask if they have agreed upon their verdict.

(*The Jury retire. When they return, all stand as the Judge re-enters the Court*)

JUDGE: Who shall speak as your Foreman?

MR BROWN: I am the Foreman, my Lord.

JUDGE: Are you agreed upon your verdict?

MR BROWN: We are.

JUDGE: How say you, Guilty or Not guilty?

MR BROWN: Not guilty, my Lord.

JUDGE: The prisoner is discharged. Next case . . .

COMPREHENSION EXERCISES

1. What are the duties of a Town Clerk?

2. Explain the terms:

   jury; assize; evidence; verdict.

3. What part does each of the following take in a trial?

   the judge; the jury; counsel for the prosecution; counsel for the defence.

4. Why did everyone stand when the Judge entered the court?

5. What does the expression 'on bail' mean?

6. What, in brief, was

   (*a*) the case against the prisoner.

   (*b*) his defence?

7. What made Mr Brown uncertain of the accused man's guilt even before he had heard his defence?

8. What is the judge's 'summing up'?

9. Why did the jury take so long to decide on their verdict?

10. Explain the expression 'to give someone the benefit of the doubt'.

SENTENCE PATTERNS

48. How to express Wishes and Preferences

(a) Normal requirements of everyday life.

Want + the thing required

What do you want?
David wants a new bicycle for Christmas.
Do you want another cup of tea?
No, I don't want any more, thank you.

Should/would like (a polite form of *want*)

Would you like a chocolate?
I should like to meet your boy-friend.
Would you like me to drive you to the station?
She would like a new hat, but she can't afford it.

(b) A desire to do something, or that someone else should do something.

Want + *to*-infinitive

Do you want to go home?
I want to visit Germany next summer.
Susan wants to finish this book before bedtime.
David wants to be a Member of Parliament one day.

Want + (pro)noun + *to*-infinitive

Mr Brown wants David to pass his examination.
Do you want me to post this letter?
I don't want you to make a mistake.
We don't want anyone to know where we have been.

(c) A desire that something was happening, or that something was true in the present or had been true in the past.

Wish + (that) + clause with verb in a Past Tense for present or future wishes and in the Past Perfect Tense for past wishes

I wish I had more money. (now)
I wish the weather was warmer. (now)

I wish we lived nearer to our friends. (now)
I wish we were going to England for our holiday. (future)

I wish I had gone to Brighton instead of to Blackpool for
my holiday. (past)
I wish I had known you were coming. (past)
He wishes he had worked harder. (past)
Tom wishes he had driven more carefully. (past)

(d) A wish or hope.

Hope + (that) + clause   *That* is usually omitted.

I hope you have a good time.
I hope (that) she arrives safely.
I hope we have enough petrol.
The prisoner hopes (that) the jury will find him innocent.

Hope + *to*-infinitive

We hope to get home before it starts to rain.
I hope to see you again soon.
Tom hopes to save enough money to get married.
We hope to visit Spain during the summer.

Hope + *for* + noun

We hope for better weather tomorrow.
The farmers hope for a good harvest this summer.
If you hope for nothing, you will not be disappointed.
He hoped for a word of thanks, but she didn't even smile.

A vain or unfulfilled hope is expressed by *If only* + clause
with verb in the Past Tense for present or future wishes and
in the Past Perfect Tense for past wishes

If only she lived a little nearer!
If only I knew his name.
If only we could get there in time.

If only we had been more careful!
If only I had known where he lived!
If only he had locked the money away safely!

(*e*) A wish expressed to others for their success or welfare.
An Imperative.

> Enjoy yourselves at the party!
> Sleep well!
> Have a nice time!

May (in more formal speech and writing, and very frequently
in prayers)

> May all go well for you.
> God save the Queen—Long may she reign!
> May God be with you!

This last has been shortened to form the everyday expression
Goodbye (God b(e with) ye)
The greetings Good morning, Good night, etc., are shortened
forms of:

> May you have a good morning, etc.

Wish + Indirect Object + Direct Object, to report a wish
expressed by others

> He wished me a happy holiday.
> They wished us long life and happiness.
> We wished them a safe journey.

(*f*) Asking others what their wishes are.

Want or *Wish* + ((pro)noun) + *to*-infinitive

> Where does she want to go for her holiday?
> Where do you want me to put this chair?
> Who do you want us to invite to the party?
>
> Do you wish to make a statement to the court?
> Do you wish me to call my next witness, my Lord?

Shall

> Shall I pour the coffee? (Do you want me to?)
> Shall we join the ladies?
> Shall I cut the grass for you?
> Shall the maid bring you an early cup of tea?

(g) Preferences.

Would rather + infinitive without *to* for preferences affecting oneself

> I would rather be happy than rich.
> We would rather go by air than by sea.

Would rather + *(that)* + clause with verb in the Past Tense for preferences affecting others

> I would rather (that) he spoke the truth.
> She would rather (that) we lived a little nearer.

> *(That* is usually omitted).

Prefer

> He prefers white wine to red.
> She prefers to do her own shopping.
> David prefers playing football to watching it.
> I prefer you to write in ink rather than in pencil.

49.   The Future Continuous Tense

The main concern of this Tense, as in all the Continuous tenses, is with a state of affairs over a period of time rather than with a single event.

> How long will you be staying in Italy?
> Will David be living with his cousins while he is in North Wales?
> I shall be working on a farm all through the summer.
> If we go by this train we shall be travelling all night.
> I shall be thinking of you while you are away.

The Future Continuous can also be used to ask questions about future intention, particularly when the speaker has some further possibility in mind.

> Will you be coming back through Paris? (If so, you could call to see a friend of mine)
> Will you be staying in England for long? (If so, you will have a good opportunity to improve your English)

Will David be calling on the Thompsons while he is in Manchester?

Will you be passing the chemist's on your way home? (if so, you can fetch me some medicine)

50.   *Used*

(a) *Used to* as a special verb. [juːst] It expresses a customary action or state in the past which has now ended.

> Mr Brown used to walk to the station every morning.
>> (but now he goes by car)
> We used to spend our holidays by the sea.
>> (but now we go elsewhere)
> David used to play football regularly.
>> (but now he doesn't)

As a special verb, *used to* should form its interrogative by inversion and its negative with *not* (*n't*).

> Used students to attend as many lectures as they do now?
> English people used not to go abroad for their holidays as often as they do now.

Forms with *do* are common in spoken questions.

> Did you used to live in Cardiff?
> Did he used to go to school with you?

and these forms with *do* are always used in short responses and question tags:

> You used to live here, didn't you?
> Did he used to live here? Yes, he did.
> He didn't use to have much money when he was at College, did he? No, he didn't.

A negative form with *never* is common in informal speech:

> I never used to like her very much.
> I never used to leave home till half past eight.
> You never used to be so unkind to me.

(b) *Used to* as an adjective with *be* and verbs of *becoming*. This adjectival construction is followed by a noun or a gerund in *-ing* and means *accustomed*.

> The Russians are used to snow in winter.
>
> In France we got used to only having rolls and coffee for breakfast.
>
> I could never get used to living in the country.
>
> He is not used to working for his living yet.

(c) *Used* as the Past Tense of the ordinary verb '*to use*' (juːzd) This is straightforward. The only point needing care is the passive form *was used to* which might be confused with the adjectival form in (b) above.

> (i) *The spade was used to dig a hole in the ground* ('juːzd).
>
> (ii) *He was used to digging, so he did not find it hard work.* ('juːst)

NEW WORDS

assize(s) (əˈsaiz(iz))
bail (beil)
bench (bentʃ)
benefit (ˈbenifit)
counsel (ˈkaunsl)
defence (diˈfens)
doubt (daut)
evidence (ˈevidəns)
existence (igˈzistəns)
foreman (ˈfoːmən)
gown (gaun)
jury (ˈdʒuəri)
justice (ˈdʒʌstis)
lawyer (ˈloːjə)
liar (ˈlaiə)
lodging (ˈlodʒiŋ)
loss (los)

mystery (ˈmistəri)
ounce (auns)
paste (peist)
proof (pruːf)
puzzle (noun and verb) (ˈpʌzl)
scale (skeil)
set (set)
shadow (ˈʃadou)
silence (ˈsailəns)
sovereign (ˈsovrin)
substance (ˈsʌbstəns)
suspicion (səsˈpiʃn)
temptation (tempˈteiʃn)
theft (θeft)
thief (θiːf)
trial (ˈtraiəl)
verdict (ˈvəːdikt)

wig (wig)
witness ('witnis)
youth (juːθ)
accuse (ə'kjuːz)
admit (əd'mit)
appoint (ə'point)
arrest (ə'rest)
claim (kleim)
defend (di'fend)
discharge (dis'tʃaːdʒ)
exist (ig'zist)
fail (feil)
nod (noun and verb) (nod)
prosecute ('prosikjuːt)
recognise ('rekəgnaiz)
slip (slip)
steal, stole, stolen, (stiːl, stoul, 'stouln)
suffer ('sʌfə)

sum up ('sʌm 'ʌp)
suspect (verb) (səs'pekt)
swear, swore, sworn (sweə, swoː, swoːn)
tempt (temt)
warn (woːn)
yield (jiːld)
absent ('absənt)
guilty ('gilti)
innocent ('inəsənt)
mysterious (mis'tiəriəs)
pale (peil)
pastey ('peisti)
severe (si'viə)
slight (slait)
stupid ('stjuːpid)
weak (wiːk)
apart (ə'paːt)

Idioms

to take a seat (tə 'teik ə 'siːt)
rose to their feet (rouz tə ðeə 'fiːt)
to call for silence (tə 'koːl fə 'sailəns)
away from home (ə'wei frəm 'houm)
to put a case (tə 'put ə 'keis)
step by step ('step bai 'step)
to tell the truth (tə 'tel ðə 'truːθ)
to speak the truth (tə 'spiːk ðə 'truːθ)
the benefit of the doubt (ðə 'benifit əv ðə 'daut)
we like to think so (wi 'laik tə 'θiŋk sou)
not an ounce of evidence (not ən 'auns əv 'evidəns)
later on ('leitər 'on)
at first sight (ət 'fəːst 'sait)

EXERCISES

A. *Write sentences expressing the following wishes. Use the method (Sentence Pattern 48) which seems best for each:*

1. for another cup of tea
2. to become Mayor of this town
3. for someone to drive more carefully
4. for someone to speak English a little better
5. for the children to enjoy themselves at the zoo
6. for God to give someone happiness
7. to live in London
8. for someone to have a happy birthday
9. for someone to arrive home in time for Christmas
10. for someone to get to the office earlier in the morning

B. *Use these nouns in sentences (twenty sentences in all), first as uncountable, then as countable nouns:*

glass; tin; stone; chocolate; wood; cake; wine; sands; cheese; fire.

C. *Write sentences in the Future Continuous Tense making use of the following ideas:*

1. living in the United States all next year.
2. a person's length of stay in England
3. the possibility of a person bringing her husband to a party
4. the possibility of a person needing the car on Sunday
5. a person working away from home all next week
6. a person staying in Switzerland for a month
7. some people working hard for an examination until the end of term
8. the likelihood of feeling tired the next day after a late night
9. the possibility of a person meeting his brother while he is in Paris
10. someone not needing his lawn mower while he is away on holiday

D. *Rewrite these sentences using a form of the verb* used:

1. We were accustomed to go to Brighton for our holidays.
2. Did you live in Edinburgh at one time?
3. It was not my habit to smoke as much then as I do now.
4. We are quite accustomed to looking after ourselves.
5. Elephants are employed in India to pull heavy loads.
6. When I was a boy, it was our habit to play cricket where those houses now stand.
7. Were you in the habit of going to the seaside every week-end?
8. I was never very fond of either of the two sisters.
9. It was their habit to spend their holidays here every year, wasn't it?
10. This umbrella hasn't been taken out very often, has it?

E. *Rewrite these sentences, using a part of the verb* do *in place of the words in italics:*

1. He *performed* his work quite satisfactorily.
2. If you've *finished* with that book, I should like to read it.
3. Have you *completed* all the exercises that were set?
4. How *are you*, Mr Brown?
5. How is he *progressing* at his new school?
6. This bad work *is not satisfactory*. You must *write* this composition again.
7. I have *cut* the lawn, but I haven't yet *tidied* the flower beds.
8. You needn't spend much money. A small present will *be sufficient*.
9. She has had her hair *dressed* in a new style.
10. He has *succeeded* much better with his English lessons this term.

F. *Express these comparisons in a different form:*

1. He is not as clever as his sister.
2. Your car is faster than mine.
3. The older he grew, the wiser he became.

4. David plays cricket better than his father.
5. A jury is not always as wise as the judge.
6. Edinburgh is farther from London than Cardiff is.
7. You can't speak English as well as I can.
8. Is Tom older than Susan?
9. David does not enjoy working in the garden as much as his father does.
10. It is warmer in summer than in winter.

G. *Give the possessive of:*

1. the palace of the Duke of Marlborough
2. a holiday of three weeks
3. at the end of one's wits
4. the shoes of the children
5. the head of King Charles
6. a hairdresser for ladies
7. a home for lost dogs
8. the daughter of Joe Smith, the policeman
9. the mother of David and Susan
10. the car of the father of David

H. *To the following add adverbs or adverb phrases of the kind suggested:*

Example:

He is coming to England (Manner, Time)
He is coming to England by air next week.

1. She walked (Manner, Place)
2. (Time) they sat (Manner, Place)
3. I (Frequency) visit my friends (Place)
4. You will (Frequency) find Joan (Place)
5. (Time) they went for a swim (Place)
6. They danced (Manner, Place, Time)
7. The Judge spoke (Manner) to the prisoner (Time)
8. (Time) the jury returned (Manner, Place)
9. He has not been (Place, Time)
10. Mr Brown used to play cricket (Manner, Time)

I. *Make these sentences negative, so that the obligation or necessity is removed but so that they do not become prohibitions:*

1. You are to be home before midnight.
2. You must work at your studies every evening.
3. People should read a newspaper from cover to cover.
4. An accused person must give evidence at his trial.
5. You will have to eat everything that is put before you.
6. I was told I ought to be in my seat as much as half an hour before the play starts.
7. Susan's got to finish all these letters before she goes home.
8. He had to run to catch his train.
9. You need a passport for every journey overseas.
10. You should buy an expensive fountain pen.

J. *Add the definite article* the *where required in these sentences:*

1. This is last time we shall see him before he leaves for United States.
2. We shall be on holiday next week, but week after that we shall be at home.
3. I travelled in third carriage from engine.
4. Narrow strip of water between France and England is called English Channel.
5. Browns take two newspapers each day, *Times* and *Daily Mail*
6. Sun rises in east and sets in west.
7. Best hotel in village is near church.
8. In August Queen goes on holiday to Scotland.
9. On arrival in United Kingdom all visitors must go through Customs.
10. It is duty of Medical Officer of Health to look after deaf and blind.

K. *Write sentences using each of the following words, first as a noun, then as an adjective:*

evil; liquid; nylon; female; salt; captive; guilty; weak; public; wealthy.

L. *Write the questions to which these might be the answers:*

1. No, I don't think he can.
2. Every three weeks.
3. Until next summer, I expect.
4. I haven't seen him for a week.
5. No, I must have left it somewhere.
6. I'm sorry, I don't know.
7. He has spent it all on books.
8. Yes, it is—if you like cold weather.
9. No, it must have been someone else.
10. They said he was guilty.

M. *Put these sentences into the passive (Book Two, Sentence Patterns 15, 16, 17)*

1. Will they sell all these cars abroad?
2. Is anyone teaching these children French?
3. No one told these workmen they could go home early.
4. Someone has sent this child to school without any breakfast.
5. The manufacturers make golf balls of rubber.
6. Someone printed this book in Holland.
7. People do not play cricket in winter in England.
8. Does anyone play football in Japan?
9. Someone will punish you if you do that again.
10. No one has swept this floor for a week.

COMPOSITION

Exercises

1. Write out, as in the conversation passage, the questioning of 'Shorty's' landlady, first by the defence counsel and then by the prosecuting counsel.

2. Imagine that you were present as a customer when an attempt was made to rob a bank. Describe what happened.

3. Write a summary of the trial of Eric Ridley in about 150 words.

What Every Husband Knows

Man wants but little here below,
He's not so hard to please;
But Woman—bless her little heart—
Wants everything she sees!

LESSON 12

House-Hunting

DURING his year of office as Mayor, Mr Carter, the Manager of the factory where Tom Smith works, had become so busy with his public duties, that he had left much of the work of running the factory to Tom. Tom had done so well that at the end of the year Mr Carter called him into his office and told him that he proposed to appoint him Assistant Manager at a higher salary. Tom was naturally very pleased—and so was Susan, for they could now make plans for getting married without further delay.

The main problem was to find a house. They were determined to start with a home of their own, and Mr Brown said that, as Tom was now likely to stay in Bishopton for some time, it would be foolish to rent a house; they should buy one, if they could find one that they liked and could afford. They would be able to pay for it with a loan from an insurance company or building society, which they could repay gradually over a number of years. So Susan and Tom started their house-hunting.

They knew exactly what they wanted: a small, modern house in a pleasant situation on the edge of the town with plenty of light and air and a good garden. But they soon found that houses for sale like this were very scarce. They spent days going from one house agent to another and looking at the houses they had for sale. But always there was something wrong: the house was ugly to look at, or was damp or in need of repair or there was dry rot or worm in the woodwork, or the plaster on the walls and ceilings was badly cracked. Susan was quite disgusted to see how some lazy people neglected their homes—scratched paint, floors unpolished, rust on bathroom taps and kitchen sinks, and nothing but rubbish, weeds and coarse grass in their gardens. Sometimes they found a house they liked, but then the price was too high.

It looked as though they would have to postpone their marriage, and Susan was almost in despair, when one day they found just what they were looking for—or rather, Mr Brown found it for them. He told them of a house which was being sold by one of the customers of his bank, an old lady named Mrs Hallam who was a widow and too old to live any longer by herself and who was going to live with her daughter in another town. Tom and Susan went to see the house and were charmed with it at once. It was a small house built of warm red brick with a beautifully cultivated garden all round it. Mrs Hallam showed them round, and the more they saw the more they were sure that this was the ideal house for them. Mrs Hallam took a great fancy to them also, and by the time their visit came to an end, she too had decided that she did not want to sell her house to anyone else but this nice young couple. So when they came to talk about price, she asked a good deal less than the house was worth.

The house had many advantages, but perhaps the most convenient thing for Susan and Tom was that Mrs Hallam was ready to move out at any time they wished. So the wedding was fixed for a date six weeks ahead, and Susan and her mother began preparations for the great event.

Tom soon found that buying the house was only the beginning of his problems. It had to be furnished. Fortunately, the place was in such a good state of repair and so tastefully decorated that they would not have much to do to it, and they were also able to buy some of Mrs Hallam's carpets and curtains. They decided they could not afford to furnish all the rooms at once. They were tempted to buy many things on hire purchase, but Mr Brown advised them not to start their married life with too large a debt to repay. By the time they had bought everything they needed, Tom found he had very little money left. But, as he said, a wife, a home and a good job are better than money in the bank.

CONVERSATION

(*Tom and Susan arrive at Mrs Hallam's house, and knock at the door. Mrs Hallam opens the door*)

SUSAN: Good morning. Mrs Hallam?

MRS HALLAM: Yes. Good morning.

SUSAN: We must apologise for disturbing you, but my father,
    Mr Brown the bank manager, told us you have this

house for sale. May we see it, please? This is my fiancé, Tom Smith.

MRS HALLAM: Certainly. Come in. Your father said I might expect a call from you. It's rather a small house, I'm afraid.

SUSAN: It's a beautiful house. We fell in love with it as soon as we saw it, didn't we, Tom?

TOM: It certainly does seem to be the sort of house we are looking for. It has a wonderful garden, too.

MRS HALLAM: Yes, the garden is one of the nicest things about it. My husband used to be very fond of gardening, and I've tried to keep it tidy. But it's getting a little too much for me now. I expect you'd like to look around.

SUSAN: Yes, please, if we may.

MRS HALLAM: This is the sitting-room. It has a french window into the garden and gets all the afternoon sun.

TOM: Are those roses from the garden?

MRS HALLAM: Yes, we have clay soil which is excellent for roses. I'm rather proud of my rose garden. Here is the dining-room and through there is the kitchen.

SUSAN: What a lovely kitchen! It'll be a pleasure to cook here. Seeing all those pots and pans with their lids shining so brightly makes me want to start straight away!

MRS HALLAM: Can she cook well, Mr Smith? I think it's so important. I remember no one taught me to cook when I was a girl, and when I got married I couldn't even bake a cake—all I could do was make tea and fry an egg. My husband was so patient, dear man, but what he must have suffered!

TOM: I think Susan can do better than that, Mrs Hallam— but whether she'll be as good a cook as her mother, remains to be seen.

MRS HALLAM: I'm sure she will. When do you intend getting married?

SUSAN: As soon as we can find a house we like—and can afford.

MRS HALLAM: Now let's go upstairs, shall we? There's one nice big bedroom and two rather small ones. And there's quite a good-sized bathroom. All the water pipes are on the inside walls so they never burst in cold weather. It's a warm, comfortable house and my husband used to say it was very well built.

SUSAN: The more I see of it, the more I like it. If we decide to buy it, when could we move in?

MRS HALLAM: As soon as you like. My daughter and my grandchildren have been trying to persuade me to come to live with them, as they think I am too old to go on living alone. So I could go at any time within the next month or two.

TOM: I think we're both agreed it's exactly the house we want, but I'm afraid the price may be more than we can afford.

MRS HALLAM: Well, let's go downstairs and talk about it over a cup of tea, shall we? I have some cakes that I baked this morning, so you can tell me whether you think I learnt to cook a little when I was married.

(A little later, after tea)

MRS HALLAM: So that's settled. Now let's go and look at the garden. There'll be mud on the paths after the rain, but some rain was badly needed after all the dry weather we've been having.

SUSAN: I like the rose bushes trained along the fence like that.

MRS HALLAM: They need some attention, I'm afraid. The insects have got at them, too. Your husband—I mean your fiancé—will have to bind them to the fence with some wire and nails. Are you fond of gardening, Mr Smith?

TOM: I've never done any. I've always lived in a town house without much of a garden, but I think I shall enjoy it. I'm sure I can count on plenty of help from Susan's father—he's an expert. And now I really think we must be going. Thank you so much for all your kindness.

SUSAN: And I promise you we'll look after your lovely house, Mrs Hallam. I'm sure we're going to be very happy here.

MRS HALLAM: I'm sure you are. Good-bye, both of you. And good luck!

COMPREHENSION QUESTIONS

1. Why were Tom and Susan so anxious to have a house of their own?
2. Why did Mr Brown consider it would be foolish for Tom and Susan to rent a house?
3. How did they propose to pay for their house?
4. What kind of house did they want?
5. What is the meaning of the terms (not used in this passage):

   suburbia; ribbon development; a green belt policy; over-spill towns?

6. What is a house agent?
7. Give the meanings of the following phrases as used in this passage:

   a good state of repair; tastefully decorated; they were tempted to buy many things.

8. Explain the meaning of the following phrases as used in these passages:

   without further delay; to take a great fancy to; almost in despair; a detached house.

SENTENCE PATTERNS

51.　　　　How to express Cause or Reason

The commonest method of expressing cause or reason is by an adverbial clause introduced by *because, as, since, seeing that, now that:*

> Susan has gone to London because she wants to buy a new coat.
> Since you have quite made up your mind, we must do as you wish.
> As it was now late, they decided to go home to bed.
> Seeing that everyone else is going home, I suppose we had better go home too.
> We shan't need such a big house now that the children have all left home.

A participial phrase is sometimes used instead of an adverbial clause:

> Feeling thoroughly bored, they decided to leave the party.
> Having finished their meal, they left the restaurant.
> Being uncertain of the way, they asked a policeman.
> Knowing he was fond of food, she cooked an excellent meal.

Another construction uses a preposition and a gerund:

> He was punished for being late.
> David was given a prize for having done well in his examination.
> He was fined for driving without a licence.
> The foreman was rewarded for inventing a safety device for the machine.

The words *cause* and *reason* may also be used:

> The reason for his failure was his continual carelessness.
> The chief cause of the strike was the bad working conditions in the factory.
> One cause of high prices is an increase in demand.
> Many accidents are caused by carelessness.
> He gave his wife's illness as a reason for his absence.

52.   Verbs of Becoming

These are verbs which show a development or change of condition (sometimes called inchoative verbs). They include:

become, get, grow and, less commonly, *come, fall, go, run, turn, wear*.

These verbs are followed by:

(a) an adjective:

> Our streets are becoming more crowded every day.
> She is getting careless in her work.
> As she grows older she becomes more loveable.
> Everything will come right in the end.
> Your work is falling short of what it should be.
> The milk will go sour if you leave it too long.
> Dogs will run wild if they have no home.
> Peeled apples soon turn brown.
> His clothes were wearing thin.

(b) a noun

> His eldest son became a doctor.
> He is getting quite a big boy, isn't he?
> She's growing a really pretty girl.

(c) a prepositional phrase

> I shall go to sleep if he talks much longer.
> They quarrelled until they nearly came to blows.
> Ice will turn to water if you heat it.
> All his hopes turned to dust and ashes.

(d) a *to*-infinitive.

> The new neighbours are getting to know one another.
> They were not very friendly at first, but now they are getting to like each other.
> This is coming to be known as a good shopping centre.
> The workmen grew to hate their foreman.

In conversation, *get* is used much more commonly than *become*, especially with the continuous tenses:

It is getting dark.
We noticed that he was getting older.
She is getting quite well known as a pianist.
You'll get used to wearing glasses in time.

The following expressions are in common use:

to come true (of dreams); to fall asleep; to fall ill; to run short; to run dry; to wear thin; to get used to; to come undone; to come right in the end; to go bad (of fruit, etc.); to go mad; to go to sleep.

53. Quantitative Adjectives

The principal quantitative adjectives in English are:

some, any, one, all, every, each, both, much, many, little, a little few, a lot of.

Some Both *some* and *any* are used when the number or quantity is uncertain. *Some* implies that what is being referred to does exist; *any* is used when the existence of what is being referred to is uncertain. This implied certainty or uncertainty underlies all the uses of *some* and *any* given below. Both *some* and *any* are used with singular uncountable nouns and plural countable nouns.

Some is used:

(*a*) in affirmative statements:

He has some interesting friends.
There are some people waiting for you in the library.
She has spilt some wine on her dress.
It needed some courage to do that.

(*b*) in imperative sentences:

Cut some flowers for me, please.
Bring me some more sheets of paper.
Give the dog some water; it's thirsty.
Would you give me some advice, please?

(c) in questions expecting the answer 'Yes':

> You have some strange people living next door, haven't you?
>
> Haven't you lost some buttons from your coat?
>
> Haven't you had some trouble with these people before?

(d) in making an offer:

> May I offer you some wine?
>
> Will you have some more tea?
>
> Would you like some matches?
>
> Can I fetch you some ice-cream?

Notice that in all these examples there is no question about the existence of what is referred to.

Any   Whilst *some* is definite, *any* is indefinite and uncertain.

Any is used:

(a) in negative sentences:

> There aren't any people living here now.
>
> We haven't any strawberries in our garden this year.
>
> I'm afraid I haven't any money left.
>
> I can't see any possibility of having a holiday next summer.

(b) in questions to which the answer is uncertain:

> Are there any people living here now?
>
> Have you any strawberries in your garden this year?
>
> Have you any money left?
>
> Is there any truth in what he says?

(c) after *hardly* and *scarcely* (here the idea is almost negative):

> He has scarcely any friends.
>
> There is hardly any sugar left.
>
> I have hardly any doubt that he did it.

(d) in conditional sentences where the speaker does not know whether or not the condition is likely to be fulfilled:

> If you have any time left, you could then visit the National Gallery.

If he gives us any trouble we will call the police.

If there are any people here who speak French will they please come forward?

But if the speaker thinks the condition is very likely to be fulfilled, *some* is often used:

If you would find us some chairs, we could sit down.

If you would lend me some money, I should be very happy.

(*e*) after words expressing doubt, wonder or uncertainty:

I doubt if you will find any shops open at this time of night.

I wonder whether you have any idea how old she is.

I'm not sure whether he will make any profit out of this deal.

One (see Sentence Pattern 4)

Notice that *one*, as an indefinite pronoun should be used only when the speaker can include himself in what is said. Thus anyone might say:

One should think before one speaks.

but a person who had not lived in England would not say:

When one has lived in England all one's life, one knows that the English climate is not as bad as some people pretend.

Each, Every, All

Each and *every* are singular and are followed by a singular verb (see Sentence Pattern 61 (*b*)); *all* is plural, and is followed by a plural verb.

Each emphasises that the people or things referred to are to be considered individually; *every* suggests a collection of single people or things.

Each boy is equally to blame.

He examined each book with the greatest care.

Every book in the library belongs to the college.

Every visitor who calls on the Mayor is treated with the same politeness.

All links together a complete group of persons or things (countable nouns).

All the boys in this school are English.

All these cars are for sale.

Notice that *all* can also be used with uncountable nouns, and is then followed by a singular verb:

All that glitters is not gold.

All this trouble was caused by one man.

Either, Neither, Both

Either, *neither* and *both* are used with two persons or things. *Either* (affirmative) and *neither* (negative) consider the two separately, and are singular; *both* considers them together, and is plural.

Either Tom or Harry is certain to be chosen captain.

Neither Tom nor Henry has a chance of being elected.

Both husband and wife are ill at the moment.

Both the copies of *David Copperfield* have been borrowed from the library.

Many, Much, A lot of

Many is used with countable nouns; *much* with uncountable nouns. *A lot of* is used colloquially with countable and uncountable nouns.

Many

Many people do not like living in the country.

He has as many friends as I have.

Have they many flowers in their garden?

How many cousins have you?

Much

Much talk wastes time.

How much money have you?

Many people say we have too much rain in England.

We haven't much time so we must hurry.

In affirmative sentences *much* is replaced by *a lot of, a good (great) deal of, plenty of*, unless *much* is the subject of the sentence or follows *how, so, as, too*. To a lesser extent this is also true of *many*, except that *a large number of* is used instead of *a great deal of*.

> The boy gave his teachers a lot of trouble.
> There was plenty of wine for everyone.
> Some people have a great deal of difficulty in learning English.
> There are a lot of people waiting to see you.
> He bought a large number of pictures he did not want.
> I have made plenty of mistakes in my time.

Little, A little, Few, A few

Little is the opposite of *much*; *few* is the opposite of *many*. Both are negative in meaning, and mean 'almost none'.

> There was little time for argument.
> There is very little sugar in this tea.
> We had little money left by the end of the holiday.
> Few people learn languages easily.
> There were very few seats empty when we arrived.
> She is a lonely woman with few friends.
> I have little hope of ever seeing her again.
> Few students get full marks in an examination.

A little and *a few* The addition of the indefinite article makes these two words positive—the presence of something is emphasised, rather than its absence.

> We haven't much milk at the moment, but I can give you a little.
> There is a little sugar in that basin in the cupboard.
> There is still a little time before the bus goes.
> I have a few biscuits here, if you would like them.
> Now that he has had a few lessons, his dancing has greatly improved.
> We invited a few friends in for dinner last evening.
> You must take a little more care with your work.
> They came to see me a few days ago.

54.

The Light, the Dark

Notice this use of the definite article with words for climate, the weather, the seasons, etc.

Children are often afraid of the dark.
We found the kitten shivering in the snow.
Come into the light so that I can see you.
The soldier fainted in the heat.
The warmth made him sleepy.
This colour may look different in the daylight.
Don't stand there in the rain. You'll get wet.
Those plants were killed by the frost last week.
The ship disappeared in the mist.
It is dangerous to drive in the fog.
They strolled along quietly in the twilight.
Our dog Spot slept peacefully in the sunshine.
She does not go out much in the winter.
We will come and see you again in the spring.
We usually go abroad during the summer.
Students come back to Oxford in the autumn.

NEW WORDS

bush (buʃ)
ceiling (ˈsiːliŋ)
clay (klei)
comfort (ˈkʌmfət)
damp (damp)
debt (det)
despair (noun and verb)
 (disˈpeə)
disgust (noun and verb)
 (disˈgʌst)
fence (fens)
fortune (ˈfɔːtjuːn)

grandchild (ˈgrantʃaild)
hammer (ˈhamə)
insect (ˈinsekt)
lid (lid)
loan (loun)
marriage (ˈmaridʒ)
mud (mʌd)
pan (pan)
pipe (paip)
plaster (ˈplaːstə)
polish (ˈpoliʃ)
pot (pot)

rent (rent)
rubbish ('rʌbiʃ)
rust (noun and verb) (rʌst)
sink (siŋk)
situation (sitju'eiʃn)
soil (soil)
tap (tap)
weed (wiːd)
widow ('widou)
worm (wəːm)
worth (wəːθ)
bake (beik)
bind, bound (baind, baund)
burst (bəːst)
crack (noun and verb) (krak)
cultivate ('kʌltiveit)
delay (noun and verb) (di'lei)
disturb (dis'təːb)
fry (frai)
furnish ('fəːniʃ)
insure (in'ʃoː, in'ʃuə)
knock (nok)

neglect (noun and verb)
  (ni'glekt)
polish ('poliʃ)
postpone (poust'poun)
repair (ri'peə)
repay (ri'pei)
rot (noun and verb) (rot)
scratch (skratʃ)
coarse (koːs)
damp (damp)
fortunate ('foːtjunət)
gradual ('gradjuəl)
ideal (ai'diːl)
lazy ('leizi)
scarce (skeəs)
tasteful ('teistful)
fortunately ('foːtʃənətli)
gradually ('gradjuli)
naturally ('natʃurəli)
scarcely ('skeəsli)
within (wið'in)

Idioms

without further delay (wið'aut 'fəːðə di'lei)
over a number of years ('ouvər ə 'nʌmbər əv 'jiəz)
house-hunting ('haus 'hʌntiŋ)
in need of repair (in 'niːd əv ri'peə)
in despair (in dis'peə)
she showed them round (ʃi 'ʃoud ðəm 'raund)
to take a fancy to someone (tə teik ə 'fansi tə 'sʌmwʌn)
a good state of repair (ə 'gud 'steit əv ri'peə)
to start straight away (tə 'staːt streit ə'wei)
it remains to be seen (it ri'meinz tə bi 'siːn)
so that's settled (sou 'ðats 'setld)
They need some attention (ðei 'niːd səm ə'tenʃn)

EXERCISES

A. *Join these pairs of statements into single sentences so that one statement is expressed as the cause of or reason for the other.* (*Sentence Pattern 52*):

1. Susan was very tired. She had been up late the night before.
2. They have decided to get married. They will have to find a house.
3. It is nearly midnight. I suppose we had better go home.
4. Tom will earn a higher salary. He has been appointed Assistant Manager.
5. They did not enjoy the party. They knew no one there.
6. The young man was praised. He had saved a child from drowning.
7. There is a scarcity of skilled workers in this industry. Prices have risen.
8. They cannot afford a large house. They will have to be content with a smaller one.
9. It has been snowing all day. We can't go for our usual walk.
10. He was short of money. He borrowed some from a friend.

B. *Use each of these expressions in a separate sentence:*

go to sleep; wear thin; fall ill; turn brown; get used to; become a teacher; grow tired of; come straight; run short; get light.

C. *Use these phrases in sentences:*

the twilight; the summer; the warmth; the spring; the dark; the rain; the ice; the lamplight; the early morning; the moonlight.

D. (a) *Write sentences in which these verbs are followed by an infinitive or by a (pro)noun and infinitive (Sentence Pattern 1):*

arrange; help; watch; expect; pretend; show how; refuse; persuade; hear; dare.

(b) *Write sentences in which these adjectives are followed by an infinitive:*

afraid; glad; cruel; stupid; willing; lucky; delighted; certain; wise; anxious.

E. *Rewrite these sentences, replacing the main verb by the verb* have:

1. She takes a bath every morning.
2. I shall order you to be punished if you do that again.
3. One must be very clever to win a scholarship to a university.
4. He is wearing a dark blue suit and a red tie.
5. We are given an examination at the end of each term.
6. They own a house in town and a cottage in the country.
7. You must get those teeth seen to before they decay.
8. You can order a meal at this restaurant until midnight.
9. We were made to open all our cases when we came through the Customs.
10. London possesses many fine parks and open spaces.

F. *Put the word* since, for *or* during *into the blank spaces in these sentences, and put the verb into the right tense:*

1. I (stay) in England . . . another four months.
2. He (not visit) our house . . . last September.
3. It (rain) . . . four hours . . . last night, but it is fine this morning.
4. It is a long time . . . I (be) last in Athens.
5. We (go) to France . . . a fortnight, and . . . that time we (visit) some friends in Nice.
6. How long have you (study) English? . . . three years.
7. I (work) in London . . . six months . . . I last saw you.
8. How long you (wait)? . . . more than half an hour.

9. How many times you (be) home . . . you first (come) to England?

10. I (sit) here . . . two hours. . . . this time I (read) three newspapers.

G. *Rewrite this report of a speech in the words the speaker actually used:*

The speaker said they had asked him to come there that evening to talk about holidays in Britain. He began by assuring them that the weather in Britain, particularly in the summer, was not nearly so bad as some people would like them to believe. (England had its fair share of sunshine, but even in the hottest summer the countryside remained green and beautiful. He knew they would all want to visit well-known places like London, Oxford and Stratford, but they must not think that those were the only places of interest Britain had to show. They should try to visit Wales and Scotland and the South-west as well. And let them not forget that if they wanted to see the Britain of the present as well as of the past, they should see something of the industrial towns of the Midlands and the North. He concluded by assuring them that if they decided to spend a holiday in Britain, they would find plenty to interest and amuse them, whatever their tastes might be.

H. *Put the words in brackets into their correct form:*

1. (Play) tennis is a pleasant form of exercise.
2. Forgive (I) (ask), but is this seat taken?
3. (Find) someone in this crowd is like (look) for a needle in a haystack.
4. It's no use (I) (go) with you to the theatre because I can't understand German.
5. Do you like (live) in the heart of the country?
6. Have you finished (write) those letters yet?
7. It is hard (believe) that she has at last decided (go) to England.
8. Do you mind (close) the window, please? I don't like (sit) in the cold.

9. He is certain (pass) his examination if he goes on (work) hard.
10. Where did you (live) before (come) to England?

I. *Rewrite these sentences, using* too *or* enough *followed by an infinitive or* for:

1. She is very old; she must not live alone.
2. This house is small; we have a large family.
3. She is not young; she can look after herself.
4. Are you so strong that you could lift that table?
5. She is so good looking that she might win the beauty competition.
6. It is early; we need not set off for the party yet.
7. I shan't go out today; it is very cold.
8. He is wise; he thinks before he speaks.
9. It is very cold today; I think we shall have snow.
10. She arrived late; we had all finished tea.

J. *Write sentences expressing the following ideas and using the word given in brackets:*

Example: Idea: Permission to leave (may)
　　　　　 Sentence: You may leave the room now.

1. The possibility that someone has missed the bus (perhaps)
2. A polite request to borrow someone's programme (might)
3. The possibility that some friends have already arrived (may)
4. The possibility that the speaker may have an increase in salary next year (possible)
5. A prohibition against talking during a lecture (must)
6. An order against driving without a licence (permit)
7. A request for permission to enter (can)
8. An enquiry about permission to smoke in the theatre (allow)
9. An enquiry about the person responsible for a prisoner's escape
10. An offer of help to carry someone's luggage (may)

K. *Tell someone to do each of the following, first as a request, then as a polite command, and finally as a direct order:*

1. to pour you another glass of wine
2. to pick up a book from the floor
3. to let you read a letter
4. to tell you the truth
5. to think before she speaks
6. to cut the grass in the garden
7. not to smoke in the dining-room
8. not to talk so loudly
9. to drive more carefully
10. to close the door quietly

L. *Give negative short responses to the following:*

1. Why have you taken my book?
2. Does Mr Brown live in London?
3. I don't take sugar in my tea.
4. You're the worst card player in the world.
5. Must we get home before midnight?
6. Ought that small child to be playing with a pen-knife?
7. Your brother is a thief.
8. The bus has already left.
9. We must finish all these exercises today.
10. Why haven't you washed your hands?

COMPOSITION

Exercises

1. Write a description of you own ideal house and garden.
2. Write the letter of thanks that Susan might write to Mrs Hallam after their visit to her house.
3. Write the conversation that might take place
   Either   between Susan and her mother
   or   between Tom and Mr Brown after the visit to Mrs Hallam's house.

LESSON 13

Sports Day at the Factory

THE visitor to Britain often comes here with a picture in his mind of 'Merry England' gained from travel posters of 'beefeaters' in their sixteenth century uniforms at the Tower of London. Life-guards in front of Buckingham Palace, ancient castles, splendid country houses and lovely old-world villages. These things are all there, and are enjoyed both by visitors and by the English themselves.

But this is not the real Britain. The Britain that grew up during the nineteenth century after the Industrial Revolution and became the wealthiest country in the world, the Britain that is still a great manufacturing nation, is something quite different. If you had looked for this other Britain forty or fifty years ago you would have found it almost entirely in the Midlands and the North—in the 'Black Country' around Birmingham, in the coalfields of Nottingham, Yorkshire and Lancashire—and also in South Wales and the Lowlands of Scotland. But the developments in electric power and the invention of new manufacturing materials such as plastics and man-made fibres have begun to change all this. Industry, and especially light industry, is being spread much more evenly over the whole country. The attraction of living in the South of England, where the climate is kinder, conditions of life are easier and the bright lights and gaiety of London are a little nearer, has led to a steady movement southward—two early examples of which were the setting up of the motor-car industry at Oxford and the electrical industry at Rugby. Now almost every town in the South of England has its one or more factories, and London is surrounded by a wide and growing belt of light industry in an astonishing variety.

One of the pleasantest features of this wider spread of industry has been the coming of the model factory. No longer is it expected that a factory will be an ugly, ill-lit place in the middle of an untidy collection of huts and disused railway-trucks. The new factories are clean and brightly painted, with plenty of windows letting in sunlight and fresh air, and often made attractive by well-kept lawns and flower-beds. Many modern factories have their own sports fields close by.

A factory of this kind is the Bishopton bicycle factory where Tom Smith is now Assistant Manager. Once every summer the firm holds a Sports Day in which all who work in the factory, from Mr Carter the Managing Director to the newest apprentice, take a keen interest. The programme is organised by the Sports and Social Committee, on which both management and workpeople are represented, and the day's events include not only athletic sports for the younger employees and games for the children, but also a flower, fruit and vegetable show for the older people, an exhibition of hobbies, and many competitions and sideshows. One of the special features of the afternoon is the tea—a splendid feast set out in huge tents, where everyone can eat as much as he likes, and where even the children come away feeling they could not swallow another mouthful.

This year Tom has taken David Brown with him, for David is anxious to see as much as he can of many different walks of life before making up his mind what he wants to do when he finishes his university course. David is much impressed with what he sees—particularly the growing confidence between managers and workpeople, so different from the bitter struggles of former times. He decided that British industry has come a long way since the days of the Industrial Revolution and the early days of the Trade Union Movement, about which he had read at school.

CONVERSATION

(Tom and David are on the factory sports field. They meet Bill Drummond, Chairman of the Sports Committee)

TOM: Hello, Bill. How's it going?

BILL DRUMMOND: Pretty well I think. Everyone seems to be enjoying the fun.

TOM: This is a friend of mine, David Brown. David, this is Mr Drummond, although everyone round here calls him Bill. As Chairman of the Sports Committee he's responsible for all that's going on this afternoon.

BILL DRUMMOND: Pleased to meet you, Mr Brown. He wouldn't be any relation to your young lady, Mr Smith, would he?

TOM: Yes. He's Susan's brother. David's at Oxford, by the way.

BILL DRUMMOND: What College, Mr Brown? I've got a boy up at Oxford at the moment. He's at Ruskin College on a trade union scholarship.

DAVID: I'm at Queen's. You've got a very good show here this afternoon, Mr Drummond.

BILL DRUMMOND: Glad you're enjoying it.

DAVID: Is this sort of thing arranged by the management?

BILL DRUMMOND: No, not entirely. The Sports Club and other welfare services are controlled jointly by the management and workpeople. We in the trade unions know that higher wages are not the only thing that matters. A man likes to feel a sense of loyalty to the organisation he works for, whether it's a private firm or a nationalised industry. He can only do that if he's treated fairly, and his position is secure, and if his working conditions are as good as they can be.

DAVID: Do you ever have a strike here?

BILL DRUMMOND: Not often, I'm pleased to say. Nobody wants to go on strike or threaten to, and it is a weapon to be used only in extreme cases where we've failed to solve our problems by discussion. In the bad old days, as you know, there was a bitter struggle between the workers and their masters. The level of wages was low, discipline in the factories was hard and a man could be dismissed at a moment's notice. Workers often looked on their employers as enemies and hated them. But those days are now gone, I'm glad to say. Both management and workpeople today realise that they need each other, and have learnt to work together peacefully, and

P.E. 3—9

any difficulties that arise are immediately referred to the Works Council. Above all, we are now almost free from the curse of unemployment. But you've come here to enjoy yourself, not to listen to a lecture from me.

DAVID: No, I'm very interested. Has the split between management and workers entirely disappeared?

BILL DRUMMOND: Not altogether, I'm afraid. Old habits die hard. There are still employers who would cheat and deceive their workers if they could, just as there are workers who are idle, or hinder production or demand higher wages than they are worth, or cause damage to machinery and materials by their carelessness. But these are exceptions. The average employer is concerned for the welfare of his employees and the average worker is ready to give a fair day's work for a fair day's pay.

DAVID: You've certainly made your factory site attractive here.

BILL DRUMMOND: We've done our best. I must say a lot has been done to remedy conditions since the old days when all factories were ugly places, surrounded by bare earth and heaps of ash. Some like that still exist, but today we make an effort to prevent factories becoming ugly and untidy. Now I expect you would like some tea: it should be ready in the tea tent by now.

. . . .

(In the tea tent David meets Mr Carter)

MR CARTER: Hello, David. Nice to see you. What do you think of our Sports Day?

DAVID: I'm thoroughly enjoying it, thank you. You people in industry certainly know how to have a good time.

MR CARTER: Oh, it's not fun and games like this every day, you know. Working in a factory can never be a soft life, but we can only get good results if everyone does his best. And we find that occasions like this not only improve friendly relations in the factory but make for higher production. We're interested in the whole lives of our workpeople—their homes, their families, their hobbies—not just in the time they spend among the grease and machines on the factory floor.

DAVID: What happens if a man becomes sick or is injured while at work?

MR CARTER: Well, everyone comes under the National Health Service of course, and there is an insurance to cover anyone who is injured. Then we have our own welfare service with a doctor and a trained nurse always in attendance. But we're more concerned with keeping our people healthy than in curing them when they're ill.

DAVID: How do you do that?

MR CARTER: We try to keep the air in the factory clean and free from harmful dust and smoke. We have an excellent canteen so that everyone has good hot meals. All our people enjoy three weeks' holiday with pay, and in addition we send our young apprentices away to camp or on walking tours or mountain climbing during the summer. But now you must excuse me. I've been asked to judge a Beauty Competition for the Prettiest Typist of the Year—and I might be glad of your help. You can come too, Tom, if you like—I think you know a pretty typist when you see one.

COMPREHENSION QUESTIONS

1. What are 'Beefeaters'?
2. What is meant by the term 'Industrial Revolution'?
3. What is 'The Black Country'?

4. Where in Britain are the chief coalfields?
5. Why has British industry tended to move southward?
6. What is meant by the term 'model factory'?
7. How are the social and welfare services at Tom's factory organised?
8. How have the relations between the management and work-people changed in recent years?
9. What is a trade union?
10. What other factors besides high wages are important to work-people in a factory?

SENTENCE PATTERNS

55.   The Use of Prepositions

The choice of the right preposition/adverb in English is difficult because usage is more often idiomatic than logical. *In, on, under, to,* etc., have distinct meanings, usually connected with move-ment or position, but they have also gained a wide range of usage having no apparent relation to their original meaning. There are no rules for this idiomatic usage: the student must learn each example separately, linking the noun or verb or adjective with its correct preposition as a single word-group.

The preposition/adverbs expressing movement or position are these:

about, above, across, along, among, at, back, backwards, before, behind, beside, between, by, down, downwards, far, forwards, from, in, in front of, into, near, of, off, on, out, out of, over, past, round, through, to, towards, under, up, upwards, with, without.

Prepositions expressing time are:

after, at, before, during, for, from, in, on, since, through, to, till, until.

The following pairs need careful attention:

(*a*) *At—in* for places.

At is used for small towns and villages and the suburbs of large towns.

> David was born at Bishopton.
> He lives at Windsor.
> They have bought a house at Highgate. (A district of London)

In is used for large towns, counties or provinces, and countries.

> He works in Birmingham, although his family live in London.
> He has a shop at Worthing, a seaside town in Sussex.
> She has been staying with some friends in Italy.

The distinction depends partly on the point of view of the speaker. The nearer he is to a place, or the more closely he is associated with it, the more likely he is to use *in* rather than *at*, however small the place may be. Thus villagers will speak of people living *in* a village a short distance away.

In—into

In is used for place where there is no suggestion of movement. *Into* is used for *place to which* and expresses movement.

> He has been ill in bed for a week.
> He undressed and got into bed.
> There were several people swimming in the pool.
> The boy jumped into the pond.

Sometimes *in* is used for movement, especially in conversation, but *into* is never used unless there is a suggestion of movement in some direction.

> The silly child fell in the mud.
> We jumped in the water, but it was terribly cold.

but we cannot say

> They were playing into the garden.

Between—among

Between is used of two only; *among* of more than two.

> The prize-money was divided between the two winners.
> In many new housing estates, very little room is left between the houses (i.e. between each house and the next).

There have been many quarrels among the members of this family.

It was nice to be back among our friends again.

With—by

These two prepositions are used with actions, *by* to introduce the person doing the action and *with* to introduce the thing or 'instrument' used to do it. *By* is sometimes used for the instrument, but *with* is never used for the person.

He was killed with a dagger.

He was killed by his best friend.

This bridge was built by the Romans with very primitive tools.

These groups of time prepositions must be distinguished:

For—since—during

For states a period of time that an action or state of affairs continues. It can be used in past, present and future sentences.

She stayed with us for a month.

I have been in England for three years.

This concert lasts for two hours.

He is coming to us for a week's holiday.

Since states a point in the past when an existing action or state of affairs started. Notice the Present Perfect or Past Perfect Tense is used in English where most languages use the Present and Present Perfect.

I have been here since last Thursday.

He has lived in France since he was a child.

We had been waiting since half past six.

I had not seen her since she was a child of ten.

During tells what happened in the course of a stated period of time.

I learnt Italian during my holidays in Italy.

We had a great deal of rain during August.

During most of my childhood we lived in London.
There was a violent storm during the night.

At, in, on.

The use of these time prepositions is idiomatic.

At night, at dawn, at sunset, at mid-day, at midnight, at noon,
at Easter, at Christmas, at New Year, at six o'clock.

In the spring, in the summer, in the autumn, in the winter,
in the morning, in the afternoon, in the evening, in January,
February, etc., in 1965.

On Monday, Tuesday, etc., on Christmas Day, on New Year's
eve, on someone's birthday, on their wedding day, on the
first of July.

Idiomatic use of Prepositions

In the following examples, the prepositions have no apparent link
with their original meaning, and are entirely idiomatic. Each
phrase must be learnt as a unit.

(*a*) Prepositions following certain verbs:

rely on, agree with, grow up, lit by, tear up, set off, quarrel
with, accuse someone of, approve of, belong to, insist on,
depend on.

(*b*) Prepositions following certain adjectives:

afraid of, familiar with, disappointed by, similar to, different
from, preferable to, responsible for, satisfied with, good
at, ashamed of, impressed by.

56.   How to express Purpose and Result

The three concepts: Reason, Purpose and Result should be
carefully distinguished:

Reason clauses and phrases tell us why something occurs; they
are concerned with the cause of an action or state of affairs and
not with the outcome or what may have followed.

He went home because he was tired.

Purpose clauses and phrases tell what someone's intention was in doing something.

He worked hard in order to pass his examination.

Result clauses and phrases state the result or outcome of some action.

He worked so hard that he passed his examination.

Purpose

(*a*) (*so as*) *to, in order to*

This construction with the infinitive is used only when the subject of the purpose verb is the same as the subject of the main verb.

In order to is more formal than *so as to*. The *so as* is often omitted:

She worked hard in order to pass her examination.
He spoke loudly in order to be heard all over the room.
She shut the gate so as to stop the children wandering into the road.
She listened carefully so as to hear every word.
He started early in order not to miss the train.
She took a taxi in order not to be late.
She pulled the curtains to keep out the sunlight.
He lit a fire to warm the room.
I bought the book to read in the train.

(*b*) *so that, so that . . . not, in order that, in order that . . . not.*

In order that is formal. Notice the use of *can, could, should* (more formal *may, might*) in the purpose clause.

Tom taught Susan to drive so that she could help him with the driving during their holiday.
His mother gave him some money so that he could go to the pictures.
Some men work hard in order that they may obtain wealth.
The wicked prince murdered his brother in order that he might become king.

(c) *For* The preposition *for* is often used to introduce an adverbial phrase showing the purpose of the main verb. The preposition *for* is often followed by a verbal noun (gerund) in —*ing*.

> He bought a boat for sailing on the river.
> She wanted some polish for cleaning the silver.
> He married her for her money.

Result

(a) *So* + adjective or adverb + *that*-clause. *That* is often omitted in conversation.

> He was so rich that he never thought about money.
> They were so hungry that they could hardly wait for their meal to be cooked.
> She was so late that we did not wait for her.
> Susan is so kind that everyone likes her.
> He worked so hard that he soon became manager.
> Susan types so quickly that she soon finishes her work.
> David drove so fast that his mother was quite frightened.

(b) *Such* + noun + *that*-clause. *That* is often omitted in conversation.

> It was such a fine day (that) we decided to go for a drive in the country.
> She was such a beautiful girl (that) people looked round at her in the street.
> He told such a strange story (that) we could hardly believe it.
> They had such a wonderful holiday (that) no one wanted to go home.

(c) When the subject of the result clause would be the same as the subject of the main clause, a construction with *too* or *enough* with a *to*-infinitive is often used.

> It was too late to go to bed. (It was so late that it was not worth going to bed.)
> He ran too fast to be caught.
> The child was too young to go to school.

It was too good a dinner to hurry over.
This is too high a mountain to climb.
This is too heavy a bag for you to carry.
He was not tall enough to reach the shelf.
Richard is not clever enough to go to a university.
He did not run fast enough to win the race.

57.   Inversion

Inversion consists in reversing the order of subject and verb in the sentence so that the verb precedes instead of following the subject. There are three principal uses of inversion in English:

(a) In forming questions.

Where a special verb alone is used, there is a straightforward inversion of subject and verb.

He is at home this evening.
Is he at home this evening?

Where a special verb is used as an auxilliary with another verb the special verb and the subject are inverted and the main verb follows.

He has finished his work.
Has he finished his work?

Where no special verb is used, a form of the special verb *do* is placed before the subject, and the infinitive without *to* of the main verb follows.

He works in London.
Does he work in London?
He lived in Bishopton.
Did he live in Bishopton?

(b) In short responses, which add something to a remark already made without repeating the remark in full. *So* is used to add to positive statements; *neither* or *nor* to add to negative statements.

"I like a lot of sugar in my tea." "So do I."
Tom can swim well, and so can Susan.

"I shan't stay here long." "Nor shall I."

"Mary has never been to Spain, and neither has John."

Notice (i) that the same rules for the use of special verbs apply here as in the question construction.

(ii) Inversion is necessary in this short response construction to distinguish it from the other short response with *so* that shows surprised agreement, where there is no inversion.

"Look. You've broken your umbrella." "So I have!"

"But John was here only last week." "You're right. So he was."

(c) Where a negative or semi-negative adverb has been brought to the beginning of a sentence for emphasis. This construction belongs to written rather than to spoken English.

Such a thing has never happened before.
Never has such a thing happened before.

He had no sooner arrived than the trouble began.
No sooner had he arrived than the trouble began.

You seldom find so many clever people in one family.
Seldom do you find so many clever people in one family.

Other front-position negative or semi-negative adverbs followed by this inversion construction are:

hardly ever, scarcely ever, nowhere, nowhere else, rarely, never before, by no means, in no circumstances, not only, little, in no other way.

NEW WORDS

apprentice (ə'prentis)
ash (aʃ)
attendance (ə'tendəns)
average ('avridʒ)
belt (belt)
camp (kamp)
coalfield ('koulfiːld)

confidence ('konfidəns)
curse (noun and verb) (kəɪs)
damage (noun and verb) ('damidʒ)
discipline ('disəplin, 'disiplin)
effort ('efət)
enemy ('enəmi)

exception (ik'sepʃn)
exhibition (eksi'biʃn)
feast (fiːst)
grease (griːs)
heap (hiːp)
hut (hʌt)
insurance (in'ʃuərəns,
   in'ʃoːrəns)
kind (kaind)
material (mə'tiːriəl)
model ('modl)
nurse (nəːs)
position (pə'ziʃn)
remedy ('remədi)
revolution (revə'luːʃn)
scholarship ('skoləʃip)
strike (straik)
track (trak)
weapon ('wepən)
welfare ('welfeə)
arise, arose, arisen (ə'raiz,
   ə'rouz, ə'rizn)
astonish (əs'toniʃ)

cheat (tʃiːt)
deceive (di'siːv)
dismiss (dis'mis)
hate (noun and verb) (heit)
hinder ('hində)
nurse (nəːs)
prevent (pri'vent)
solve (solv)
split (split)
swallow ('swolou)
threaten ('θretn)
athletic (aθ'letik)
bitter ('bitə)
disused (dis'juːzd)
former ('foːmə)
idle ('aidl)
joint (dʒoint)
model ('modl)
plastic ('plastik)
private ('praivit)
secure (si'kjuə)
steady ('stedi)
even ('iːvn)

Idioms

close by ('klous 'bai)
different walks of life ('difrənt 'woːks əv 'laif)
How's it going? ('hauz it 'gouiŋ)
not the only thing that matters (not ði 'ounli θiŋ ðət 'matəz)
in the good (bad) old days (in ðə 'gud (bad) ould 'deiz)
at a moment's notice (ət ə 'moumənts 'noutis)
old habits (ways) die hard ('ould habits (weiz) 'dai 'haːd)
We've done our best (wiːv 'dʌn auə 'best)
to make an effort (tə 'meik ən 'efət)
to have a good time (tə 'hav ə gud 'taim)

EXERCISES

A. *Fill in the blanks in these sentences:*

1. The result was very different . . . what we had expected.
2. She ran . . . the house followed . . . a barking dog.
3. He was impressed . . . the way . . . which those responsible . . . the sports had organised the events.
4. He was born . . . York, . . . the North . . . England, but now he has settled down . . . our village.
5. When people grow . . . they are not usually afraid . . . being alone . . . the dark.
6. We can ensure peace . . . the nations by the peoples . . . the world getting . . . know one another.
7. I cannot approve . . . your belonging . . . this club until I know a little more . . . it.
8. He was ashamed . . . being beaten . . . the examination . . . his younger brother.
9. . . . last summer, she stayed . . . us . . . a month . . . our house . . . the country.
10. I don't want to quarrel . . . you . . . your birthday . . . such an unimportant matter.

B. *Express each of the following in another way without altering the meaning (Sentence Pattern 57):*

1. He telephoned to enquire if his wife was ready to leave.
2. He came home early so that he would have plenty of time to dress for dinner.
3. He was such a kind man that everyone loved him.
4. He wanted a pump for blowing up his bicycle tyre.
5. These books are too heavy for you to carry.
6. She shouted in order to make herself heard.
7. They hurried so that they would not be late.
8. She sings so beautifully that we could listen to her for hours.
9. He is rich enough to buy the largest house in town.
10. He went to the library to read in peace.

C. *Write sentences beginning with these abverbs:*

hardly ever; never before; nowhere; in no other way; little;
no sooner; never; seldom; scarcely ever; nowhere else;
rarely; in no circumstances; not only.

D. *Add the definite or indefinite article* (the, a, *or* an) *as required
in these sentences:*

1. At grocer's shop in Bishopton belonging to Mr Green,
   Mrs Brown bought pound of butter and tin of soup.
2. This is most interesting book I have had from college
   library.
3. They crossed Channel in boat belonging to British Railways.
4. Police are looking for man with finger missing from left
   hand.
5. Lighted firework should never be held in hand.
6. Tom bought Susan box of chocolates before play started.
7. He went to United States for holiday at end of his
   examinations.
8. Solomon was wisest man world has ever seen.
9. 'Friend in need is friend indeed.'
10. 'Bird in hand is worth two in bush.'

E. (*a*) *Form abstract nouns from the following:*

child; kind; honest; young; advise; patient; captive; high;
long; broad; know; treat; strong; exist; just; silent; thief;
invent; employ; grow; manager.

(*b*) *Give the collective noun for:*

people watching a play in the theatre
those deciding a prisoner's guilt or innocence
group playing together in a game
father, mother and their children
large number of people in the street
collection of books
students being taught together in one room

the Prime Minister and those who hold office under him
elected representatives who control the affairs of a town or
county
those who belong to a group holding similar political views

F. *Change the verbs in these sentences into the Present Tense:*

1. He hoped the lecturer would not mind his being late.
2. She seemed cross when she could not get her own way.
3. The egg I was eating tasted bad.
4. I heard she was leaving the office to get married.
5. He wanted to see the man who had bought the house next door.
6. Did you recognise the man who was sitting next to you?
7. I noticed that she was wearing a new hat.
8. We could see that he disliked us.
9. Susan wished she could have gone to the theatre with Tom.
10. The children saw and heard much more than their parents thought they did.

G. *Put the given verb into the right tense in these sentences:*

1. If I (be) you, I (change) my doctor.
2. Supposing he (not arrive), what you (do).
3. They (win) the match last week if they (play) better.
4. We (go) to Italy next summer if we (afford) it.
5. We should be glad if you (send) these goods as soon as possible.
6. I should have paid his fare if I (have) enough money.
7. We (go) for a picnic tomorrow provided it (keep) fine.
8. I gave the poor man money on condition that he (buy) food with it.
9. You (have) a holiday today so long as you (work) harder tomorrow.
10. I (have) a holiday in Russia next year if I (save) enough money for the journey.

H. *Express these sentences in another way without altering the meaning (Sentence Pattern 39):*

1. He is going to the Argentine on business next month.
2. I am willing to lend you my bicycle if you promise to look after it.
3. You shall finish this work today, no matter what you may say.
4. If the police ask you questions, will you answer?
5. He is determined to have his own way.
6. She has made up her mind to sell her house and live abroad.
7. I cannot agree to your marrying a man without money or prospects.
8. Are you sure he's going to leave school at the end of this term?
9. Have the workpeople in this factory decided to go on strike?
10. I mean to learn English really well before I go back to my own country.

I. *Use the following adverbs in sentences:*

never; always; hardly; fast; gradually; merely; sometimes; nowhere; usually; aside.

J. *Rewrite the following sentences, using a sentence pattern with* It *as subject:*

1. We are likely to have rain tomorrow.
2. One should not worry about the future.
3. We are told that she is now living in Warsaw.
4. I doubt whether we shall win any gold medals in these Olympic Games.
5. By chance I have the seat next to yours at the concert.
6. There doesn't seem to be any doubt that someone has made a mistake.

7 Ankara is a long way from Rome.

8. We do not know whether the plane hit a mountain or broke up in the air.

9. One has difficulty in pleasing everyone all the time.

10. We had a fine day for the sports, and everyone enjoyed himself.

K. *Express these wishes or preferences in a different way, without altering the meaning:*

1. Do you want another cup of coffee?
2. If only I had a little more money!
3. Have a good holiday!
4. May you always be happy!
5. I prefer living in the country to living in the town.
6. Do you wish to see the Principal?
7. I wish I could swim.
8. I would rather not answer that question.
9. Would you like to stay here for the night?
10. Do you hope for a fine day tomorrow?

L. *Complete these sentences by adding the main clause:*

Example: . . . to keep the house warm.
         They lit a big fire to keep the house warm.

1. . . . so they could visit the Shakespeare Theatre.
2. . . . in order to be able to get married.
3. . . . to save himself from falling.
4. . . . to take them to the station.
5. . . . for copying his lesson notes.
6. . . . so that she would not have to do any housework.
7. . . . in order to learn English.
8. . . . to cut the lawn.
9. . . . for cleaning his car.
10. . . . to save time.

COMPOSITION

Exercises

1. Write a favourable reply to the letter asked for in Lesson 10, Composition Exercise 2 (page 208).
2. Write a lively account of some open-air festival or celebration that you have witnessed in your own country.
3. You have been invited to give a short talk to a group of people of your own age about your favourite game or sport. Write out what you would say.

An artist was re-painting the sign outside an inn. When he had finished, the landlord came out to look at the result. He said:

"You should have left more room between coach and and and and and horses."

Can you punctuate this to make sense?

LESSON 14

Susan's Wedding

Susan's wedding-day had arrived at last and the Browns'
home was in a state of great excitement. The house was full
of aunts and uncles, nieces, nephews and cousins, who had
gathered to mark the occasion, the men looking a little self-
conscious in their 'morning dress'—the black tail-coat,
striped trousers, grey gloves and tall silk hat, that English-

men still wear for such occasions. Mrs Brown was upstairs with the bride and bridesmaids, amid much laughing and joking, 'putting the finishing touches', as she called it—busy with a needle and thread and scissors sewing on a button that had come off a glove here and replacing the ribbon on a bunch of flowers there.

Meanwhile Tom, the anxious bridegroom, was waiting in Bishopton Church, which was already nearly filled with guests and well-wishers. With him was Susan's brother David, whom he had chosen as his 'best man' because he had no brothers of his own. From time to time David fingered the wedding ring in his waistcoat pocket, to be sure it would be ready for him to hand to the bridegroom at the right moment. At last the organ began to play the familiar tune which signals the arrival of the bride, and Tom could not resist the temptation to look round over his shoulder as Susan came slowly up the aisle with her hand on her father's arm. She looked very beautiful, he thought, in her long white dress and veil with its crown of orange blossom and the pearl necklace given to her by her grandmother; and he could hardly believe she was the same person whom he had seen only the day before in paint-spotted slacks, helping him to move furniture in their new home.

* * * *

And now the marriage service, with its holy and ancient words, was over. Tom had promised to give her all his worldly goods (he smiled to himself as he remembered how little in the way of 'worldly goods' he had in the bank at the moment) and Susan had promised to love, honour and obey 'until death us do part', and on the third finger of her left hand was the gold ring that made them man and wife. As the organ played Wagner's *Bridal March* and Susan walked back down the aisle, this time with her hand on her husband's

arm, she smiled happily at the many friends who had come
to see her married. Outside the church in the bright sunlight
the cameras were raised and the confetti showered on them
as they climbed into their white-ribboned car, which was to
take them to the wedding reception in the Royal Hotel.
Here the bride, with a little assistance from the bridegroom,
cut the huge wedding cake. Then came the moment which
Tom had been fearing—the moment when he would have to
make a speech. But in the end he found with relief that he
did better than he or Susan had dared to hope he would,
and his performance was loudly applauded by a sympathetic
audience.

When the speeches were over, and the messages of good
wishes from the friends and relatives who could not be
present had been read, the young couple set off on their
honeymoon. They had talked a great deal about where they
would go, but all the suggestions had seemed too expensive.
Then one day Tom's father had said: "You only have one
honeymoon—so go where you would like, and your Mother
and I will pay for it as an extra wedding-present." That had
made the choice easier. Susan said she wanted to go where
she could bathe, or sail on the blue waters of a sheltered bay
or lie at ease on the shore in the rays of a sun that shone all
day long out of a cloudless heaven. Tom said he wanted to
go somewhere interesting and new to them so that they would
bring back with them memories that they would never forget. So they had decided to go to Greece, which they felt sure
would give them both all that they wanted.

As they left the house for the station many of their friends
were there to see them off. Confetti and rice were thrown
over them again and someone had put a notice 'Just Married'
on the back of the car. Later on they would find that the
bridesmaids and the best man had scattered confetti in their
baggage too.

When the last guest had gone and David had caught his train back to Oxford and Mr and Mrs Brown were left alone, the house seemed very quiet and empty. Mrs Brown went into Susan's room to tidy up, and when her husband found her there a little later there were tears in her eyes. He put his arm gently round her shoulders. "Don't cry," he said. "They'll soon be back."

CONVERSATION

(*At Susan's wedding Mr Brown rises to propose a toast to the bride and bridegroom*)

MR BROWN: Ladies and gentlemen—my very good friends. This is, of course, a day of joy and gladness for us all —but particularly for my wife and me. We have seen our dear daughter married to the man she loves and to whom we know we can entrust her with confidence. But I am sure you will understand me when I say that this joy is mixed with a touch of sadness, for us. When you have had someone you love living with you for twenty years, have seen her grow up from babyhood to childhood, and from childhood to womanhood, it is not easy to get used to the idea that she is not going to live there any more. Yet this does not prevent us from wishing them well with all our hearts.

Secure in their love for each other, Susan and Tom start out on their married life with every chance of happiness—which is so much more than wealth or rank or title—and that this happiness may grow and continue is, I am sure, the wish of us all here today. Life will not always be plain sailing for them—perhaps it would not be a good thing if it were. But so long as they face their difficulties together nothing can really harm them.

Those who make speeches on occasions such as this are supposed, I believe, to make jokes and tell amusing stories. I am not going to do this. Instead I am going to ask you to rise and drink with me to Susan and Tom, the bride and bridegroom—may they be blessed with long life, health and every happiness together.

(*Tom replies*)

TOM: Ladies and gentlemen: First I should like to say how pleased Susan and I are to see so many of you here at our wedding, and how grateful we are for the many generous gifts you have given us. My wife and I—it will be a long time, I'm sure, before I can say that quite as naturally as Susan's father does—my wife and I will be delighted if you will visit us in our new home—but as it's not very big, please don't all arrive on our door-mat at the same time!

The proposer of this toast, with his customary generosity, has said some very kind things about me, for which I thank him. I can only trust that Susan will continue to be as happy with me as her parents have always made her at home, and that my new father and mother will consider that they have not lost a daughter but gained a son.

Before I sit down, I should like to thank David, my best man, for having the ring ready at the right moment —and for all the good advice he has given me on how to manage Susan. And my wife has asked me to thank her three lovely bridesmaids whose beauty and charm have delighted us all.

(*And so, as David, the 'best man', rises to read the telegrams of congratulation from their many friends, we say Good-bye to the Brown family, who have helped us through these three books in our efforts to learn* Present Day English)

COMPREHENSION QUESTIONS

1. What is 'morning dress'?
2. Explain the term 'best man' at a wedding.
3. What is the 'aisle' of a church? What other parts of a church can you name?
4. Where will you find the marriage service as used in English churches?
5. Who was Wagner?
6. What is 'confetti'?
7. Why did Tom and Susan decide to go to Greece for their honeymoon?
8. Why did Mr Brown think Tom and Susan would live happily together?
9. What is a bridesmaid, and what are her duties at a wedding?
10. Give the meaning of the following phrases as used in this passage:

    looking a little self-conscious; could not resist the temptation; to propose a toast; life will not always be plain sailing.

SENTENCE PATTERNS

58.　　　　　How to express Concession

Concession constructions are used to express the idea that something is true in spite of what can be said to the contrary or on the other side: the concession phrase or clause makes the necessary allowances. The most usual ways of expressing concession are these:

(a) *Although*

> Although she is over eighty, she can still read without glasses.
> Although April is here the weather is still quite cold.
> Although this student works hard he is not making much progress.
> Tommy can read well, although he is only five.

She is taking the examination this summer, although she does not expect to pass.

Though is often used instead of *although*, particularly in conversation.

(b) *May*

The Thompsons may live in a small house, but they are quite well off.

He may be only a child, but that is no reason why he should behave so rudely.

He may be a clever doctor, but I don't think he can cure this patient.

You may have learnt these words last night, but you don't know them now.

(c) *Matter*

No matter how hard he works his employer is never satisfied.

No matter what anyone says, you are not to leave this house.

It doesn't matter where you go in Europe, you will find someone who speaks English.

It doesn't matter how bad a reputation an accused person may have, he is treated as innocent until he is proved guilty.

(d) *-ever*

Wherever a criminal may hide, the law will catch up with him.

Whatever you say, I shall still do as I like.

However often I tell him, he still forgets.

However hard he works, he can't do all that digging in one day.

(e) *Even if*

Even if you told me so a thousand times, I shouldn't believe you.

Even if he does live in Edinburgh, that doesn't make him a Scotsman.

I wouldn't do that even if you offered me a thousand pounds.

59. How to express Probability

(a) *Going to* + infinitive. This is the most usual way of expressing strong probability, something the speaker considers is very likely to happen. This is used very frequently with impersonal *It*.

> It is going to snow before long.
> Those two are going to fight before long.
> It's going to be a fine day tomorrow; look at that red sky.

Sometimes a warning is included in the statement.

> You're going to slip in a minute, if you're not careful.
> Mr Brooke's business is going to suffer if he's away from the office much longer.
> Look out, that child's going to fall off that wall.

(b) *Must* also expresses strong probability.

> It must be time for lunch; I'm hungry.
> You must have heard of him. He's the best known dance-band leader in England.
> This must be the author you were telling me about.
> I must have left my suitcase at the airport.

(c) *Should, ought to*, expresses what the speaker thinks will probably happen as a result of what he has seen or been told.

> He ought to pass his examination without much trouble (if he continues to work as he is doing now).
> You ought to (should) be there before dark (if you start at the agreed time).
> She ought to (should) be a famous singer one day (if she is as good as she seems).

(d) *Probable, probably, likely, chance.*

> It is probable that the government will reduce the rate of income tax in the next few months.
> He probably wants to borrow some money from you.
> The price of silver is likely to go up again before long.
> There is a good chance that Tom will be appointed manager next year.

60.   Agreement

The function of a single word in English depends usually on its place in the sentence rather than on inflexions or a change in the *form* of the word. In the three sentences

Tom gave his friend a new bicycle.
His friend gave Tom a new bicycle.
Tom gave a friend his new bicycle.

the same words are used in the same form; the differences in meaning depend on the position of those words in the sentence. For this reason, we do not need to worry very much about agreement in English. The ordinary adjective does not agree with its noun; with very few exceptions, the same form of the verb is used for singular and plural and for all three persons. There are, however, some instances of agreement in English, the most important of which are these:

(*a*) Agreement of Subject and Verb. Because verbs have a special form for the third person singular of the Present Tense, it is important to see that the subject and verb agree in number.

> *The cleverest boy in each class receives a prize at the end of the year* (not *receive*).

Special care is needed where there is more than one subject. When two or more subjects are linked by *and*, the verb is plural; but where a singular subject has other nouns linked to it by *with*, *as well as*, *together with*, the verb is singular in agreement with the singular subject.

> The Queen, with her husband and children, was present at the concert (not *were present*).
> The castle, as well as many cottages nearby, was destroyed in the fire (not *were destroyed*).

Collective nouns, too, require care. As a rule, collective nouns are singular, because they collect a number of similar things into one group.

> The government has agreed to reduce income tax.

> The sports committee was asked to arrange a dance for the workpeople.

But where the speaker or writer is thinking more of the individual persons or things that make up the group than of the group itself, the collective noun may be regarded as plural, and is then followed by a plural verb.

> The committee were unable to agree.
> This football team play in blue shirts.

Once the decision has been taken, the number of the collective noun must not be changed within the same sentence. Thus, in the sentence

> The government is determined to carry out this policy but have not said when the new law will come into force.

have should be *has*, because the sentence begins by treating the collective noun *government* as singular. There are one or two 'nouns of multitude' (*a number of*, *a lot of* are the most common) which are usually treated as plural, although they are singular in appearance:

> There were a large number of people present.
> A lot of things have happened since I last saw you.

(b) Singular Distributives

Each, *every*, *either*, *neither* and *any* are singular, for they divide (or distribute) a group of people or things into single units, taking one at a time. The verb following these distributives will, therefore, also be singular.

> Each of you is to blame for what has happened.
> Everyone must do what he thinks right.
> Either of these two roads leads to Manchester.
> Neither of the boys was very good at arithmetic
> Anyone is allowed to enter if he can afford to pay.

(c) Relative Pronouns

We saw in Lesson 9 that the choice of the relative to be used in any sentence—or indeed whether a relative pronoun

is to be used at all—depends on the work the relative is doing
in its clause. The *number* of the relative pronoun (singular or
plural) depends on the noun or pronoun to which it relates.
(This is called its *antecedent*.) Since there is no change in the
form of the relative itself to show whether it is singular or
plural, its number does not always matter. But if the relative
is the subject of a following Present Tense verb, the rule
becomes important, because that verb must agree with its
subject, the relative, which in turn will agree with its antecedent. Some examples will make this clear:

He is one of the bravest men who have ever lived.

(*Have* not *has*, because *who* is plural in agreement with its
antecedent *men*.)

*This is one of the most extraordinary things that have hap-
pened in recent years.*

(*Have* not *has* because *that* is plural in agreement with its
antecedent *things*.)

61. Meaning and Stress

Stress plays an important part in English. A difference in stress
can affect both the sound of a word and the meaning of a sentence.
A variation in the syllable on which the stress falls in a word is
used to distinguish the different functions that word may have in a
sentence (e.g. noun or verb). In the following pairs, the first is a
noun, the second a verb. Notice here that the presence or absence
of stress often affects the quality of the vowel sound:

próduce—prodúce; prógress—progréss; súrvey—survéy; ré-
fuse—refúse; cóntent—contént; récord—recórd; cónduct—
condúct; présent—presént; óbject—objéct; ínsult—insúlt.

Stress shift and change of vowel are also found where one word
is formed from another by the addition of a suffix, e.g. *admire—
admiration; compose—composition.*

NEW WORDS

aisle (ail)
arrival (ə'raivl)
assistance (ə'sistəns)
audience ('oːdiəns)
babyhood ('beibihud)
baggage ('bagidʒ)
bay (bei)
blossom ('blosəm)
bride (braid)
bridegroom ('braidgruːm)
bridesmaid ('braidzmeid)
bunch (bʌntʃ)
button ('bʌtn)
childhood ('tʃaildhud)
confetti (kən'feti)
crown (kraun)
ease (iːz)
generosity (dʒenə'rositi)
gentleman ('dʒentlmən)
gladness ('gladnis)
heaven ('hevn)
honeymoon ('hʌnimuːn)
mark (noun and verb) (maːk)
mat (mat)
message ('mesidʒ)
moon (muːn)
necklace ('neklis)
needle ('niːdl)
nephew ('nevjuː)
niece (niːs)
organ ('oːgən)
pearl (pəːl)
rank (raŋk)
ray (rei)

reception (ri'sepʃn)
relief (ri'liːf)
rice (rais)
scissors ('sizəz)
shore (ʃoː)
shower ('ʃauə)
stripe (straip)
sympathy ('simpəθi)
tail (teil)
tear(s) ('tiə(z))
title ('taitl)
tune (tjuːn)
uncle ('ʌŋkl)
veil (veil)
waistcoat ('weiskout)
womanhood ('wumənhud)
applaud (ə'ploːd)
bathe (beið)
bless (bles)
march (noun and verb) (maːtʃ)
obey (ə'bei)
rejoice (ri'dʒois)
relieve (ri'liːv)
replace (ri'pleis)
resist (ri'zist)
sew, sewed, sewn (sou, soud,
    soun)
shelter (noun and verb) ('ʃeltə)
conscious ('konʃəs)
customary ('kʌstəm(ə)ri)
generous ('dʒenərəs)
grateful ('greitful)
sympathetic (simpə'θetik)
meanwhile ('miːnwail)

Idioms

to mark the occasion (tə 'maːk ði ə'keiʒn)
putting the finishing touches ('putiŋ ðə 'finiʃiŋ 'tʌtʃiz)
from time to time (frəm 'taim tə 'taim)
to make a speech (tə 'meik ə 'spiːtʃ)
to see them off (tə 'siː ðəm 'of)
to get used to (tə get 'juːst tə)

EXERCISES

A. *Express the idea of concession in these sentences in a different way without altering the meaning:*

1. Even if the book does belong to you, that is no reason why you should spoil it.

2. You may think you are as strong as a horse; you still can't lift that box.

3. Johnny always takes great care of his mother, although he is only six.

4. However late he goes to bed at night, he is always up early in the morning.

5. It doesn't matter what you say, I still won't lend you the money.

6. Even if she does wear expensive furs, that doesn't make her a lady.

7. You may have been born in England, but you don't speak the language very well.

8. Wherever you may have hidden the jewels, I shall still find them.

9. No matter how hard a person tries, he cannot be sure of succeeding.

10. Although it has been so cold lately, most people have kept fit and well.

B. *Write sentences expressing the probability of the following:*

1. a fall of snow before morning.
2. that Mr X will be the next Prime Minister.
3. that John will do well in his next examination.
4. that the speaker has picked up the wrong suitcase.
5. that there will be a strike at the factory shortly.
6. Susan and Tom's happiness in the future.
7. a long, cold winter.
8. that someone is old enough to retire.
9. our money lasting till the end of our holiday.
10. that Mr Brown will win first prize for his vegetables at next year's Flower Show.

C. *Make any corrections you think necessary in these sentences:*

1. The factory, with all its machines, tools and store sheds, were destroyed in the fire.
2. This is one of the most interesting books that has ever been written.
3. That is the man who we met yesterday at John's party.
4. Neither father or son reached their home that night.
5. The committee is considering your letter and they will write to you shortly.
6. Any of these coats are cheap enough for you to afford.
7. I don't like these sort of people.
8. I met yesterday a man from my home country.
9. A lot of people have praised this artist for his paintings.
10. The chairman, as well as most other people at the meeting, are agreed that the secretary behaved badly.

D. *Use the following words in sentences (eighteen sentences in all), first as nouns and then as verbs. Mark the syllable on which the stress falls in each:*

progress; content; produce; permit; record; refuse; conduct; present; object.

E. *Write sentences expressing the following ideas and using the word
   given in brackets:*

   1. Polite request to borrow a newspaper (might)
   2. Refusal to allow some friends to pay for themselves (let)
   3. The possibility that someone may be right (possible)
   4. Granting permission to leave early (permission)
   5. Agreeing to someone's spending their money how they
      please (may)
   6. Asking for permission to ask a question (can)
   7. Prohibiting passengers from getting off a moving bus
      (must)
   8. Forbidding students to speak any other language but
      English in class (allow)
   9. The possibility of meeting some friends at a party (might)
  10. Possibility that a missing handbag has been stolen
      (perhaps)

F. *Write sentences in the Future Continuous making use of the
   following ideas (Sentence Pattern 50):*

   1. the possibility of someone coming to England next year
   2. the length of David's stay at the university
   3. an enquiry about Mrs Brown shopping in Bishopton
      tomorrow
   4. the determination of the speaker to work hard all next
      term
   5. someone will sing in a series of concerts in London shortly
   6. the possibility of someone having dinner on the train
   7. a denial that Tom will stay the night
   8. the possibility of the Brown's buying a new house next
      year
   9. an enquiry about the place where Susan's wedding
      reception will be held
  10. the time of someone's arrival in Warsaw

G. *Use each of these expressions in a separate sentence:*
     come true; fall asleep; run dry; come undone; come right

in the end; go bad; grow dark; go mad; fall short of; turn to.

H. *Express the idea of cause or reason in these sentences in a different form without altering the meaning:*

1. As we have a busy day tomorrow I think we will go to bed early.
2. Wishing to make a good impression, Tom brought Mrs Brown some flowers.
3. He was sent to prison for stealing a watch.
4. This cold weather has been the cause of much illness.
5. He lost his job through repeated lateness.
6. David will not need so much money now he is living at home.
7. Seeing a policeman outside the house, we knew that something had happened.
8. The chief reason for his success was his own hard work.

I. *Write the remarks to which each of the following might be a short response:*

1. Oh, did she?
2. You did, did you?
3. Neither do I.
4. So does Tom.
5. Nor can Joan.
6. Oh, must I!
7. So will Mary.
8. So I have!
9. But we *didn't*.
10. Oh yes I can.

COMPOSITION

Exercises

1. Write the speech you think David. the 'best man' might have made on behalf of the guests at Susan's wedding.
2. Write a composition on 'Marriage Customs', comparing English customs with those in your own and any other countries you know.
3. Write a letter from Mrs Brown to one of her women friends, describing Susan's wedding.

LIST OF SENTENCE PATTERNS

Note: There is a reference index to the Exercises in Teacher's Book Three.

LIST OF IRREGULAR VERBS

This list includes all the Irregular Verbs introduced in Books One, Two and Three of the Course. Special Verbs are marked thus *

Present	Past	Past Participle
arise	arose	arisen
bear	bore	borne
beat	beat	beaten
become	became	become
begin	began	begun
bind	bound	bound
bite	bit	bitten
blow	blew	blown
break	broke	broken
bring	brought	brought
burst	burst	burst
buy	bought	bought
*can	could	
catch	caught	caught
choose	chose	chosen
come	came	come
cost	cost	cost
creep	crept	crept
cut	cut	cut
deal	dealt	dealt
dig	dug	dug
*do	did	done
draw	drew	drawn
drink	drank	drunk
drive	drove	driven

Present	Past	Past Participle
eat	ate	eaten
fall	fell	fallen
feed	fed	fed
feel	felt	felt
fight	fought	fought
find	found	found
fly	flew	flown
forbid	forbad(e)	forbidden
forget	forgot	forgotten
forgive	forgave	forgiven
freeze	froze	frozen
get	got	got
give	gave	given
go	went	gone
grind	ground	ground
grow	grew	grown
hang	hung	hung
*have	had	had
hear	heard	heard
hide	hid	hidden
hit	hit	hit
hold	held	held
hurt	hurt	hurt
*is	was	been
keep	kept	kept
know	knew	known
lay	laid	laid
lead	led	led
leave	left	left
lend	lent	lent
let	let	let

Present	Past	Past Participle
lie	lay	lain
lose	lost	lost
make	made	made
*may	might	
mean	meant	meant
meet	met	met
*must		
*ought		
pay	paid	paid
put	put	put
read (ri: d)	read (red)	read (red)
ride	rode	ridden
ring	rang	rung
rise	rose	risen
run	ran	run
say	said	said
see	saw	seen
sell	sold	sold
send	sent	sent
sew	sewed	sewn
shake	shook	shaken
*shall	should	
shine	shone	shone
show	showed	shown
shut	shut	shut
sing	sang	sung
sit	sat	sat
sleep	slept	slept
slide	slid	slid
sow	sowed	sown
speak	spoke	spoken

Present	*Past*	*Past Participle*
spell	spelled, spelt	spelled, spelt
spend	spent	spent
spill	spilled, spilt	spilled, spilt
spin	spun	spun
split	split	split
spread	spread	spread
stand	stood	stood
steal	stole	stolen
strike	struck	struck (stricken)
swear	swore	sworn
sweep	swept	swept
swell	swelled	swollen
swim	swam	swum
take	took	taken
tear	tore	torn
tell	told	told
think	thought	thought
throw	threw	thrown
understand	understood	understood
upset	upset	upset
wake	woke	woken
wear	wore	worn
weave	wove	woven
*will	would	
win	won	won
write	wrote	written

COMPOSITION NOTES

KEY TO PHONETIC SYMBOLS

Vowels and Diphthongs

iː	siː	see, sea	θin	thin
i	siks	six	ðiːz	these
e	ten	ten	sed	said
a	bad	bad	pak	pack
aː	haːd	hard	faːst	fast
o	hot	hot	wot	what
oː	doː	door	koːt	caught
u	tuk	took	put	put
uː	buːt	boot	juː	you
ʌ	sʌn	son, sun	kʌt	cut
əː	səː	sir	fəːst	first
ə	ˈmʌðə	mother	ˈsistə	sister
ei	keim	came	eit	eight
ou	ʃou	show	nou	no, know
ai	lait	light	main	mine
au	kau	cow	raund	round
oi	toi	toy	boi	boy
iə	niə	near	hiə	here, hear
eə	peə	pear, pair	weə	where
uə	ʃuə	sure	juə	you're

Consonants

t	teik	take	put	put
d	dog	dog	had	had
p	pen	pen	map	map
b	buk	book	ˈteibl	table
k	ˈkofi	coffee	buk	book
g	gou	go	dog	dog
f	foː	four	haːf	half
v	ˈveri	very	hav	have
m	ˈmʌðə	mother	kʌm	come

n	nain	nine	hand	hand
ŋ	siŋ	sing	'rʌniŋ	running
l	luk	look	dol	doll
θ	θin	thin	sauθ	south
ð	ðis	this	'faːðə	father
s	siks	six	buks	books
z	rouz	rose	dogz	dogs
ʃ	ʃal	shall	fiʃ	fish
ʒ	'pleʒə	pleasure	'viʒn	vision
tʃ	matʃ	match	'kwestʃn	question
dʒ	bridʒ	bridge	peidʒ	page
r	rʌn	run	tə'morou	tomorrow
w	woːl	wall	wen	when
j	jiə	year	jes	yes
h	hand	hand	hot	hot

WORD LIST

ability (əˈbiliti)
able (ˈeible)
absent (ˈabsnt)
absolutely (absəˈluːtli)
accident (ˈaksidənt)
act (akt)
active (ˈaktiv)
according (əˈkɔːdiŋ)
   accordingly (əˈkɔːdiŋli)
account (əˈkaunt)
accuse (əˈkjuːs)
accustom (əˈkʌstəm)
actual (ˈaktjuəl)
   actually (ˈaktjuəli)
administration (ədminisˈtreiʃn)
   administrative
      (ədˈministrətiv)
admit (ədˈmit)
adopt (əˈdopt)
advance (ədˈvaːns)
advantage (ədˈvaːntidʒ)
adventure (ədˈventʃə)
advice (ədˈvais)
agent (ˈeidʒənt)
agenda (əˈdʒendə)
agriculture (ˈagrikʌltʃə)
ahead (əˈhed)
air (eə)
airman (ˈeəmən)
aisle (ail)
alderman (ˈɔːldəmən)
amazing (əˈmeiziŋ)
ambition (amˈbiʃn)
amount (əˈmaunt)
anaesthetic (ˈanəsˈθetik)
ancient (ˈeinʃnt)
anger (ˈaŋgə)
angle (ˈaŋgl)
annoy (əˈnoi)
apart (əˈpaːt)
apologise (əˈpolədʒaiz)
   apology (əˈpolədʒi)
appear (əˈpiə)

applaud (əˈplɔːd)
apply (əˈplai)
appoint (əˈpoint)
appreciate (əˈpriːʃieit, əˈpriːsieit)
apprentice (əˈprentis)
approve (əˈpruːv)
arch (aːtʃ)
arise (əˈraiz)
   arose (əˈrouz)
   arisen (əˈrizn)
army (aːmi)
around (əˈraund)
arrest (əˈrest)
arrival (əˈraivl)
arrow (ˈarou)
art (aːt)
architect (ˈaːkitekt)
article (ˈaːtikl)
artificial (aːtiˈfiʃl)
artistic (aːˈtistik)
ash (aʃ)
aside (əˈsaid)
assembly (əˈsembli)
assistance (əˈsistəns)
assize (əˈsaiz)
assure (əˈʃɔː, əˈʃuə)
astonish (əˈstoniʃ)
athletic (aθˈletik)
attack (əˈtak)
attempt (əˈtempt)
attend (əˈtend)
   attendance (əˈtendəns)
attention (əˈtenʃn)
attract (əˈtrakt)
audience (ˈɔːdiəns)
automatic (ɔːtəˈmatik)
avenue (ˈavinju)
average (ˈavridʒ)
avoid (əˈvoid)
awake (əˈweik)
awkward (ˈɔːkwud)
axe (aks)

babyhood ('beibihud)
baggage ('bagidʒ)
bail (beil)
bake (beik)
balance ('baləns)
balcony ('balkəni)
bar (baː)
bare ('beə)
barrel ('barəl)
base (beis)
bathe (beið)
battle ('batl)
bay (bei)
beak (biːk)
beam (biːm)
bear ('beə)
   bore (boː)
   borne (boːn)
beard ('biəd)
beast (biːst)
beat (biːt)
   beaten ('biːtn)
beer ('biə)
beg (beg)
behave (bi'heiv)
being ('biːiŋ)
belt (belt)
bench (bentʃ)
beneath (bi'niːθ)
benefit ('benifit)
berry ('beri)
bind (baind)
birth (bəːθ)
bishop ('biʃəp)
bite (bait)
bitter ('bitə)
bless (bles)
blind (blaind)
block (blok)
blood (blʌd)
blossom ('blosəm)
boast (boust)
book-stall ('bukstoːl)
bold (bould)
bone (boun)
border ('boːdə)

bottom ('botm)
brass (braːs)
brave (breiv)
breadth (bredθ)
breeze (briːz)
bribe (braib)
bride (braid)
bridegroom ('braidgruːm)
bridesmaid ('braidzmeid)
brilliant ('briljənt)
broad (broːd)
bunch (bʌntʃ)
bundle ('bʌndl)
burst (bəːst)
bury ('beri)
   buried ('berid)
bush (buʃ)
button ('bʌtn)
by-pass ('baipaːs)

cage (keidʒ)
calculate ('kalkjuleit)
camel ('kaml)
camp (kamp)
campaign (kam'pein)
canal (kə'nal)
candidate ('kandideit)
captain ('kaptin)
captive ('kaptiv)
   captivity (kap'tiviti)
career (kə'riə)
carnation (kaː'neiʃn)
case (keis)
cat (kat)
cattle ('katl)
cauliflower ('koliflauə)
cause (koːz)
caution ('koːʃn)
cave (keiv)
ceiling ('siːliŋ)
ceremony ('seriməni)
chairman ('tʃeəmən)
chapel ('tʃapl)
charm (tʃaːm)
chat (tʃat)
chatter ('tʃatə)

cheat (tʃiːt)
chest (tʃest)
cheque (tʃek)
chief (tʃiːf)
childhood ('tʃaildhud)
choir ('kwaiə)
circulate ('səːkjuleit)
citizen ('sitizn)
civic ('sivik)
civilise ('sivilaiz)
claim (kleim)
claw (kloː)
clay (klei)
climate ('klaimit)
cloth (kloθ)
coarse (koːs)
coin (koin)
collar ('kolə)
collect (kə'lekt)
colony ('koləni)
column ('koləm)
combination (kombin'eiʃn)
  combine (kəm'bain)
comedy ('komədi)
comfort ('kʌmfət)
command (kə'maːnd)
commerce ('koməːs)
common ('komən)
community (kə'mjuːniti)
companion (kəm'panjən)
compete (kəm'piːt)
competition ('kompə'tiʃn)
  competitor (kəm'petitə)
complain (kəm'plein)
complete (kəm'pliːt)
complicated ('komplikeitid)
compose (kəm'pouz)
concern (kən'səːn)
condition (kən'diʃn)
confess (kən'fes)
confetti (kən'feti)
confidence ('konfidəns)
confirm (kən'fəːm)
confuse (kən'fjuːz)
congratulate (kən'gratjuleit)
connect (kə'nekt)

conquer ('koŋkə)
conscience ('konʃəns)
conscious ('konʃəs)
Conservative (kən'səːvətiv)
consider (kən'sidə)
  considerable (kən'sidərəbl)
consignment (kən'sainmənt)
constable ('kʌnstəbl)
contain (kən'tein)
content (adj.) (kən'tent),
  (noun) ('kontent(s))
continue (kən'tinju)
  continuous (kən'tinjuəs)
control (kən'troul)
convenience (kən'viːniəns)
  convenient (kən'viːniənt)
cool (kuːl)
copper ('kopə)
copy ('kopi)
corporation (koːpə'reiʃn)
correct (kə'rekt)
correspondent (koris'pondənt)
council ('kaunsil)
  councillor ('kaunsilə)
counsel ('kaunsəl)
county ('kaunti)
courage ('kʌridʒ)
court (koːt)
crack (krak)
crash (kraʃ)
cream (kriːm)
creature ('kriːtʃə)
creep (kriːp)
critic ('kritik)
crop (krop)
cross (kros)
crown (kraun)
cruel ('kruːəl)
crush (krʌʃ)
cultivate ('kʌltiveit)
cure ('kjuə)
curious ('kjuriəs)
current ('kʌrənt)
curse (kəːs)
curve (kəːv)
customary ('kʌstəmri)

cylinder ('silində)

daffodil ('dafədil)
damage ('damidʒ)
damp (damp)
danger ('deindʒə)
deaf (def)
deal (diːl)
dealer ('diːlə)
death (deθ)
debt (det)
decay (di'kei)
deceive (di'siːv)
decision (di'siʒn)
declare (di'kleə)
decrease (di'kriːs)
deed (diːd)
deep (diːp)
deer ('diə)
defeat (di'fiːt)
defence (di'fens)
    defend (di'fend)
delay (di'lei)
delicate ('delikət)
delight (di'lait)
    delighted (di'laitid)
deliver (di'livə)
    delivery (di'livəri)
demand (di'maːnd)
deposit (di'pozit)
descend (di'send)
describe (dis'kraib)
    description (dis'kripʃn)
desert (noun) 'dezət, (verb)
    di'zəːt)
deserve (di'səːv)
desire (di'zaiə)
despair (dis'peə)
detail ('diːteil)
develop (di'veləp)
    development (di'veləpmənt)
devil ('devl)
diary ('daiəri)
dictaphone ('diktəfoun)
dictate (dik'teit)

direct (di'rekt)
direction (di'rekʃn)
difficult ('difiklt)
dip (dip)
disappoint (disə'point)
discharge (dis'tʃaːdʒ)
discipline ('disiplin)
discount ('diskaunt)
discover (dis'kʌvə)
discuss (dis'kʌs)
    discussion (dis'kʌʃn)
disease (di'ziːz)
disgust (dis'gʌst)
dismiss (dis'mis)
distinguish (dis'tiŋgwiʃ)
district ('distrikt)
disturb (dis'təːb)
disused (dis'juːzd)
ditch (ditʃ)
dive (daiv)
dock (dok)
dollar ('dolə)
donkey ('doŋki)
double ('dʌbl)
doubt (daut)
drag (drag)
drain (drein)
    drainage ('dreinidʒ)
drawer (droː)
drown (draun)
duly ('djuːli)
duty ('djuːti)

eager ('iːgə)
earnest ('əːnist)
earth (əːθ)
ease (iːz)
editor ('editə)
educate ('edjukeit)
    education (edju'keiʃn)
effect (i'fekt)
effort ('efət)
elder ('eldə)
elderly ('eldəli)
elect (i'lekt)

election (i'lekʃn)
elegance ('eligəns)
 elegant ('eligənt)
elephant ('elifənt)
empire ('empaiə)
employ (im'ploi)
 employer (im'ploiə)
 employment (im'ploimənt)
encourage (in'kʌridʒ)
enemy ('enəmi)
enormous (in'oɪməs)
enquire (in'kwaiə)
 enquiry (in'kwairi)
enter ('entə)
entire (in'taiə)
 entirely (in'taiəli)
envelope (*noun*) ('envəloup)
envy ('envi)
equal ('iɪkwl)
equally ('iɪkwəli)
escape (is'keip)
essence ('esəns)
essential (i'senʃl)
exact (ig'zakt)
 exactly (ig'zaktli)
example (ig'zaɪmpl)
exceed (ik'siɪd)
exception (ik'sepʃn)
exhibition ('eksi'biʃn)
exist (ig'zist)
 existence (ig'zistəns)
expand (iks'pand)
expect (iks'pekt)
experiment (iks'perimənt)
expert ('ekspəɪt)
explode (iks'ploud)
explore (iks'ploɪ)
export (*noun*) ('ekspoɪt),
 (*verb*) (eks'poɪt)
express (iks'pres)
extend (iks'tend)
 extent (iks'tent)
extraodrinary (iks'troɪdinri)
extreme (iks'triɪm)
even ('iɪvn)
evil ('iɪvl)

fade (feid)
fail (feil)
faint (feint)
fairy ('feəri)
faith (feiθ)
false (foɪls)
fame (feim)
familiar (fə'miljə)
faraway ('faɪrəwei)
farther ('faɪðə)
fate (feit)
favour ('feivə)
fear (fiə)
feast (fiɪst)
feather ('feðə)
feature ('fiɪtʃə)
fellow ('felou)
female ('fiɪmeil)
fence (fens)
festival ('festivəl)
fever ('fiɪvə)
fiancé(e) (fi'aɪnsei)
fibre ('faibə)
fierce ('fiəs)
figure ('figə)
file (fail)
fix (fiks)
flame (fleim)
flash (flaʃ)
flavour ('fleivə)
flesh (fleʃ)
float (flout)
flood (flʌd)
flour ('flauə)
flow (flou)
flutter ('flʌtə)
fog (fog)
fold (fould)
fool (fuɪl)
foolish ('fuɪliʃ)
forbid (fə'bid)
 forbad(e) (fə'bad)
 forbidden (fə'bidn)
force (foɪs)
foreman ('foɪmən)
forest ('forist)

form (foːm)
former (ˈfoːmə)
fortunate (ˈfoːtjunət)
  fortunately (ˈfoːtjunətli)
fortune (ˈfoːtjuːn)
foundation (faunˈdeiʃn)
foundry (ˈfaundri)
frequent (ˈfriːkwənt)
fry (frai)
fun (fʌn)
furnish (ˈfəːniʃ)
further (ˈfəːðə)

gain (gein)
gap (gap)
general (ˈdʒenrl)
generosity (dʒenəˈrositi)
  generous (ˈdʒenərəs)
gentleman (ˈdʒentlmən)
giant (ˈdʒaiənt)
gladness (ˈgladnis)
goat (gout)
God (god)
gown (gaun)
grace (greis)
  graceful (ˈgreisful)
gradual (ˈgradjuəl)
  gradually (ˈgradjuəli)
grain (grein)
grand (grand)
  grandchild (ˈgrantʃaild)
grateful (ˈgreitful)
grave (greiv)
grease (griːs)
greet (griːt)
grind (graind)
group (gruːp)
growth (grouθ)
guess (ges)
guilty (ˈgilti)

habit (ˈhabit)
hall (hoːl)
hammer (ˈhamə)
harm (haːm)
  harmful (ˈhaːmful)
haste (heist)

hate (heit)
heading (ˈhediŋ)
headline (ˈhedlain)
heal (hiːl)
heap (hiːp)
heat (hiːt)
heaven (ˈhevn)
height (hait)
helmet (ˈhelmit)
hesitate (ˈheziteit)
hill (hil)
hinder (ˈhində)
hire (ˈhaiə)
  hire-purchase (ˈhaiəˈpəːtʃəs)
hobby (ˈhobi)
hollow (ˈholou)
holy (ˈhouli)
honey (ˈhʌni)
honeymoon (ˈhʌnimuːn)
honour (ˈonə)
hook (huk)
horn (hoːn)
horizon (həˈraizn)
human (ˈhjuːmən)
humble (ˈhʌmbl)
hump (hʌmp)
hut (hʌt)

ideal (aiˈdiəl)
idle (ˈaidl)
illegal (iˈliːgl)
illness (ˈilnis)
imitate (ˈimiteit)
immediate (iˈmiːdiət)
immense (iˈmens)
import (*noun*) (ˈimpoːt),
    (*verb*) (imˈpoːt)
impress (imˈpres)
  impression (imˈpreʃn)
  impressive (imˈpresiv)
improve (imˈpruːv)
include (inˈkluːd)
incoming (ˈinkʌmiŋ)
increase (*noun*) (ˈinkriːs),
    (*verb*) (inˈkriːs)
independent (indiˈpendənt)

indoors (in'doːz)
industry ('indəstri)
   industrial (in'dʌstriəl)
influence ('influəns)
inform (in'foːm)
injure ('indʒə)
   injury ('indʒəri)
ink (ink)
inland ('inland)
innocent ('inəsənt)
insect ('insekt)
inside (in'said)
install (in'stoːl)
instant ('instənt)
instrument ('instrəmənt)
insult (noun) ('insʌlt), (verb)
   (in'sʌlt)
insure (in'ʃoː, in'ʃuə)
   insurance (in'ʃoːrəns,
   in'ʃuərəns)
intelligent (in'telidʒənt)
intend (in'tend)
interest ('intrəst)
interfere (intə'fiə)
international (intə'naʃnl)
interrupt (intə'rʌpt)
interval ('intəvl)
invalid ('invəlid)
invent (in'vent)
   invention (in'venʃn)
invoice ('invois)
item ('aitəm)
ivory ('aivəri)

jam (dʒam)
jaw (dʒoː)
jealous ('dʒeləs)
joint (dʒoint)
joke (dʒouk)
journalism ('dʒəːnəlizm)
   journalist ('dʒəːnəlist)
judge (dʒʌdʒ)
jug (dʒʌg)
jungle ('dʒʌŋgl)
jury ('dʒuːri)
justice ('dʒʌstis)

keen (kiːn)
keyboard ('kiːboːd)
kind (kaind)
kingdom ('kiŋdəm)
knock (nok)
knot (not)
knowledge ('nolidʒ)

Labour ('leibə)
lace (leis)
ladder ('ladə)
landlord ('landloːd)
lamp (lamp)
launch (loːntʃ)
lawn (loːn)
lawyer ('loːjə)
lazy ('leizi)
lead (liːd)
   led (led)
leader ('liːdə)
leave (liːv)
lecture ('lektʃə)
   lecturer ('lektjərə)
leg (leg)
legal ('liːgl)
level ('levl)
liar ('laiə)
Liberal ('libərəl)
liberty ('libəti)
licence ('laisəns)
lid (lid)
likely ('laikli)
limb (lim)
limit ('limit)
line (lain)
link (liŋk)
liquid ('likwid)
list (list)
literature ('litəritʃuə)
   literary ('litərəri)
load (loud)
loan (loun)
local ('loukl)
lock (lok)
lodging ('lodʒiŋ)
loose (luːs)

lorry ('lori)
loss (los)
loyal ('loiəl)
   loyalty ('loiəlti)
lung (lʌŋ)

mad (mad)
magazine (magə'ziːn)
mail (meil)
main (mein)
majority (mə'dʒoriti)
male (meil)
management ('manidʒmənt)
manufacture (manju'faktʃə)
march (maːtʃ)
mark (maːk)
marriage ('maridʒ)
mass (mas)
mat (mat)
material (mə'tiːriəl)
mayor (meə)
mean (miːn)
meanwhile ('miːn'wail)
mechanic (mi'kanik)
medical ('medikl)
melt (melt)
memory ('mem(ə)ri)
mention ('menʃn)
merchant ('məːtʃənt)
mercy ('məːsi)
mere (miə)
   merely ('miəli)
merry ('meri)
message ('mesidʒ)
metal ('metl)
mild (maild)
mill (mil)
million ('miljən)
miner ('mainə)
   mining ('mainiŋ)
minister ('ministə)
miserable ('mizrəbl)
mix (miks)
model ('modl)
moderate ('modərət)
modern ('modən)

modest ('modist)
monk (mʌŋk)
monkey ('mʌŋki)
monument ('monjumənt)
moon (muːn)
moral ('morəl)
moreover (moː'rouvə)
motion ('mouʃn)
mould (mould)
mount (maunt)
mouse (maus)
mud (mʌd)
multiply ('mʌltiplai)
murder ('məːdə)
museum (mju'ziːəm)
mystery ('mist(ə)ri)
mysterious (mis'tiːriəs)

nail (neil)
nasty ('naːsti)
nation ('neiʃn)
   nationalise ('naʃnəlaiz)
native ('neitiv)
nature ('neitʃə)
   natural ('natrəl)
   naturally ('natʃurəli)
neat (niːt)
   neatly ('niːtli)
necessary ('nesəsri)
neck (nek)
necklace ('neklis)
needle ('niːdl)
neglect (ni'glekt)
nephew ('nevju)
net (net)
newcomer ('njukʌmə)
niece (niːs)
noble ('noubl)
nod (nod)
nomination (nomin'eiʃn)
none (nʌn)
nonsense ('nonsəns)
noon (nuːn)
nose (nouz)
note (nout)
notice ('noutis)

WORD LIST

305

nowhere ('nouweə)
nuisance ('njuːsəns)
nurse (nəːs)
  nursery ('nəːsri)
nut (nʌt)
nylon ('nailən)

oak (ouk)
oar (oː)
obey (ə'bei)
object (noun) ('obdʒekt), (verb) (əb'dʒekt)
  objection (əb'dʒekʃn)
observe (əb'zəːv)
obtain (əb'tein)
occasion (ə'keiʒn)
ocean ('ouʃn)
offend (ə'fend)
official (ə'fiʃl)
  officially (ə'fiʃəli)
omit (ou'mit)
operation (opə'reiʃn)
opinion (ə'pinjən)
opponent (ə'pounənt)
opportunity (opə'tjuːniti)
opposite ('opəzit)
ordinary (oːdinri)
organ ('oːgən)
organise ('oːgənaiz)
  organisation (oːgənai'zeiʃn)
origin ('oridʒin)
ounce (auns)
outgoing ('autgoiŋ)
outlook ('autluk)
outspoken (aut'spoukən)
overcome (ouvə'kʌm)
overseas (ouvə'siːz)
owe (ou)

pad (pad)
pain (pein)
pale (peil)
pan (pan)
pardon ('paːdən)
parlour ('paːlə)
parrot ('parət)

particular (pə'tikjulə)
paste (peist)
  pastey ('peisti)
patient ('peiʃnt)
  patience ('peiʃəns)
patriotic (patri'otik)
pattern ('patəːn)
pause (poːz)
paw (poː)
payment ('peimənt)
pearl (pəːl)
peculiar (pi'kjuːliə)
per cent (pə'sent)
permanent ('pəmənənt)
permit (noun) ('pəːmit), (verb) (pə'mit)
person ('pəːsən)
  personal ('pəːɪsnəl)
persuade (pə'sweid)
pet (pet)
pigeon ('pidʒən)
pile (pail)
pin (pin)
pink (piŋk)
pipe (paip)
pit (pit)
place (pleis)
plain (plein)
plant (plaːnt)
plantation (plaɪn'teiʃn)
plaster ('plaɪstə)
plastic ('plastik)
plough (plau)
plum (plʌm)
poison ('poizn)
polar ('poulə)
polish ('poliʃ)
political (pə'litikl)
policy ('polisi)
pool (puːl)
population (popju'leiʃn)
port (poːt)
position (pə'ziʃn)
possess (pə'zes)
poster ('poustə)
postpone (poust'poun)

pot (pot)
poverty ('povəti)
power ('pauə)
  powerful ('pauəful)
practical ('praktikl)
praise (preiz)
pray (prei)
preach (priːtʃ)
precious ('preʃəs)
prejudice ('predʒudis)
preserve (pri'səːv)
president ('prezidənt)
press (pres)
pretend (pri'tend)
prevent (pri'vent)
pride (praid)
priest (priːst)
primary ('praiməri)
prince (prins)
print (print)
prison ('prizn)
private ('praivit)
probable ('probəbl)
  probably ('probəbli)
problem ('probləm)
process ('prouses)
procession (prou'seʃn)
profit ('profit)
prompt (prompt)
proof (pruːf)
proper ('propə)
  properly ('propəli)
property ('propəti)
propose (prə'pouz)
prosecute ('prosikjuːt)
protect (prə'tekt)
prove (pruːv)
provide (prə'vaid)
provincial (prə'vinʃl)
provision (prə'viʒn)
prune (pruːn)
public ('pʌblik)
punctual ('pʌŋktjuəl)
pump (pʌmp)
purpose ('pəːpəs)
puzzle ('pʌzl)

qualify ('kwolifai)
quality ('kwoliti)
quantity ('kwontiti)
quite (kwait)
quote (kwout)

rabbit ('rabit)
rake (reik)
rank (raŋk)
rapid ('rapid)
rat (rat)
rate (reit)
raw (roː)
ray (rei)
reach (riːtʃ)
real (riːl)
realise ('riːəlaiz)
reason ('riːsən)
  reasonable ('riːznəbl)
receipt (ri'siːt)
recent ('riːsənt)
reception (ri'sepʃn)
recognise ('rekəgnaiz)
reduce (ri'djuːs)
refer (ri'fəː)
reflect (ri'flekt)
refresh (ri'freʃ)
regard (ri'gaːd)
regiment ('redʒəmənt)
regret (ri'gret)
regular ('regjulə)
rejoice (ri'djois)
relief (ri'liːf)
  relieve (ri'liːv)
religion (ri'lidʒən)
remain (ri'mein)
remarkable (ri'maːkəbl)
  remarkably (ri'maːkəbli)
remedy ('remədi)
rent (tent)
repair (ri'peə)
repay (ri'pei)
replace (ri'pleis)
reply (re'plai)
  replied (ri'plaid)

report (ri'po:t)
  reporter (ri'po:tə)
represent (repri'zent)
  representative (repri'zentətiv)
reproduce (ri:prə'dju:s)
republic (ri'pʌblik)
reputation (repju'tei∫n)
request (ri'kwest)
rescue ('reskju:)
resign (ri'zain)
  resignation (rezig'nei∫n)
resist (ri'zist)
respect (ri'spekt)
responsible (ri'sponsibl)
rest (rest)
result (ri'zʌlt)
retire (ri'taiə)
revenge (ri'vendʒ)
review (ri'vju:)
revolution (revə'lu:∫n)
reward (ri'wo:d)
rheumatism ('ru:mətizm)
ribbon ('ribən)
rid (rid)
ripe (raip)
  ripen ('raipn)
rise (raiz)
  rose (rouz)
  risen ('rizn)
risk (risk)
rival ('raivl)
roar (ro:)
rod (rod)
root (ru:t)
rope (roup)
rose (rouz)
rot (rot)
rotary ('routəri)
rough (rʌf)
roundabout ('raundəbaut)
route (ru:t)
row (rou)
rub (rʌb)
rubbish ('rʌbi∫)
ruin(s) ('ru:in(z))
ruler ('ru:lə)

rust (rʌst)

sacred ('seikrid)
sacrifice ('sakrifais)
sail (seil)
sake (seik)
salmon ('samən)
salt (solt)
sample ('sa:mpl)
scale (skeil)
scarce (skeəs)
  scarcely ('skeəsli)
scatter ('skatə)
scene (si:n)
scholar ('skolə)
  scholarship ('skolə∫ip)
science (saiəns)
scissors ('sizəz)
scold (skould)
scorn (sko:n)
scrape (skreip)
scratch (skrat∫)
sea-port ('si:po:t)
search (sə:t∫)
seed (si:d)
secondary ('sekəndri)
secret ('si:krit)
secure (si'kju:ə)
seize (si:z)
select (si'lekt)
sense (sens)
  sensible ('sensibl)
set (set)
settle ('setl)
  settlement ('setlmənt)
severe (si'vi:ə)
sew (sou)
shadow ('∫adou)
shake (∫eik)
shallow ('∫alou)
shape (∫eip)
sharp (∫a:p)
  sharply ('∫a:pli)
shell (∫el)
shelter ('∫eltə)
shield (∫i:ld)

shift (ʃift)
ship (ʃip)
　shipment (ˈʃipmənt)
shock (ʃok)
shoot (ʃuːt)
　shot (ʃot)
shore (ʃoː)
shower (ˈʃauə)
show (ʃou)
shriek (ʃriːk)
sick (sik)
sign (sain)
silence (ˈsailəns)
similar (ˈsimilə)
simple (ˈsimpl)
sincere (sinˈsiːə)
　sincerely (sinˈsiːəli)
sink (siŋk)
situation (sitjuˈeiʃn)
skill (skil)
skin (skin)
slave (sleiv)
slide (slaid)
slight (slait)
slip (slip)
snake (sneik)
social (ˈsouʃəl)
society (səˈsaiəti)
soft (soft)
soil (soil)
solemn (ˈsoləm)
solid (ˈsolid)
solve (solv)
song (soŋ)
sore (soː)
sort (soːt)
soul (soul)
sour (ˈsauə)
souvenir (suːvəˈniːə)
sovereign (ˈsovrin)
sow (sou)
spare (ˈspeə)
speed (spiːd)
spill (spil)
　spilled (spild)
　spilt (spilt)

spell (spel)
　spelled (speld)
　spelt (spelt)
spire (spaiə)
spirit (ˈspirit)
spite (spait)
split (split)
staff (staːf)
stain (stein)
staircase (ˈsteəkeis)
standard (ˈstandəd)
star (staː)
state (steit)
　stately (ˈsteitli)
steady (ˈstedi)
steal (stiːl)
steam (stiːm)
steep (stiːp)
steer (stiːə)
stem (stem)
stick (stik)
stiff (stif)
stock (stok)
storm (stoːm)
straw (stroː)
strawberry (ˈstroːbri)
strength (streŋθ)
stretch (stretʃ)
strict (strikt)
strike (straik)
string (striŋ)
strip (strip)
stripe (straip)
stroke (strouk)
struggle (ˈstrʌgl)
stupid (ˈstjuːpid)
style (stail)
substance (ˈsʌbstəns)
suffer (ˈsʌfə)
suiting (sjuːtiŋ)
sum (sʌm)
support (səˈpoːt)
　supporter (səˈpoːtə)
supply (səˈplai)
　supplied (səˈplaid)
surely (ˈʃoːli, ˈʃjuəli)

surround (sə'raund)
suspect (*noun*) ('sʌspekt),
    (*verb*) (səs'pekt)
    suspicion (səs'piʃn)
swallow ('swolou)
swan (swon)
sway (swei)
swear ('sweə)
sweat (swet)
swell (swel)
swerve (swəːv)
sword (soːd)
sympathy ('simpəθi)
    sympathetic (simpə'θetik)
system ('sistəm)

tail (teil)
tame (teim)
tap (tap)
    tapped (tapt)
tasteful ('teistful)
tax (taks)
tear(s) (*noun*) (tiːə(z))
tease (tiːz)
technical ('teknikl)
technology (tek'nolədʒi)
telegraph ('teligraːf, 'teligraf)
telephonist (tel'efənist)
teleprinter ('teliprintə)
temper ('tempə)
tempt (tempt)
    temptation (temp'teiʃn)
tend (tend)
tender ('tendə)
term (təːm)
test (test)
textiles ('tekstailz)
theft (θeft)
therefore ('ðeəfoː)
thick (θik)
thief (θiːf)
thorn (θoːn)
thought (θoːt)
thread (θred)
threaten ('θretn)
throat (θrout)

thumb (θʌm)
thunder ('θʌndə)
thus (ðʌs)
tight (tait)
tin (tin)
tip (tip)
title ('taitl)
toe (tou)
ton (tʌn)
total ('toutl)
tough (tʌf)
tour ('tuːə)
towards (tə'woːdz)
track (trak)
traffic ('trafik)
train (trein)
translate (trans'leit, trəns'leit)
trap (trap)
treasure ('treʒə)
    treasurer ('treʒərə)
treat (triːt)
    treatment ('triːtmənt)
tremble ('trembl)
trial (trail)
trick (trik)
trim (trim)
trip (trip)
tropical ('tropikl)
trowel ('trauəl)
trunk (trʌŋk)
trust (trʌst)
truth (truːθ)
tune (tjuːn)
tunnel ('tʌnl)
typist ('taipist)

ugly ('ʌgli)
uncle ('ʌŋkl)
union ('juːniən)
universe ('juːnivəːs)
unload (ʌn'loud)
upkeep ('ʌpkiːp)
upper ('ʌpə)
upset (ʌp'set)
upward(s) ('ʌpwəd(z))
urge (əːdʒ)

valley ('vali)
value ('valju)
variety (və'raiəti)
   various ('veəriəs)
veil (veil)
verdict ('vəːdikt)
verse (vəːs)
vessel ('vesəl)
victory ('viktri)
view (vjuː)
violent ('vaiələnt)
virtue ('vəːtju)
voice (vois)
voyage ('voiidʒ)

wage(s) (weidʒ(iz)
waist (weist)
   waistcoat ('weiskout,'weskət)
wander ('wondə)
war (woː)
warn (woːn)
waste (weist)
wayside ('weisaid)
weak (wiːk)
wealth (welθ)
   wealthy ('welθi)
weapon ('wepən)
weave (wiːv)
   wove (wouv)
   woven ('wouvn)
weed (wiːd)

week-end ('wiːkend)
weigh (wei)
welfare ('welfeə)
wheat (wiːt)
whip (wip)
whisper ('wispə)
whole (houl)
wicked ('wikid)
widow ('widou)
width (widθ)
wig (wig)
wing (wiŋ)
wipe (waip)
wire (waiə)
wise (waiz)
within (wið'in)
witness ('witnis)
womanhood ('wumənhud)
worm (wəːm)
worship ('wəːʃip)
worth (wəːθ)
   worthy ('wəːði)
wound (wuːnd)
wreck (rek)

yield (jiːld)
youth (juːθ)

zero ('ziːrou)
zoological (zuːˈlodʒikl)

NAMES OF PLACES

Africa ('afrikə)
Bath (baːθ)
Bedford ('bedfəd)
Blenheim Palace
('blenəm 'palis)
Bradford ('bradfəd)
Bristol ('bristl)
Broadway ('broːdwei)
Burford ('bəːfəd)
Cambridge ('keimbridʒ)
Canada ('kanədə)
Canterbury ('kantəbri)
Cheddar ('tʃedə)
Chepstow ('tʃepstou)
Christ Church ('kraistʃəːtʃ)
Cotswolds, The ('kotswouldz, ðə)
Dunstable Downs ('dʌnstəbl
'dauns)
Eton ('iːtn)
Fairford ('feəfəd)
Gloucester ('glostə)
Gloucestershire ('glostəʃiə)
Grantchester ('grantʃistə)
Greece (griːs)
Guildford ('gilfəd)
Irwell (river) ('əːwel)
Japan (dʒə'pan)
Japanese (dʒapə'niːz)
Jesus (College) ('dʒiːzəs)
Lake Windermere ('leik
'windəmiːə)
Lancashire ('laŋkəʃiə)
Lancastrian (laŋ'kastriən)
Lowlands ('louləndz)
Magdalen (College) ('moːdlin)

Marlborough ('moːbrə,
'moːlbrə)
Mersey (river) ('məːzi)
Monmouth ('mʌnməθ)
Monmouthshire ('mʌnməθʃiə)
Morecambe ('moːkum)
Newport ('njuːpoːt)
Norman ('noːmən)
Northampton (noː'θamtən)
Ottawa ('otəwə)
Pennines ('penainz)
Pulteney (Bridge) ('pʌltni)
Regent's Park ('riːdʒənts
'paːk)
Rhondda ('ronðə, 'rondə)
Rome (roum)
Roman ('roumən)
Ruskin (College) ('rʌskin)
Severn (river) ('sevən)
Swansea ('swonzi)
Tewkesbury ('tjuːksbri)
Tintern Abbey ('tintəːn 'abi)
Wadham (College) ('wodəm)
Warwick ('worik)
Wells (welz)
Whipsnade ('wipsneid)
Wigan ('wigən)
Windsor ('winzə)
Woburn ('woubən)
Woodstock ('wuːdstok)
Worcester ('wustə)
Wye (river) ('wai)
York Minster ('joːk 'minstə)
Yorkshire ('joːkʃə)

BOYS' NAMES

Albert (Bert) ('albət) (bəːt)
Alan ('alən)
Bernard ('bəːnəd)
Charles (Charlie) (tʃaːlz)
　　　('tʃaːli)
Christopher (Chris) ('kristəfə)
　　　(kris)

Edward (Ted) ('edwəd) (ted)
Eric ('erik)
Herbert (Bert) ('həːbət) (bəːt)
Owen ('ouin)
Richard (Dick) ('ritʃəd) (dik)
Rupert ('ruːpət)

FAMILY NAMES

Anderson ('andəsən)
Bennett ('benit)
Collins ('kolinz)
Deacon ('diːkən)
Dickens ('dikinz)
Douglas ('dʌgləs)
Drummond ('drʌmənd)
East (iːst)
Foster ('fostə)
Granger ('greindʒə)
Hallam ('haləm)
Hardy ('haːdi)
Hathaway ('haθəwei)
Kipling ('kipliŋ)
Llewellyn (luːˈelin)

Morgan ('moːgən)
Morris ('moris)
Nicholson ('nikəlsən)
Parsons ('paːsənz)
Pickwick ('pikwik)
Reynolds ('renəldz)
Ridley ('ridli)
Saunders ('soːndəz)
Sawyer ('soːjə)
Ward (woːd)
Warner ('woːnə)
Williams ('wiljəmz)
Wordsworth ('wəːdzwəθ)
Yardley ('jaːdli)